ANALYTICS, POLICY, AND GOVERNANCE

ANALYTICS, POLICY, AND GOVERNANCE

EDITED BY
**JENNIFER BACHNER, BENJAMIN GINSBERG,
AND KATHRYN WAGNER HILL**

Yale

UNIVERSITY PRESS

New Haven and London

Yale University Press books may be purchased in quantity for
educational, business, or promotional use. For information,
please e-mail sales.press@yale.edu (U.S. office) or
sales@yaleup.co.uk (U.K. office).

Designed by Newgen.
Set in Joanna and Futura type by Newgen.

Printed in the United States of America.

Library of Congress Control Number: 2016950785
ISBN: 978-0-300-20839-9 (paperback : alk. paper)

A catalogue record for this book is available from the British
Library.

This paper meets the requirements of ANSI/NISO
Z39.48-1992 (Permanence of Paper).

10 9 8 7 6 5 4 3 2 1

Contents

ANALYTICS, POLICY, AND GOVERNANCE

Introduction

Jennifer Bachner

Data have been collected and analyzed for millennia, but never before have these processes been so ubiquitous. Data journalism, with its focus on eye-catching visualizations and infographics, is transforming an industry from mere collection of information to effective presentation. Businesses rigorously analyze consumers' browsing and purchasing histories to optimize sales and marketing. Likewise, the governance of a nation increasingly relies on the collection and analysis of data, energizing the field of government analytics. Federal and state agencies employ quantitative methods to conduct program evaluations. Policy debates overflow with statistical arguments. Campaigns mine voter data to micro-target potential supporters. Data-driven decision making holds the promise of making our government more efficient, more effective, and more responsive to our most critical needs.

PURPOSE OF THE VOLUME

This text takes the reader on a journey across the data revolution in government. Over the course of this journey, the reader will come to appreciate not only the breadth of analytical methods used in the public sector but also the policy implications and ethical issues raised by those methods. We anticipate that some readers will consume the book as a whole, building their knowledge of analytics brick by brick. There is a logical ordering to the chapters, and the information is presented in a cumulative manner. Other readers, however, will choose to read a subset of chapters, and they have been written to accommodate this approach. Each chapter stands on its own, though some of the more advanced topics presume a basic understanding of statistics. There are entire literatures on each of the topics discussed in the volume, but we have prioritized breadth to give the reader an expansive understanding of the ways in which data and analytics are being used to transform civil society. The book is best viewed as a jumping-off platform for those who are interested in the field. We anticipate that some readers will become particularly inspired by one or two of the methods or issues discussed and seek out additional resources in those areas. We also expect this volume to be especially useful as an introductory text for students preparing for careers in government and business in which an understanding of analytics has become highly desirable.

The book is intended for consumers, producers, and students of quantitative knowledge. For those who consume empirical research, the volume provides clear explanations of how foundational and emerging analytical methods are currently being used in the public sector. The reader who is new to the field will come away with a strong conceptual understanding of how sophisticated methods, such as instrumental variables, geospatial analysis, and machine learning, are used. Armed with this understanding, readers will find that previously inaccessible research is comprehensible. A reader who was previously intimidated by a research article replete with complicated tables and figures will, upon completing the volume, have the confidence and skills needed to understand—and perhaps even refute!—that article's key methodological arguments and results.

For those who plan to produce original research, the volume provides details about how various analytical methods are implemented and the types of questions each method can be used to answer. For example, a researcher focused on classic multivariate regression might find that some questions are better answered using social network analysis or geolocation data. As a researcher's toolkit expands, so does his or her ability to answer meaningful questions related to public policy, politics, and governance.

Beyond providing the reader with a survey of analytical methods, the book discusses the policy context in which data are stored, transferred, and analyzed as well as the accompanying ethical concerns. As with the emergence of all new fields, the growth of big data has activated concerns with government overreach and generated calls for greater oversight. Both individuals and organizations are deeply concerned about the protection of their data and continue to look to all levels of government to provide a coherent legal and regulatory framework governing their use.

It is useful at this point to define what is meant by analytics and to distinguish it from statistics. Whereas statistics refers to the analysis of data, analytics encompasses a much broader set of skills related to the translation of numbers into information. Analytics refers not only to the methods of data analysis and presentation but also to collecting and managing increasingly massive datasets, mining the data to detect meaningful patterns, visualizing the data to illuminate relationships, and communicating the findings to broad audiences. In short, analytics is about converting data into practical knowledge that can be acted upon by decision makers.

Yesterday's statisticians were, generally speaking, tasked with performing hypothesis tests and presenting results in tabular form. Today's data scientists—those in business and government charged with conducting analytics—use an array of innovative techniques and data from a multitude of sources to advance the missions of their organizations.

The term "big data" is widely used to refer to the exponential growth in the size of datasets. A few years ago, a dataset with a few hundred thousand observations was considered large, particularly in the context of the traditional Neyman-Pearson framework of statistical significance. As the ease of data collection and storage has increased, so has the amount of available data. Computer-assisted programs collect a tremendous amount of data every second of every day. They scrape websites for text documents, track web users' activity, gather location information from cell phones and cars, store satellite imagery, and collect data on commercial transactions. It is estimated that 2.5 quintillion bytes of data are created each year.[1]

Big data is typically distinguished from other data by three key characteristics.[2] First, big data is *voluminous* as a result of new data collection instruments and the ability to store the massive amount of collected data. Second, big data has a high *velocity*, meaning the data are collected and managed at high speeds. Third, big data has *variety*, meaning the data exist in various formats and structures. Owing to these three characteristics, big data poses unique challenges with respect to data management, analysis, and presentation. This volume discusses several techniques that are particularly useful for making sense of big data, such as text analysis and machine learning.

Most of the concepts and methods presented in the following chapters, however, are relevant to datasets of all sizes. When conducting a causal study, for example, considerations about selection bias and measurement are essential regardless of whether the dataset has 10,000 or 10 million observations. The use of big data does not eliminate the need to understand fundamental principles of statistical analysis, many of which are discussed in this volume.

It is also important to remember that numbers themselves have little inherent value. As Harvard political scientist Gary King has emphasized, the real value of big data is in the analytics.[3] Datasets are only as valuable as the knowledge that can be gleaned from them. Moreover, he warns of "big data hubris."[4] The use of a supersized dataset does not render unimportant other aspects of research design, including concept operationalization and measurement, satisfaction of statistical assumptions, and external validity. To translate data into actionable information, data scientists must have a firm understanding of statistical methods and the substantive issues at hand—this allows data scientists to make good judgments throughout the research process. With this in mind, consider some of the ways analytics is reshaping critical areas of governance.

ANALYTICS AND LAW ENFORCEMENT

Law enforcement agencies have embraced analytics as a means of both preventing and solving crime.[5] Using predictive analytics, several police departments have re-allocated their limited resources to deter criminal behavior in the most efficient manner possible. In California, the Santa Cruz Police Department, for example, uses hot-spot mapping to identify the areas with the highest probability of crime occurring during a specific time frame. These maps, which officers receive at the beginning of their shifts, inform decision making about which areas to patrol most heavily, resulting in decreased criminal activity.

The Baltimore County Police Department in Maryland has also relied heavily on data and analytics. This agency has experienced particular success with using pattern analysis when trying to apprehend serial offenders. In a series of convenience store robberies, police implemented a journey-to-crime analysis. They plotted the robberies on a map and identified the center of minimum distance (CMD). Under the assumption that the CMD was the offender's origin, police analyzed possible routes from the CMD to the crime locations and zeroed in on a street likely to be used by the suspect. Police paired this analysis with a contour map that indicated the probability of criminal apprehension based on past crime data. Combining this information prompted police to conduct a stakeout of the street, and, indeed, they were able to take the suspect into custody.

A third analytical method employed by modern police agencies is social network analysis. This type of analysis uses information about a suspect's personal connections, including family, friends, enemies, and professional associations. In Virginia, the Richmond Police Department has effectively used social network analysis for several purposes. In one case, police were searching for a homicide suspect but running out of leads. They constructed a social network of the suspect's positive relationships and contacted individuals to whom the suspect might turn for help. These individuals were told that the suspect was wanted by the police and to report any contact immediately. Within hours, police had completely shut down the suspect's social resources, and, with no safe haven, the suspect turned himself in.

ANALYTICS AND FOREIGN AID

Data and analytics are increasingly relied upon to determine allocations of aid money for foreign governments and non-profits. The Millennium Challenge Corporation (MCC), for example, incorporates a tremendous amount of data into its analyses about which countries are good candidates for development grants. The core criterion used for selection is a country's scorecard performance. Countries are evaluated on 20 indicators in three policy categories: just ruling, investment in the people, and economic freedom. To be eligible for a grant, a country must score above the median (in its income group) on at least half of the indicators. Further, the country must score above the median on the corruption indicator and above a particular threshold on either the democratic rights or civil liberties indicator.

After a country has been deemed eligible based on its scorecard, MCC performs a series of analyses to further evaluate the potential impact of an investment. MCC first conducts a constraint analysis to identify the hindrances to economic growth. This analysis informs the type and structure of the investment program developed for that country. In addition, MCC uses analytics to identify the immediate, intermediate, and ultimate impacts of an investment program. Whereas many donor organizations stop after identifying immediate impacts, MCC believes it is essential to map out the expected long-term impacts to ensure that scarce dollars are put to their best use. Finally, MCC conducts a cost-benefit analysis to determine exactly who will benefit from a proposed project and the magnitude of that benefit.

As with all research, judgments made by the researchers throughout the process can greatly influence the conclusions reached. Measuring corruption, for example, is not a straightforward task. Corruption, by definition, is illegal and (usually) hidden from plain sight. As such, it is difficult to measure. It is critical, however, that MCC base its investment decisions largely on some measure of corruption to ensure support for countries that respect the rule of law and human rights. MCC currently relies on survey data to construct its measure of corruption. Survey data, of course, are subject to a host of well-known limitations.[6] For this reason, MCC has partnered with several other organizations to form the Governance Data Alliance. Together, members are working to uncover data that can be used to determine which countries are truly committed to fighting corruption and establishing a culture of government transparency.[7]

ANALYTICS AND HEALTH CARE

The high and rising cost of health care has prompted providers, insurers, pharmaceutical companies, and the government to use data and analytics to identify cost-saving measures. Currently, health care expenditures constitute 17.9 percent of U.S. gross domestic product—more than in any other country.[8] In terms of government expenditures, health care constituted 27 percent of the 2015 federal budget. For this reason, the Centers for Medicare and Medicaid Services (CMS) implemented data-reliant programs to reduce fraud and improve the quality of outcomes for patients.

In 2012, CMS implemented several new technologies to fight fraud and abuse.[9] The Automated Provider Screening (APS) system leverages a variety of data sources, such as licensing information and criminal records, to identify ineligible providers. The Fraud Prevention System (FPS) uses predictive analytics on fee-for-service claims "to identify aberrant and suspicious billing patterns."[10] Potentially problematic claims are not reimbursed and are instead investigated by CMS. In its second year of implementing these systems, CMS estimated saving $210.7 million in fraudulent payments and took administrative action against 938 providers. As a next step, CMS is working to share its systems with state Medicaid agencies. Improved data and technology sharing across all levels of government will accelerate the effectiveness of government efforts to reduce payments made in error.

In addition to reducing fraud, CMS is implementing alternatives to its primary fee-for-service model as a cost-saving and quality-enhancing effort in the delivery of health care. Under the fee-for-service model, providers are compensated for services to patients regardless of outcomes. To create a better incentive structure, CMS is leveraging data to shift to payment models that are tied to health improvement.[11] The availability of health data from electronic health records and better sharing of clinical results have facilitated both causal and predictive analyses: researchers can determine which treatments produced positive effects in the past and which are likely to produce good results in the future. A payment model that is based on what works will benefit both the country's finances and public health.

UNCOVERING POLICY SOLUTIONS WITH DATA

The preceding examples are just a few of the many new ways in which government entities are using data and analytics to serve and protect citizens. The Department of Defense and the Department of Homeland Security are using geospatial data to develop sophisticated maritime monitoring programs to prevent terrorist activity (over 90 percent of world trade travels by sea).[12] The Small Business Administration uses analytics to inform its credit risk management strategy, and the Securities and Exchange Commission uses analytics to identify brokerage firms heading toward default. Examples of agencies relying on data and analytics to advance their goals truly abound.

In a governance context, the real value of data is the policy implications we can glean from the results of an analysis. In many instances, data have helped researchers debunk common myths or misperceptions about the true cause of an undesirable outcome. For example, many news commentators bemoan the increase in student debt levels over the past decades under the assumption that the typical student borrower is crushed by debt and hindered from achieving his or her personal and professional goals. The numbers, however, indicate that the increase in student debt is attributable to the increase in educational attainment and that these higher levels of education have led to higher lifetime earnings.[13] In consequence, policy makers should focus less on policies aimed at *all* student borrowers and more on providing a safety net for the borrowers whose bet on higher education does not yield expected returns. A targeted approach may avoid the unintended consequences of a broad-based approach, which could exacerbate rather than solve over-borrowing by students and inflating tuition by universities. Accurate analytics regarding who is suffering under the current student loan framework (and why) can help policy makers craft laws and regulations that address the real problem.

For another example of the importance of careful use of analytics, consider the emphasis placed by many researchers on race when analyzing outcomes related to health and education. In the voluminous literature that attempts to estimate the causal effect of race, this characteristic is usually treated as a unidimensional, fixed variable. In short, race is generally considered to be a single (i.e., non-aggregate) measure. From a policy perspective, however, it may be more useful to treat race as a composite variable (like socioeconomic status)—a "bundle of sticks" that includes skin color, dialect, religion, neighborhood, and region of ancestry.[14] The disaggregation of race into its constitutive components allows researchers to identify opportunities for effective policy formulation.

STRUCTURE OF THE VOLUME

The volume is divided into three parts. The first part, "Engaging the Data," covers foundational topics in statistical analysis: measurement and causal inference. In the policy and governance realm, it is essential that researchers understand the challenges associated with operationalizing concepts and quantifying causal relationships. Chapter 1 tackles measurement issues and introduces item response scaling—a means of measuring latent variables using multiple observed variables. This tool is useful for capturing variables that cannot be directly measured, such as the political awareness of citizens or the responsiveness of elected officials. To quantify these concepts, researchers can combine multiple measures to form a scale that permits a comparison of units. For example, one way to measure the political ideologies of members of Congress is to combine their roll call votes into a single scale and draw conclusions about their relative ideological positions (e.g., Senator A is the 75th most conservative senator). As the availability of data grows, so does the opportunity for researchers to combine a variety of measures to capture abstract yet policy-relevant concepts.

Chapter 2 addresses causal inference using observational data. Much of policy research is aimed at understanding causal relationships. Federal agencies often seek to determine, for example, whether a program has had its intended effects. Often these evaluations rely on observational (rather than experimental) data to identify causal effects. The overarching challenge with using observational data is disentangling correlational relationships from causal relationships. Using appropriate statistical tools, however, researchers can tease out true causal effects and, as a result, help policy makers craft more effective interventions. This chapter lays out the counterfactual reasoning framework for understanding causal inference questions and explains how tools such as matching (a form of data preprocessing) and instrumental variables can improve the accuracy of causal estimates derived from regression models.

Chapter 3 focuses on causal inference using experimental data. When identifying causal effects, experiments are considered the gold standard because of their strong internal validity. Conducting a valid experiment, however, can be quite tricky in the social sciences. This chapter explains the critical assumptions that must be met for an experiment to generate unbiased results. For example, the researcher must ensure that the treatment of any subject does not influence the behavior of another subject. But imagine an experiment in which students are treated with different curricula. If a student in the treatment group shares what she learned with a student in the control group, this assumption is violated. These and the other concepts discussed in the chapter are applied to several voter mobilization experiments, including one that uncovers the strong influence of social accountability on motivating citizens to go to the polls.

Part 2, "Emerging Data Sources and Techniques," examines methods on the cutting edge of data science. These methods allow researchers to gather and analyze vast amounts of data from the web and elsewhere, and, often, to perform analyses with a data-driven (rather than theory-driven) approach. Chapter 4 offers an introduction to the techniques associated with network analysis and then applies these techniques to the study of immigration lobbying. The authors use a network analysis to quantify the relative interest of different sectors in proposed immigration reforms and the intensity of this interest. The findings reveal that immigration lobbying comprises five key interest clusters (agricultural visas, seasonal visas, high-skill visas, family issues, and pathways to citizenship), and interest in high-skill visas generates the most lobbying activity. The analysis thus illuminates an underlying structure to the seemingly chaotic buzz of Washington lobbying.

Chapter 5 focuses on the use of geocoded data for social and policy research. In past decades, researchers have been limited to predefined units such as counties and census tracts. When analyzing these units, it is usually assumed that all individuals within a unit possess the same characteristics, an assumption that can lead to suboptimal policy recommendations. Technological advances, such as smartphones, mitigate the need to aggregate demographic characteristics to arbitrarily high levels. Researchers can use new geolocation data to better understand demographic patterns and track dynamics in these patterns. This ability has important implications for the provision of public goods by local governments. For example, the city of Boston, Massachusetts, uses a Street Bump smartphone app to collect data on road conditions. The city government uses the collected data to identify problem areas and initiate repairs. More broadly, researchers can use this dataset to study government responsiveness and the distribution of public resources among constituent groups.

Text analysis, discussed in chapter 6, is a means of translating verbal and written communications into quantitative data. One of the key benefits of relying on text for data is its availability. Nearly all aspects of policy making and governance can be captured with text. For example, legislator policy preferences are captured in speeches and press releases, and agency agendas are captured in regulations and even social media postings. The challenge with text analysis is converting this qualitative information into valid, reliable quantitative data. A text analysis must confront issues related to varying file formats, the segmentation of large files into meaningful units, the selection of features, and the stemming of words. Each of these steps requires sound judgment by the researcher to satisfactorily answer the question at hand.

Chapter 7 explores advances in machine learning, which is the use of algorithms by computers to learn from data. The applications of machine learning in the modern era are numerous: fraud detection, facial recognition, predictive pricing, hospital readmission, sales of illegal goods, voting behavior, and graduation rates. Machine learning algorithms can be classified as either supervised or unsupervised. With supervised learning, the researcher models an outcome of interest, such as whether a patient was readmitted to a hospital. With unsupervised learning, the researcher examines data with no specific outcome in mind. For example, a researcher might use a clustering algorithm to identify policy interests among a network of Washington lobbyists. Broadly speaking, machine learning methods are ideal for making sense of the vast amounts of information now available for analysis.

The final part in this volume, "Implications for Governance," discusses the policy, ethical, and governance issues raised by the public sector's heavy reliance on data and analytics. Chapter 8 focuses on data-related outcomes and processes. The chapter begins by describing the various ways in which governments, at all levels, are collecting, disseminating, and using data—these are the outcomes of the explosive availability of data. The governing structure that oversees these outcomes, however, is still in its infancy. Federal and state governments must strike a delicate balance between preserving individual data ownership and harnessing the power of data for the public good. President Barack Obama attempted to navigate these waters through the Open Government Initiative (of which open data is a big part) and the proposed Consumer Privacy Bill of Rights. The goals of guaranteeing individual privacy, increasing government transparency, and protecting the public are difficult, and yet critical, to pursue simultaneously.

Chapter 9 discusses the privacy concerns associated with the aggregation of individuals' "digital crumbs." As technology is integrated into all aspects of daily life, so is the availability of data about individuals' private lives, including their relationships, opinions, financial transactions, and location history. This chapter outlines six specific concerns associated with the rise of big data: informed consent when collecting data, the option to remain anonymous, omnipresent surveillance, preservation of individual autonomy, protection of due process, and ownership of data. These six concerns have guided policy discussions surrounding big data. Existing laws are underdeveloped and will need to be reevaluated in the coming years. Given the lack of a coherent regulatory framework, consumers must rely on technology and competition as alternative means of protecting individual privacy. Technological protection includes tags with expiration dates and encryption.

Competition on the basis of privacy policies and notices may also offer increased protection for individuals, if consumers are concerned enough to read the policies and understand their options.

Finally, chapter 10 offers concluding insights about the balance between the government's imperative to collect and protect information on the one hand and the power of the citizenry on the other. Citizens' ability to influence government depends on their having the privacy and knowledge necessary to organize effectively. The government, however, continually encroaches on average Americans' privacy and limits the information available to them through extensive surveillance and classification programs. While some measure of secrecy by the government is needed to ensure Americans' safety, a reasonable level of transparency must be maintained to preserve democratic governance.

Taken together, the chapters in this volume cover both the mechanics and the policy concerns of government analytics in the era of big data. An effective data scientist must be a master of many things: he or she must have a deep substantive knowledge of the topic under study and be able to perform an analysis, communicate the results in a compelling manner, and comply with relevant laws, regulations, and ethical boundaries. Through reading this text, we expect readers will be well on their way to becoming well-rounded social scientists.

NOTES

1. Kevin C. Desouza, *Realizing the Promise of Big Data: Implementing Big Data Projects* (Washington, DC: IBM Center for the Business of Government, 2014).

2. Frauke Kreuter, Marcus Berg, Paul Biemer, Paul Decker, Cliff Lampe, Julia Lane, Cathy O'Neil, and Abe Usher, *AAPOR Report on Big Data* (Princeton, NJ: Mathematica Policy Research, 2015).

3. Gary King, "Big Data Is Not About the Data!," http://gking.harvard.edu/files/gking/files/evbase-gs.pdf.

4. David Lazer, Ryan Kennedy, Gary King, and Alessandro Vespignani, "The Parable of Google Flu: Trap Is Big Data Analysis," *Policy Forum* 343 (2014): 1203–1205.

5. Jennifer Bachner, *Predictive Policing: Preventing Crime with Big Data and Analytics* (Washington, DC: IBM Center for the Business of Government, 2013).

6. See, for example, Robert Groves, Floyd Fowler, Mick Couper, James Lepkowski, Eleanor Singer, and Robert Tourangeau, *Survey Methodology* (Hoboken, NJ: Wiley, 2009).

7. Millennium Challenge Corporation, "Governance Data Alliance," https://www.mcc.gov/pages/activities/activity/fighting-corruption-governance-data-alliance.

8. World Bank, "Health Expenditure," http://data.worldbank.org/indicator/SH.XPD.TOTL.ZS?order=wbapi_data_value_2012+wbapi_data_value+wbapi_data_value-last&sort=desc.

9. Centers for Medicare and Medicaid Services, *Medicare and Medicaid Fraud Prevention* (Washington, DC: Department of Health and Human Services, Centers for Medicare and Medicaid Services, 2013).

10. Centers for Medicare and Medicaid Services, *Report to Congress: Fraud Prevention System—Second Implementation Year* (Washington, DC: Department of Health and Human Services, Centers for Medicare and Medicaid Services, 2014).

11. Executive Office of the President, *Big Data: Seizing Opportunities, Preserving Values* (Washington, DC: Executive Office of the President, 2014).

12. Matt Alderton, "Watching the Waters," *Trajectory* 4 (2014): 16–21.

13. Beth Akers and Matt Chingos, *Is a Student Loan Crisis on the Horizon?* (Washington, DC: Brookings Institution, 2014).

14. Maya Sen and Omar Wasow, "Race as a 'Bundle of Sticks': Designs That Estimate Effects of Seemingly Immutable Characteristics," *Annual Review of Political Science* 19 (June 2016), http://www.annualreviews.org/doi/abs/10.1146/annurev-polisci-032015-010015.

I ENGAGING THE DATA

CHAPTER ONE Measuring Political and Policy Preferences Using Item Response Scaling

Joshua D. Clinton

IN THIS CHAPTER

In this chapter, I discuss how statistical measurement models can be applied to extract meaning from a series of related measures to address important political questions with both practical and academic applications. Using a series of examples involving lawmaking in the U.S. Congress, the staffing of the federal bureaucracy, and the analysis of expert opinions, I demonstrate how a statistical measurement model can be used to provide important insights into the structure of observed data.

INTRODUCTION

It is easier than ever to acquire data on an unprecedented scale. These data are also thought to hold tremendous potential for unlocking previously hard-to-assess truths about our world. For those interested in questions related to the production and assessment of public policy, the ability to characterize current and past conditions, and the consequences and implications of various policies and events, access to data is unprecedented. Paradoxically, the amount of available data may also be paralyzing; too many measures and indicators may obscure and complicate our ability to extract the core underlying relationships because of uncertainty as to which measure—or measures—to use.

If what we are interested in is observable and measurable—for example, growth in per capita gross domestic product or the number of riders taking mass transit—then conventional statistical methods are appropriate and often easily used to characterize and analyze the observed variation. If, however, our interest lies in something less tangible—say, the extent to which a community's "happiness" is improving, the overall policy preferences of a congressional district, the level of democracy within a country, the insulation of a particular federal agency, or the effectiveness of various legislators—it may be less clear how to make the required comparisons.[1] Moreover, even if we are interested in assessing readily observable actions and outcomes, characterizing the underlying structure of the data in a principled manner may be difficult if there is a multitude of relevant measures.

As our access to data increases and our ability to measure and quantify aspects of interest improves, so too does the number of measures and comparisons that can be made. Insofar as we cannot identify a single best measure of interest, how might we make use of multiple existing measures to best assess the underlying characteristic of interest? For example, how can we identify the relative aptitude of applicants to a public policy school? Or identify which members of a legislature are most pivotal for passing a piece of legislation? Or characterize the policy preferences of bureaucrats and agencies?

Statistical measurement models are increasingly vital for empirically oriented policy analysts who find themselves confronted with an ever-increasing number of measures that they must characterize and evaluate. When correctly and appropriately applied, these models provide a principled way of analyzing multiple measures to identify and characterize the core underlying tendencies.

In this chapter, I briefly describe a statistical measurement model based on item response theory and provide some illustrative examples of how this approach can be used to characterize features relevant for public policy analysis. Entire books, chapters, and papers have been written on these models, but the goal of this chapter is to introduce the main intuition behind the models and to motivate their use by showing how they can be applied to questions that are relevant to the practice and analysis of public policy.[2] In so doing, I do not discuss the computation involved in the analysis and interpretation of the models, but there are many programs devoted to such tasks.[3]

Despite the potential of these models to use multiple measures to learn about hard-to-measure concepts, they are not magic, and there is no guarantee that they will necessarily produce the quantity that is most desired by the policy analyst. The ability of statistical measurement models to extract meaningful information from the data depends critically on the validity of the assumptions used in the statistical models, the information contained in the measures being analyzed, and the substantive information used by the analyst to construct the model. While there are great opportunities for such models to help identify trends from a host of related measures, the ability to do so is not unlimited, and the applicability of the statistical model and the meaning of the resulting estimates depend heavily on the substantive knowledge of the policy analyst performing the analysis.

In this chapter, I first describe the idea of "latent" traits, show why they are relevant for the analysis of public policy, and discuss how we might think about characterizing such traits using the analogy of administering a standardized test to assess students' aptitude. I then show how this intuition can be applied to three examples: (1) determining which senator to lobby in the 2009 Affordable Care Act debate, (2) comparing the policy preferences of career executives relative to elected officials in the United States, and (3) using experts to describe the policy preferences of the federal bureaucracy—before offering some concluding thoughts about the use of statistical measurement models for the study of public policy.

THE IMPORTANCE OF MEASURING LATENT TRAITS FOR PUBLIC POLICY

Much of what we are interested in measuring in public policy cannot be directly quantified. This is true if we are observers interested in characterizing political situations (e.g., How conservative are elected officials? How politically aware are citizens? How efficient is a particular government agency?), or if we are government officials interested in assessing conditions in the polity and the consequences of policy interventions (e.g., the "happiness" of citizens or the overall desirability of a policy reform based on several measures). Unlike quantities that can be directly and easily measured, such as the outside temperature or the number of cars using a roadway on a particular day, some concepts of interest in public policy cannot be directly measured easily. Given the rapid growth in the amount of available data, even if we lack a single clear observable measure of the quantity we care about, we sometimes have many measures that we think are related to the unobservable aspect of interest. Statistical measurement models provide us with the ability to use the measures we can observe to learn about features that are thought to be related to the measures we observe.

For example, suppose that we are working for an interest group and we want to identify which elected officials have the most moderate policy preferences. How might we use the set of votes we observe from the elected officials to make this determination? Or, alternatively, imagine you are serving in a newly elected governor's office and you are conducting a survey of supposed experts to determine the extent to which various bureaucratic agencies are more or less ideological in the policies they pursue. How should you combine the various opinions you gather when some experts are probably better than others, but it is not entirely clear which experts are better than others? Or perhaps you are the chief of staff for an elected representative and you are trying to assess the extent to which citizens are aware of various features of a recently enacted policy, or their propensity to engage in political activism. How might you use a battery of survey questions to measure political interest?

Statistical measurement models are certainly not new, and they go by a host of names depending on the particular assumptions and academic disciplines in which they are employed. Various formulations of latent variable models include structural equation modeling, item response theory, and factor analysis, and they have been used in nearly every social science discipline.[4] There are subtle differences among the various statistical measurement models, but they all share a basic underlying structure. All of the models posit that the measures we observe are related to an underlying concept, but that the precise nature of the relationship may vary across the measures with some measures being more or less related to the underlying concept.

PROVIDING SOME INTUITION FOR THE APPROACH: ASSESSING APTITUDE

To provide some intuition for statistical measurement models, suppose that you are in charge of a government agency and you have been tasked with hiring individuals who are knowledgeable and competent. Or perhaps you are running the admissions of a public policy school and you want to admit students with the greatest aptitude. Competence and aptitude are often hard to assess, and they are not something we can directly observe. We think that we can observe aspects that are related to the presence or absence of these traits in an individual, but unlike quantities such as height and weight, there is no clear measure of an individual's aptitude. As a result, we often rely on heuristics such as prior experience, letters of recommendation, and past performance to help identify which applicants possess the most aptitude.

Even with such information, there are non-trivial difficulties with assessing the competence or aptitude of an applicant. Even if an individual's experiences provide an accurate assessment of aptitude or competence, it is difficult to compare applicants because individuals have different experiences and opportunities. Because of this difficulty, we often use standardized formal examinations to provide another measure of traits that can be hard to evaluate. In fact, one of the first applications of statistical measurement models was an attempt to measure intelligence.[5] These models are still used by the Educational Testing Service to construct the SAT. While acknowledging that it can be difficult to write questions that accurately reveal aptitude or competence, thinking about the properties we would want such questions to have helps motivate the intuition behind statistical measurement models.

First, we would want to ask questions where the ability to provide the correct answer depends primarily on the trait of interest, be it competence or aptitude. For example, if aspects unrelated to a test taker's aptitude affect the probability of observing a correct response (e.g., personal background), the question will not accurately measure aptitude. The requirement that the probability of correctly answering a question depends primarily on the latent trait of interest is known as *item discrimination* in the item response framework. Questions with high item discrimination are questions for which individuals with different aptitudes will have different probabilities of providing correct answers, and questions with low item discrimination are those in which the variation in answers is unrelated to individual aptitude; a test composed entirely of questions with low item discrimination will provide little, if any, information about the actual aptitude of the test takers. Giving test takers a test about chemistry, for example, will not reveal much about their knowledge of politics. In addition to asking questions whose answers depend primarily on the aptitude or competence of test takers, we may also want to account for the possibility that the probability of observing a correct response may differ across questions and it may be unrelated to the test takers' aptitude. In the language of item response theory, questions may vary in their *item difficulty*.

To describe more precisely how we might use these concepts to measure a latent trait, let us consider the mathematical relationship between them. Recalling the motivational example, suppose that you are in charge of constructing an entrance exam to determine the students with the highest aptitude for the study of public policy, or a civil service exam designed to identify those with the most competence. In either case, you are interested in measuring the latent trait of the test takers, which we will denote as x_i. Because we cannot directly observe x_i, we want to administer a test of T items and use the responses to that test to estimate the latent trait x_i for each test taker.

For each of the T items, we observe every test taker i providing an answer on item t that can be classified in terms of a binary response [e.g., "correct" (1) vs. "incorrect" (0); "competent" (1) vs. "incompetent" (0)]. For the resulting binary outcome y_{it}, we can express the probability of observing a "correct" or "competent" (i.e., $y_{it} = 1$) response by every test taker i on every item t as[6]

$$\Pr(y_{it} = 1) = F(\alpha_t + \beta_t x_i)$$

where $F(\ )$ is a cumulative distribution function (typically either a standard normal or a logistic), x_i is the unknown aptitude of member i that we are interested in characterizing, α_t denotes the probability of providing a correct answer on question t regardless of a test taker's aptitude (item difficulty), and β_t indicates how much the probability of providing a correct answer varies depending on changes in competence (item discrimination).

If a test item is sufficiently easy and every test taker is able to provide a correct answer regardless of the test taker's actual aptitude (i.e., $y_{it} = 1$ for all individuals i on item t), α_t will be exceptionally high and $\beta_t = 0$. If so, the probability of a correct answer will be unrelated to the aptitude of the test takers—$\Pr(y_{it} = 1) = F(\alpha_t)$—and we will subsequently be unable to learn about an individual's aptitude x_i because the item is too easy. Conversely, an item may be too hard for the test takers and if everyone gets the item wrong, it will not be useful for ranking the test takers' aptitude. If so, α_t will be exceptionally low and $\beta_t = 0$. These cases are extreme examples, but they illustrate the concept of item difficulty discussed previously.

If the variation in the probability of "correct" responses ($y_{it} = 1$) is perfectly correlated with the variation in individual aptitude x_i and test takers with higher aptitudes are more likely to provide a "correct" response than test takers with lower aptitudes on the item, β_t will be very high. This is a situation with high item discrimination—and responses to item t are very useful for ranking test takers according to their aptitude x_i. The benefit of the statistical measurement model is that it allows for both possibilities to be true. Items may vary in both their difficulty (α_t) and their ability to discriminate between various levels of the latent trait (β_t), and our estimation of the latent trait x_i that uses the items can account for the characteristics of the items being used.

At this point, you may be wondering why you need a model. Why not just add up the number of correct answers to assess the aptitude of a test taker? There are several reasons why a statistical measurement model is often preferable to adding up the number of items that are correctly answered.

First, if different tests are given to different individuals—perhaps because we want to vary the test across time to prevent cheating—and we are interested in comparing scores across tests, it is important to account for the possibility that some tests may be harder than others. Adding up the number of correct answers will not account for the fact that some items may be more or less difficult, and different tests may therefore also be more or less difficult depending on the items that are asked. By determining the item difficulty and item discrimination of every item being asked in each test, the statistical measurement model allows us to calibrate responses across different tests (so long as a few conditions are satisfied). Because the model explicitly accounts for possible variation in the items being used, it is possible to make comparisons across tests.

Second, we can also use the model to learn about the structure of the responses we observe. While the discussion so far presumes that you know what the latent dimension of interest is—that is, aptitude or competence—suppose th t you thought it were possible that several latent traits might structure the pattern of responses you observe. For example, in addition to assessing aptitude, maybe you are also interested in assessing the motivation of the test takers by asking several onerous items such that the answers to the test questions might depend on both the aptitude and the motivation of the test takers. If so, we can extend the model to reflect the fact that responses depend on multiple latent traits so long as a few conditions are satisfied. Put differently, we can use statistical measurement models to learn the number of latent traits that are responsible for the observed variation and how each item relates to each of the latent traits.[7]

There are many details and nuances involved in the application of these models, but having sketched out the intuition behind such models using the analogy of constructing a test, let us now see how this tool can be used to help us better understand the practice and performance of public policy.

EXAMPLE 1: RANKING LEGISLATORS AND THE POLITICS OF THE 2009 HEALTH CARE DEBATE

Suppose it is 2009 and you are a lobbyist concerned with the upcoming debate on the Affordable Care Act. Or perhaps you are an advisor to President Barack Obama interested in enacting health care reform, or you are a member of the Office of the Whip in either the majority or minority party and you are trying to identify the impediments to health care reform. Regardless of your position in the debate, you know that passing anything in the U.S. Senate is going to require 60 votes to invoke cloture and end an attempted filibuster. But who do you need to lobby on this vote? Which senator is most likely to be the 60th most liberal senator—and thus the senator whose vote will be pivotal for invoking cloture (or not)? How similar are the policy preferences of these senators to the policy preferences of the average Democrat in the Senate?

The framework provided by the item response models discussed previously provides a principled way of answering all of these questions. What we seek is a measure of every member's policy preferences—which we can summarize in terms of their most preferred ideal point x_i. If we think of political outcomes as being described by a ruler ranging from extremely liberal outcomes to extremely conservative outcomes, the ideal point for member i can be thought of as measuring the location of every member on that scale.

While we cannot directly observe members' policy preferences (because they are a set of beliefs that exist only in their heads), we can observe the actions that they take in Congress. One activity that we can observe is roll call voting behavior on issues that come to the floor. Insofar as we think that the votes are being cast in ways that reflect the latent ideology of the members (x_i), we can extend the test-taking example from the prior section to estimate the policy preferences of the members who cast roll call votes. That is, we can treat members of Congress as test takers who take a "test" on political ideology, with the "questions" being their votes on particular legislation.

By thinking of members of Congress as test takers and the votes they cast for policy outcomes as surveys about their conservativeness, we can use the item response model presented earlier to estimate their policy preferences. Subsequently, we gain more insight into which members have the highest probability of being pivotal for invoking cloture (i.e., Who needs to be lobbied?) and how dissimilar they are from their caucus (i.e., How hard do they need to be lobbied?).

To make the connection explicit, we observe every member of the Senate i in 1 ... 100 voting either "yea" (1) or "nay" (0) on each vote t (out of T total observed votes). If we assume that members vote for policies that are closest to their ideal point, x_i—which is where Senator i is located along a liberal–conservative scale—the probability of observing a "yea" vote by member i on vote t (i.e., $y_{it} = 1$) can be expressed as

$$\Pr(y_{it} = 1) = F(\alpha_t + \beta_t x_i)$$

where the item difficulty parameter α_t denotes the probability of voting "yea" on vote t regardless of a member's ideal point, and β_t describes how much the probability of voting "yea" depends on the member's ideal point. Even though we no longer have "correct" answers as we did when applying the model to a test-taking situation, we can accomplish an analogous interpretation by defining whether conservative policy outcomes are greater than or less than 0. For example, we can define conservative policy outcomes to be associated with positive ideal points by constraining the ideal point of then Senate minority leader Mitch McConnell (R-KY) to be greater than 0. If we do so, then $\beta_t < 0$ if vote t involves a vote on a liberal proposal, which means that $\beta_t x_i < 0$ for conservative members with ideal points $x > 0$ and they will therefore have a lower probability of voting "yea" on the liberal proposal than liberal members with $x < 0$, that is, $\beta_t x_i > 0$. Similarly, votes on conservative proposals will generate votes with $\beta_t > 0$, which will flip the relative probabilities, and votes that are unrelated to ideology—such as so-called "hurrah" votes on which all members agree—will produce estimates such that $\beta_t = 0$.

Figure 1.1 presents the results from analyzing all 696 roll call votes cast in the 112th U.S. Senate that enacted the Affordable Care Act employing the model of Clinton, Jackman, and Rivers as implemented using the ideal function in the pscl package for R.[8] The resulting ideal point estimates are normalized to have a mean of 0 and a variance of 1, so the estimated policy preferences will roughly range from -2 (a point associated with the voting behavior of more liberal members) to $+2$ (a point associated with the voting behavior of more conservative members). Senators' ideal points are plotted along the bottom axis, along with the density of ideal points

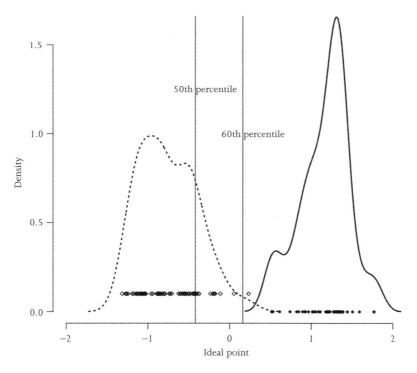

Figure 1.1. Distribution of ideal points in the 112th U.S. Senate

by party. Figure 1.1 reveals that every Democrat votes in a more liberal manner than the most moderate Republican, and whereas Democrats are fairly evenly spread out, between -1.25 and -0.5 on the liberal side of the spectrum, most Republicans are located in the neighborhood of 1.25. The vertical lines denote the median senator (i.e., the 50th percentile), as well as the location of the 60th percentile, which is the ideal point of the senator needed to overcome a conservative filibuster. Ending debate in the U.S. Senate in order to vote on the policy requires the support of at least 60 senators; consequently, those located near the right-most vertical line are critical for enacting policy.

If you are interested in figuring out who should be lobbied to ensure that cloture is invoked and a filibuster does not occur, you need to determine which senators are most likely to be critical for that vote; after all, you do not want to spend your time lobbying members who will almost surely oppose (or support) the cloture vote. Figure 1.2 uses the ideal points summarized in figure 1.1 to identify the members who are most likely to be the 60th most liberal member responsible for invoking cloture by plotting the estimated rank of each senator along with the 95 percent regions of highest (posterior) probability. These are the members whose votes are required to end debate in the Senate and proceed to a vote.

An absolutely critical aspect of statistical analysis is the ability to quantify our uncertainty about a measured quantity. The National Institute of Standards and Technology is quite explicit about the need to quantify our uncertainty, noting that "a measurement result is complete only when accompanied by a quantitative statement of its uncertainty. The uncertainty is required in order to decide if the result is adequate for its intended purpose and to ascertain if it is consistent with other similar results." A benefit of the statistical measurement model we present is that it is possible to explore how certain we are of our estimates.

Figure 1.2 reveals, for example, that Senator Bill Nelson (D-FL) is the senator whose ideal point is closest to the 60th percentile in the U.S. Senate. There is, however, a considerable amount of uncertainty in this assessment: we cannot be sure that he isn't actually either the 55th or the 65th most liberal. Therefore, there is likely a need to target multiple members to be sure that the pivotal senator is lobbied. While we can be confident that Senator Amy Klobuchar (D-MN) is more liberal than the 60th most liberal senator and that Senator Maria Cantwell (D-WA) is more conservative than the 60th most liberal, there are a range of senators who might plausibly be the 60th most liberal senator. Any senator whose range of possible ranks includes 60 is a possible candidate for being pivotal. Using this

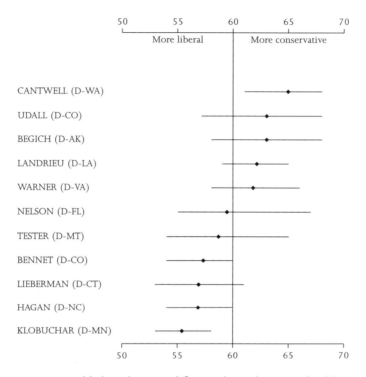

Figure 1.2. Senators most likely to be critical for invoking cloture on health care

same framework, we could easily examine other political incidents—for example, the impeachment trial of President Bill Clinton—or the preferences of other political elites such as U.S. Supreme Court justices.[9] In addition, we can use these tools to assess important areas of inquiry such as how well elected officials reflect the views of their constituents, how much political polarization exists among elected elites, and how policy preferences affect lawmaking behavior.[10]

EXAMPLE 2: ANALYZING THE OPINION OF THE PUBLIC AND ELITES: MEASURING THE POLITICAL PREFERENCES OF CAREER EXECUTIVES IN THE U.S. BUREAUCRACY

To illustrate the model more concretely, suppose that you are a member of the Executive Office of the President and you are trying to assess the political beliefs of career bureaucrats and how those beliefs compare to the beliefs of members of Congress. Bureaucrats may vary greatly in their experience in politics and their interactions with political elites in accordance with their position in the bureaucracy.

How to best make comparisons between bureaucrats and between bureaucrats and members of Congress, therefore, is not immediately obvious.

One possibility would be to survey bureaucrats, possibly using questions common to many surveys given to the general public.[11] That is, ask them a variant of the following: "In general, would you describe your political views as (1) 'very conservative,' (2) 'conservative,' (3) 'somewhat conservative,' (4) 'moderate,' (5) 'somewhat liberal,' (6) 'liberal,' (7) 'very liberal,' or (8) 'don't know.'" While this question may be acceptable for the general public, you may worry about the usefulness of such a question when applied to individuals who are more closely attuned to politics than the general public. What exactly does "very conservative" mean for an employee in the Department of Homeland Security, and does that meaning differ for an employee in the Department of Agriculture? Are bureaucrats thinking of the same policy areas when responding to this broadly worded question? Moreover, what is the policy difference between "very conservative" and "somewhat conservative" (or "very liberal" and "somewhat liberal")? Are these differences meaningful across individuals? Making inferences using responses to this question requires us to assume that these aspects are equivalent, but we do not know for certain whether this is true.[12]

A further limitation is that even if bureaucrats have a shared conception of ideology and what it means to be "very" or "weak," how should we compare the survey results to the ideology of members of Congress? How do the political views of a bureaucrat who thinks of himself as "liberal" compare to those of President Obama? Or Congresswoman Nancy Pelosi? While some have tried to ask members of Congress about their ideology—see, for example, the Political Courage Test administered by Project Vote Smart—it is unclear how the responses of legislators compare to generic political questions that are asked of bureaucrats.[13]

Given the important role that federal bureaucrats play in the implementation of public policy, some scholars have attempted to locate the policy preferences of career bureaucrats relative to those of elected officials by asking bureaucrats how they would have voted on 14 issues that were considered in the previous Congress.[14] By collecting measures on how bureaucrats would have voted on these issues, we can better relate the political ideologies of these two groups and avoid the ambiguities of interpreting what it means to indicate that a respondent is "conservative." For example, bureaucrats were asked, "We are also interested to know your personal opinion about several key votes in Congress in the last few years. Specifically, would you have supported the following measures? A bill to permanently reduce estate taxes: (1) 'yes,' (2) 'no,' or (3) 'not sure.' " Table 1.1 presents the full set of questions that were asked in the *Survey on the Future of Government Service*.

Even if we ask career executives these questions, how should we analyze the resulting responses? One possibility would be to simply add the responses together to create a scale for the number of "liberal" (or "conservative") responses. While this may at first seem like the obvious solution, there are several complications that quickly emerge. First, it may not be obvious which outcomes are "liberal." Consider, for example, how bureaucrats might respond when asked their opinions on "a bill to ensure access to federal courts for individuals who challenge government use of eminent domain to take their property." Which is the liberal outcome? Second, even if it were possible to identify the liberal and conservative responses associated with each question, is ideology additive? That is, is a person who responds with the liberal outcome on seven items necessarily seven times more liberal than a person who responds with the liberal outcome only once?

We can use the statistical measurement model presented earlier to perform this task. Recall that the basic model assumes that

$$\Pr(y_{it} = 1) = F(\alpha_t + \beta_t x_i)$$

where, in this case, y_{it} indicates that bureaucrat i is in agreement with item t, x_i indicates bureaucrat i's most preferred policy outcome, α_t measures the probability that bureaucrats support the policy being asked about in item t regardless of their policy preferences, and β_t reflects the extent to which the support for the policy varies depending on their most preferred policy. Note that unlike the case of trying to construct an additive scale based on the number of "correct" answers, when we use a statistical measurement model, we do not need to determine which answers are "liberal" or "conservative" beforehand. Given the model for a "yes" response, the model will use the observed responses to find the variation that best differentiates between the responses. Both "yes" and "no" answers can be associated with conservative views because the model can adjust the sign for α_t and β_t to ensure that positive values of x are associated with conservative views. (To be clear, this also illustrates a potential issue with any model. We assume that the variation that we recover is based on ideological differences, but nothing ensures that this is the case. An important job of the analyst is to think carefully about what the model is actually estimating when interpreting the results.)

An important limitation of the statistical measurement model is that because we are estimating everything—after all, the only data we are using are data on

Table 1.1. Questions asked of executive officials in the U.S. federal bureaucracy in *Survey on the Future of Government Service*

In addition to the general political background of elected officials, we are also interested to know your personal opinion about several key votes in Congress in the last few years. Specifically, would you have supported the following measures?

	Yes	No	Not sure
A bill to authorize electronic surveillance of suspected terrorists without obtaining court approval (502/HR5825)			
A bill to ensure access to federal courts for individuals who challenge government use of eminent domain to take their property (511/HR4772)			
Efforts to amend the Constitution to prohibit desecration of the U.S. flag (189/SJRes12)			
A bill to require photo identification and proof of citizenship for voters in a federal election (459/HR4844)			
A bill to create federal grants to support sex education programs (214/S403)			
A bill to halt deployment of space-based missile defense systems (142/HR5122)			
A bill to increase the minimum wage to $7.25 per hour in two years (179/S2766)			
A bill to prohibit funds for contracts with companies that incorporate offshore to avoid U.S. taxes (275/HR5576)			
A measure to amend the Constitution to define marriage as the union of a man and a woman (378/HJRes88)			
A bill to permit federal funds for embryonic-stem-cell research (206/HR810)			
Confirmation of Samuel Alito as an associate justice on the Supreme Court (1/.)			
A bill to make it a federal crime to take a minor across state lines to obtain an abortion without parental notification or consent (216/S403)			
A bill to establish English as the national language and require immigrants to pass proficiency tests (131/S2611)			
A bill to permanently reduce estate taxes (315/HR5638)			

the set of responses—the meaning of the scale that we recover can sometimes be difficult to interpret. The model is able to extract the characteristic that is most responsible for the variation that we observe and it is able to rank-order individuals according to that characteristic, but it is up to the analyst to interpret the meaning and importance of the characteristics that are estimated. While in this case we think it is reasonable to assume that bureaucrats' answers are largely structured by their policy preferences, nothing in the model technically ensures that we can equate x with policy preferences, since the model is only interested in finding the latent trait that best differentiates between the responses of different individuals. Relatedly, the scale that is recovered does not have any real meaning apart from measuring the extent to which individuals are differentiated. While we can be certain that a policy preference of 1 differs from a policy preference of -1, what policies someone with a policy preference of 1 would support is unclear. (In principle, we can use the statistical model to evaluate the likelihood of supporting various policy outcomes given a set of item parameters to help interpret the meaning of the scale, or we can use the estimates from prominent political leaders to help define what differences in the estimates imply about the nature of political conflict.)

If we treat the responses of 1,889 bureaucrats who answered at least 2 of the 14 questions in the survey as equal to the congressional role call votes cast by members of the U.S. House and Senate, we get the estimates plotted in figure 1.3. For each member of the U.S. House (top), U.S. Senate (middle), or career executive in the federal bureaucracy (bottom), we can use the statistical measurement model to estimate not only their most preferred policy position (solid circle) on a scale that ranges from very liberal (-3) to very conservative (3) but also how certain we are about each characterization (the gray horizontal line around each point).[15]

Substantively, we can conclude several things. First, most bureaucrats are estimated to have policy preferences located near 0 based on the responses they provide, but the preferences of elected officials are typically considerably more extreme: note the absence of any ideal points in either the House or the Senate near 0. While there are certainly some bureaucrats who are as ideologically extreme as members of Congress, most bureaucrats express views on policy that place them between the two parties in Congress regardless of whether we consider the House or the Senate. Second, while career bureaucrats appear to have more centrist policy views in general, we are far less certain about the preferences of bureaucrats than we are about those of members of Congress. This is largely because bureaucrats are far more likely to answer that they "don't know" what they think about a particular policy than members of Congress

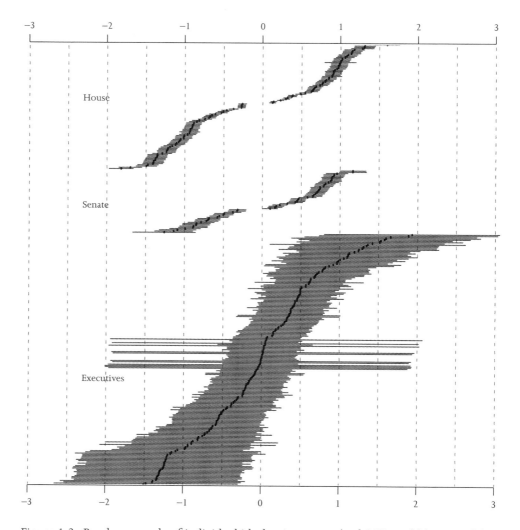

Figure 1.3. Random sample of individual ideal point means (and 95% credible intervals)

are to miss a vote. For example, for a few bureaucrats, we are entirely uncertain as to what their most preferred policy is; it could be anything from −2 to 2 because they answered so few questions.

Besides simply comparing how the policy views of bureaucrats compare to those of elected officials, there are a host of interesting questions and analyses that the ability to measure bureaucrats' policy preferences allows, such as those related to congressional oversight, bureaucratic performance, and other issues that are centrally related to policy making and government activity.[16] Approaches based on similar ideas can also be used to assess critical issues related to the separation of powers and representation.[17]

EXAMPLE 3: ACCOUNTING FOR "EXPERTISE": ANALYZING EXPERT OPINION

Because the statistical measurement model allows for some items to be more or less related to the underlying concept of interest—for example, some votes may be more ideological than others and some test questions may be more related to aptitude than others—the model can also be used to combine and evaluate the available information. Suppose, for example, that you are involved in a project that requires collecting the opinions of several policy experts and you must decide how to use and analyze the experts' opinions. It is certainly likely that even if the experts all agree on what is being measured, there are still likely to be differences in the ratings that they provide. If so, you are confronted with the following critical question: Do the differences in expert ratings reflect genuine differences in the outcome of interest, or are the differences due to differences in the quality (or taste) of the experts themselves? In other words, does expert disagreement reflect differences in the quality of raters, or does it primarily reflect uncertainty about what is being rated?

To illustrate how expert responses can be analyzed using a statistical measurement model to account for the consequences of differences between raters, consider an example from Clinton and Lewis.[18] Clinton and Lewis were interested in characterizing the ideological leanings of government agencies using the knowledge of 37 experts working in universities, think tanks, and the media. Each expert was presented with the following: "Please see below a list of United States government agencies that were in existence between 1988 and 2005. I am interested to know which of these agencies have policy views due to law, practice, culture, or tradition that can be characterized as liberal or conservative. Please place a check mark (✓) in one of the boxes next to each agency—(1) 'slant liberal,' (2) 'neither consistently,' (3) 'slant conservative,' or (4) 'don't know.'" Twenty-six experts responded to the inquiry, and the goal was to use the experts' ratings of the 82 departments and agencies in existence between 1988 and 2005 to construct an estimate of agency ideology while allowing for the possibility that some experts may provide more useful determinations than others.

Whereas the focus of example 1 was on estimating senators' ideal points—the xs in the statistical model—the focus here is on the estimates related to how well the rater's determination corresponds to the relationship suggested by the other raters. While the actual statistical model is slightly different because the outcome is an ordered variable with three categories—"slant liberal," "neither consistently," and "slant conservative"—the intuition is the same as the binary model discussed earlier.[19]

With several ratings and the assumption that a majority of the raters are able to correctly identify the variation of interest, the same model that is used to locate legislators can also be used to combine expert ratings and effectively "rate the raters."[20] Building on the intuition of example 1, instead of thinking about senators casting votes and using the votes that are cast to make inferences about the senators, we can think about the experts' views as the "votes" that are being voted upon by the objects we are interested in evaluating. That is, we can think of the agency being rated by the experts as the elite official in the earlier examples indexed by i and the rating of a particular expert t as the observed vote. In terms of the measurement model,

$$\Pr(y_{it} = \text{slants liberal}) = F(\alpha_t + \beta_t x_i)$$

where, in this example, each expert t is equivalent to a test question and we are interested in learning about the agency's ideology x_i from these "test questions" while accounting for the fact that raters may differ in their standards and quality even if they are all responding to the same latent input.

As before, the model produces a series of estimates (and estimates about how certain we are about those estimates for each agency). Table 1.2 reports some of those estimates arranged from most liberal (negative) to most conservative (positive). Some agencies are clearly thought to be more liberal in their policy mandate than others—for example, the Peace Corps is unambiguously more liberal than the Department of Defense. Other agencies, such as the Department of Transportation and the National Aeronautics and Space Administration, are thought to be non-ideological.

In this case, however, we are also likely interested in assessing the performance of the individual experts whose insights were used to construct the rating. To do so, we can compare the probability that each expert rates an agency as "slants liberal," "neither consistently," or "slants conservative" for every possible value of agency ideology relative to the rating given by other experts. This allows us to see how the standards of different experts compare to the average rating and whether some experts behave differently from the others. So-called characteristic curves describe

Table 1.2. Expert ratings of average agency policy preferences, 1988–2005

Agency	Mean	2.5% CI	97.5% CI
Peace Corps	−1.72	−2.49	−1.02
Consumer Product Safety Commission	−1.69	−2.42	−0.99
Equal Employment Opportunity Commission	−1.58	−2.28	−0.97
Occupational Safety and Health Review Commission	−1.52	−2.25	−0.82
Department of Labor	−1.43	−2.03	−0.81
Department of Housing and Urban Development	−1.33	−1.93	−0.80
Department of Health and Human Services	−1.32	−1.91	−0.78
Department of Education	−1.22	−1.78	−0.75
Environmental Protection Agency	−1.21	−1.74	−0.72
National Foundation on the Arts and the Humanities	−1.00	−1.52	−0.54
Social Security Administration	−0.45	−0.78	−0.10
National Labor Relations Board	−0.27	−0.58	0.05
Department of State	−0.27	−0.58	0.04
National Aeronautics and Space Administration	−0.07	−0.38	0.24
Federal Election Commission	0.05	−0.27	0.35
Department of Transportation	0.07	−0.23	0.36
Federal Emergency Management Agency	0.08	−0.19	0.37
Federal Trade Commission	0.12	−0.19	0.47
Department of Agriculture	0.16	−0.16	0.50
Department of Veterans Affairs	0.23	−0.12	0.55
Federal Communications Commission	0.32	0.02	0.62
Department of Energy	0.35	0.01	0.68
Department of Justice	0.37	0.05	0.67
Trade and Development Agency	0.40	−0.34	1.18
Department of the Interior	0.47	0.14	0.81
Securities and Exchange Commission	0.73	0.38	1.11
Department of Homeland Security	0.88	0.51	1.26
Department of the Treasury	1.07	0.68	1.48
Small Business Administration	1.17	0.72	1.67
Department of Commerce	1.25	0.80	1.75
National Security Council	1.40	0.91	1.87
Office of National Drug Control Policy	1.77	1.04	2.47
Department of Defense	2.21	1.49	3.06

Notes: Agencies are ordered from most liberal to most conservative according to the (posterior) mean estimate. The 95% HPD (highest posterior density) interval is also reported. Estimates reflect the ratings of 26 experts.

the probability that a rater will place an agency with a given true ideology into each of the possible classifications. Note that similar analyses can be performed in any of the previous examples—we can see how well each item/vote/question relates the latent quantity being studied to the probability of observing a positive response (e.g., a "correct" vote, a "yea" vote, or a "liberal" survey response).

Figure 1.4 plots the characteristic curves of four selected experts. As we can see, there is significant variation across the experts in terms of their scoring of agency ideology. The x-axis describes the ideology of a true agency, and the y-axis describes the probability of that expert providing each of the three possible rankings (which must sum to 1 for a selected agency ideology). For example, consider the rankings of expert 22. If the agency's true ideology is −1, the expert has roughly a 95 percent chance of rating the agency as "slants liberal," roughly a 5 percent chance of rating the agency as "neither consistently" liberal nor conservative, and a fraction of a percentage of rating the agency as "slants conservative." However, if the agency's true ideology is 0, then the expert is most likely to rate the agency as "neither consistently" (roughly a 40 percent chance), and she is equally less likely to rate the agency as either "slants liberal" or "slants conservative" (30 percent chance of each).

Expert 12's rankings are very similar to those of expert 22, but expert 12 is always more likely to choose either "slants liberal" or "slants conservative" than "neither consistently"; even if the true agency ideology is 0, "neither consistently" is never the most probable ranking for this expert. In contrast to experts 12 and 22, expert 6 is most likely to respond "neither consistently" for every agency whose true ideology is less than 1. Finally, expert 19 is most likely to give a rating of "slants conservative" regardless of the agency ideology; her ranking is completely unresponsive to the true agency ideology.

Collectively, given the set of rankings we receive, the views of expert 19 stand apart from the others in that the ratings of expert 19 appear to have no relationship to the quantity we are interested in. Not only is there no systematic variation in the rankings she reports, but there is also no relationship between the ideology of an agency in the views of the other experts and expert 19's rankings. In contrast, for the other three experts, as the true ideology of the agency increases, so too does the probability of observing a "slants conservative" response.

Thus, the statistical measurement model provides one way to aggregate the opinions of experts in a way that allows us to determine if some experts are more informative than others. In hindsight, for example, we can see that expert 22's

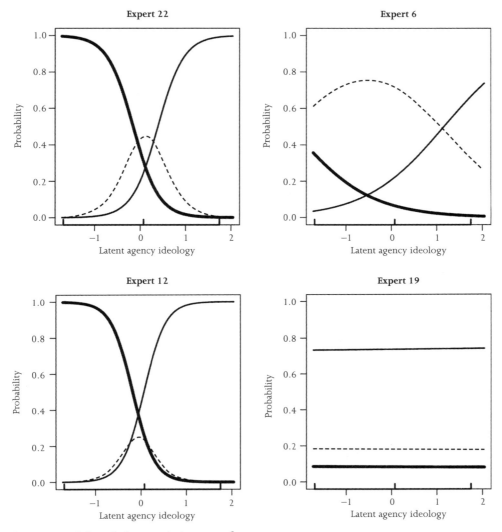

Figure 1.4. Selected characteristic curves for experts

Note: The thick solid line denotes the probability of the expert designating an agency with the given policy preference as "slants liberal," the dashed line denotes the probability of the expert indicating "neither," and the thin solid line denotes the probability of a "slants conservative" rating.

determinations are far more informative than those of expert 19 (or even expert 6) in terms of providing rankings that vary in ways that reflect the true ideology of agencies. This is important because if we are interested in using the ratings to assess agency ideology, we may wish to account for the differential ability of experts.

To be clear, we can only infer what agency ideology is likely to be based on the underlying pattern that best explains the variation we observe in the ratings themselves. As a result, if most of the ratings themselves are completely unrelated to the concept we are interested in the model, we will not be able to magically recover what we are interested in. The statistical model is aimed at extracting a parsimonious structure from the observed data, but if the observed data are not meaningful, then so too will be the estimates that are extracted from the model. Put differently, while the model provides an ability to determine which experts may be better positioned than others, this assessment is based on an evaluation of how well the experts' ratings compare to the underlying structure based on the collective responses—not some objective criteria. As a result, if most of the ratings are ill informed or even mistaken, the statistical model will be unable to identify the few experts who have it right. If, however, most of the experts are able to get it right but some may be better than others, then the model can identify which experts are best able to characterize the variation.

CONCLUSION

The availability of data has had a tremendous impact on both the study and the practice of public policy. Individuals interested in characterizing outcomes or the circumstances surrounding the adoption, implementation, and alteration of public policies now frequently have a large number of observable features that can be used to reach data-driven conclusions and assessments. Despite the availability of data, however, it is often still the case that either we have multiple measures of the feature of interest and it is unclear as to which measure is unambiguously "best," or else we have multiple measures that are related to the concept we are interested in but we lack a direct measure of that concept.

In either of these circumstances, a statistical measurement model can be useful for analyzing the structure of the observed data and extracting the core tendencies. Moreover, the model is suitably flexible so that the same underlying model can be readily applied to a variety of different situations; the examples discussed in this chapter, for example, show how it can help in analyzing questions on an exam, a series of elite decisions, an opinion survey, and the ratings provided by experts. While there are many details involved in the implementation of statistical measurement models that the chapter omits, hopefully you get a sense of what such models can offer to those interested in analyzing data relevant for public policy.

That said, it is important to emphasize that while statistical measurement models are powerful in terms of being able to provide insights that may otherwise be either elusive or unwieldy, the results are only as good as the assumptions of the statistical measurement model. The assumptions made by the model are certainly less stringent than those that are implied by attempts to aggregate measures by treating every item as equally informative and taking an average or a sum, but we can only learn about traits that are already in the data structure. Relatedly, while statistical measurement models are able to generate estimates of the latent trait (labeled x in the preceding examples), they do not reveal what the actual meaning of x is. It is incumbent on the analyst to interpret what x means substantively. For example, does the x estimated from elite behavior in example 1 reflect the personal policy preferences of the senator, or does it reflect other factors (e.g., the policy preferences of voters)? Does the x being measured by responses to a series of test items measure just aptitude, or does it also reflect educational opportunities (or aptitude given the educational opportunities of the test taker)? Using a statistical measurement model is only the first step in thinking through what the results do or do not reveal. The critical issues related to the interpretation of what is found are issues that cannot be "solved" statistically.

If careful attention is given to what the estimated parameters actually mean, statistical measurement models can provide a powerful tool to those who are interested in analyzing the wealth of data that now often surrounds issues involving public policy. When appropriately estimated and interpreted, these models provide the ability to summarize underlying features of the data and to characterize aspects that are important but unobserved to make novel conclusions and characterizations about the policy-making process and its outcomes.

NOTES

1. For examples, see Matt S. Levendusky, Jeremy C. Pope, and Simon Jackman, "Measuring District-Level Partisanship with Implications for the Analysis of U.S. Elections," *Journal of Politics* 70, no. 3 (2008): 736–753; Dan Pemstein, Stephen Meserve, and James Melton, "Democratic Compromise: A Latent Variable Analysis of Ten Measures of Regime Type," *Political Analysis* 18, no. 4 (2010): 426–449; Jennifer L. Selin, "What Makes an Agency Independent?," *American Journal of Political Science* 59, no. 4 (2015): 971–987; and Craig Volden and Alan E. Wiseman, *Legislative Effectiveness in the United States Congress: The Lawmakers* (New York: Cambridge University Press, 2014).

2. See, for example, Valen E. Johnson and James H. Albert, *Ordinal Data Modeling* (New York: Springer, 2000); Frank B. Baker and Seock-Ho Kim, *Item Response Theory: Parameter Estimation Techniques*, 2nd ed. (Boca Raton, FL: CRC Press, 2004); Andrew Gelman and Jennifer Hill, *Data Analysis Using Regression and Multilevel/Hierarchical Models* (New York: Cambridge University Press, 2006); Simon Jackman, "Measurement," in *The Oxford Handbook of Political Methodology*, ed. Janet M. Box-Steffensmeier, Henry

E. Brady, and David Collier (New York: Oxford University Press, 2008), 119–151; and Simon Jackman, *Bayesian Analysis for the Social Sciences* (New York: Wiley, 2009).

3. The models in this chapter were implemented in R using either pscl or MCMCpack assuming a mean of 0 and a variance of 1. pscl developed by Simon Jackman, "Classes and Methods for R Developed in the Political Science Computational Laboratory, Stanford University," version 1.4.6; and MCMCpack developed by Andrew D. Martin, Kevin M. Quinn, and Jong Hee Park, "MCMCpack: Markov Chain Monte Carlo in R," *Journal of Statistical Software* 42, no. 9 (2011): 1–21.

4. For structural equation modeling, see Kenneth A. Bollen, *Structural Equations and Latent Variables* (New York: Wiley, 1989). For item response theory, see Baker and Kim, *Item Response Theory*. For factor analysis, see Harry H. Harman, *Modern Factor Analysis*, 3rd ed. (Chicago: University of Chicago Press, 1976).

5. Charles Spearman, "'General Intelligence,' Objectively Determined and Measured," *American Journal of Psychology* 15, no. 2 (1904): 201–292.

6. The model has been generalized to allow for continuous and ordered responses as well. See, for example, Kevin M. Quinn, "Bayesian Factor Analysis for Mixed Ordinal and Continuous Responses," *Political Analysis* 12, no. 4 (2004): 338–353.

7. This is similar to exploratory factor analysis.

8. Joshua D. Clinton, Simon Jackman, and Doug Rivers, "The Statistical Analysis of Roll Call Voting: A Unified Approach," *American Political Science Review* 98, no. 2 (2004): 355–370.

9. See, for example, Anthony M. Bertelli and Christian R. Grose, "The Spatial Model and the Senate Trial of President Clinton," *American Politics Research* 34, no. 4 (2006): 535–559; and Andrew D. Martin and Kevin M. Quinn, "Dynamic Ideal Point Estimation via Markov Chain Monte Carlo for the U.S. Supreme Court, 1953–1999," *Political Analysis* 10, no. 2 (2002): 134–153.

10. For investigations into these questions, see Stephen Jessee, "Spatial Voting in the 2008 Presidential Election," *American Political Science Review* 103, no. 1 (2009): 59–81; Joseph Bafumi and Michael C. Herron, "Leapfrog Representation and Extremism: A Study of American Voters and Their Members of Congress," *American Political Science Review* 104, no. 3 (2010): 519–542; Nolan McCarty, Keith T. Poole, and Howard Rosenthal, *Polarized America: The Dance of Ideology and Unequal Riches* (Cambridge, MA: MIT Press, 2006); Keith Poole and Howard Rosenthal, *Ideology and Congress* (New Brunswick, NJ: Transaction, 2007); and Gregory J. Wawro and Eric Schickler, *Filibuster: Obstruction and Lawmaking in the U.S. Senate* (Princeton, NJ: Princeton University Press, 2007).

11. For surveys of bureaucrats, see Joel D. Aberbach and Bert A. Rockman, *In the Web of Politics* (Washington, DC: Brookings Institution, 2000); and Robert Maranto and Karen M. Hult, "Right Turn? Political Ideology in the Higher Civil Service, 1987–1994," *American Review of Public Administration* 34, no. 2 (2004): 199–222.

12. Henry E. Brady, "The Perils of Survey Research: Inter-Personally Incomparable Responses," *Political Methodology* 11, no. 3 (1985): 269–291.

13. For examples, see Stephen Ansolabehere, James M. Snyder Jr., and Charles Stewart III, "Candidate Positioning in U.S. House Elections," *American Journal of Political Science* 45, no. 1 (2001): 136–159; Stephen Ansolabehere, James M. Snyder Jr., and Charles Stewart III, "The Effects of Party and Preferences on Congressional Roll-Call Voting," *Legislative Studies Quarterly* 26, no. 4 (2001): 533–572; and Boris Shor and Nolan McCarty, "The Ideological Mapping of American Legislatures," *American Political Science Review* 105, no. 3 (2001): 530–551.

14. Joshua D. Clinton, Anthony Bertelli, Christian Grose, David E. Lewis, and David C. Nixon, "Separated Powers in the United States: The Ideology of Agencies, Presidents and Congress," *American Journal of Political Science* 56, no. 2 (2012): 341–354.

15. Because a Bayesian methodology is used, what is graphed is actually the posterior mean for each bureaucrat as well as the region of highest posterior density. See Jackman, *Bayesian Analysis for the Social Sciences*, for example, for more discussion on the use and interpretation of Bayesian statistics.

16. See, for example, Clinton et al., "Separated Powers in the United States"; and Anthony M. Bertelli and Christian R. Grose, "Secretaries of Pork? A New Theory of Distributive Politics," *Journal of Politics* 71, no. 3 (2009): 926–945.

17. For example, Michael A. Bailey and Forrest Maltzman, *The Constrained Court: Law, Politics, and the Decisions Justices Make* (Princeton, NJ: Princeton University Press, 2011). See also Bafumi and Herron, "Leapfrog Representation and Extremism."

18. Joshua D. Clinton and David E. Lewis, "Expert Opinion, Agency Characteristics, and Agency Preferences," *Political Analysis* 16, no. 1 (2008): 3–20.

19. Quinn, "Bayesian Factor Analysis."

20. For work evaluating movie critics, see, for example, Michael Peress and Arthur Spirling, "Scaling the Critics: Uncovering the Latent Dimensions of Movie Criticism with an Item Response Approach," *Journal of the American Statistical Association* 105, no. 489 (2010): 71–83. For work identifying notable legislation, see, for example, Joshua D. Clinton and John S. Lapinski, "Measuring Legislative Accomplishment, 1877–1994," *American Journal of Political Science* 50, no. 1 (2006): 232–249.

CHAPTER TWO Causal Inference with Observational Data

Justin Esarey

IN THIS CHAPTER

Much of our interest in studying the world stems from the desire to change that world through political and technological intervention. If we wish to change social outcomes, we must understand how these changes are precipitated by factors under our control. But a central aphorism of social science is that correlation is not necessarily causation: when we observe that two things are associated, it does not logically imply that changes in one of them cause changes in the other. There are many alternative explanations for an observed relationship that must be ruled out before causality can be inferred. Experimental methods (covered elsewhere in this volume) allow us to rule out many of these alternatives via random assignment of the treatment and strict control of other factors in the environment. The subject of this chapter, and in large measure the subject of most research into quantitative analysis and research design, is what we can do to rule out these alternatives when we cannot conduct an experiment.

WHAT IS "CAUSAL INFERENCE"?

As Sekhon[1] notes in his essay on causal inference, every student of statistics quickly learns the aphorism that "correlation is not causation." Yet a great deal of research in the social sciences is aimed precisely at inferring causal relationships from empirical observation. Through clever research design and careful statistical modeling, we try to identify the hidden causal relationships embedded in the correlations that we can see. In this sense, a great deal of the work of policy scholars and those in allied fields (political science, economics, sociology, etc.) could be considered part of a grand tradition in causal inference with many approaches and variations.

At present, *causal inference* tends to have a much more specific meaning. The term is now strongly linked to what is referred to[2] as the "credibility revolution" in empirical social science, a movement designed to improve the robustness and overall believability of quantitative research. As Angrist and Pischke describe, the sensitivity of non-experimental findings to model assumptions and disagreement between non-experimental studies and experimental studies of the same phenomena led many social scientists to re-examine their methodologies with an eye toward producing more robust inferences from non-experimental data.

The result of this "credibility revolution" in social science is a renewed interest in particular epistemological frameworks, research designs, and statistical models that are aimed at producing reliable causal inferences. The process begins with the following question: What effect does imposing some treatment T have on an outcome of interest y? A policy scholar answering the question using a *causal inference* approach must first specify the conditions required to infer what changes in y are caused by T. These conditions are usually derived from a definition of causality and associated epistemological framework, such as those proposed by Rubin[3] or Pearl.[4] The person moves on to propose a research design and analytical strategy under which the necessary conditions for causal inference can be met; this proposal is collectively referred to as an *identification strategy*.[5] Generally speaking, the strategy is to mimic the conditions of an ideal experiment to maximize the validity of a causal inference. Where possible, the strategies explicitly include experimental techniques such as random assignment to a treatment and strict control over external influences. When this is not possible, the strategies attempt to reconstruct the features of an ideal experiment by using instrumental variables, matching procedures, or other strategies to imitate experimental conditions.

While causal inference is of interest to all social scientists, it has a special value for policy-oriented academics and practitioners. Policy work is fundamentally about using targeted interventions to produce better social and economic outcomes. This goal leads naturally to an interest in determining and measuring how much these interventions actually change outcomes. The driving question of policy research is often "How much should I expect a new program or policy to change an outcome of interest?"[6] The causal inference framework is designed to answer just this sort of question.

In this chapter, I explain the counterfactual reasoning framework that underlies causal inference according to the Rubin causal model and link this framework to the known advantages of experiments for causal inference. I describe three common procedures for causal inference in observational (viz., non-experimental) data: matching methods, regression models with controls, and instrumental variables models. The goal of the chapter is to compile and summarize some of the basic ideas of causal inference as they are presented in a variety of sources and to relate these ideas to the problems of policy analysis.[7]

Throughout my exposition, I tie the discussion of causal inference to a policy-relevant question: How much does a high school education increase income for those who receive it? This question is interesting from the perspective of causal inference because income and education are difficult to disentangle. Although education increases one's own income, many confounding factors (such as innate ability) probably cause both.[8] Using U.S. Census data originally collected by Angrist and Krueger,[9] I show how matching, regression, and instrumental variables approaches can be used to recover the causal effect of a high school education on (log) weekly wage.

COUNTERFACTUAL REASONING AND AVERAGE TREATMENT EFFECTS

The Rubin causal model[10] is built on the idea of *counterfactual* reasoning: the causal effect of a treatment T is equivalent to the difference between what an outcome y would be in the presence of T compared to the outcome in its absence. Under some conditions, we can obtain a reliable estimate of this effect with empirical observation.

The Rubin Causal Model

For a particular individual observation i, the causal effect of T on y is[11]

$$y_i(T=1,X) - y_i(T=0,X) \tag{1}$$

where X includes any influences on y other than the treatment T. This equation says that the causal effect of a treatment on some unit is the difference between what we observe for that unit when the treatment is applied and what we observe for that same unit when the treatment is *not* applied.

The fundamental problem of causal inference tells us that we can never observe this causal effect directly because we cannot simultaneously observe the same unit with and without the treatment condition.[12] Even if we observe the same unit at different times, influences on the unit that are included in X (including its past history with the treatment condition) have changed in the interval between the two observations; it is not a comparison of identical units.

We may, however, be able to observe a collection of units that are, on average, the same except for the presence or absence of the treatment. This will give us the average treatment effect (ATE) on the population that is represented by this sample. Consider[13] taking expectations over i for equation (1):

$$ATE = E\left[y_i\left(T=1,X\right) - y_i\left(T=0,X\right)\right]$$
$$= E\left[y_i\left(T=1,X\right)\right] - E\left[y_i\left(T=0,X\right)\right]$$

and then taking expectations over X:

$$ATE = E\left[E\left[y_i\left(T=1,X\right)|X\right]\right] - E\left[E\left[y_i\left(T=0,X\right)|X\right]\right]$$
$$= E\left[y|T=1\right] - E\left[y|T=0\right] \tag{2}$$

Note that I drop the individual indexing for conciseness in places where it can be inferred. This tells us that we might be able to estimate the average causal effect of a treatment in some population by comparing the average outcome of treated units to the average outcome of non-treated units in a sample from that population. Although we cannot simultaneously observe a single unit with and without the treatment, we *can* simultaneously observe a group with the treatment that is functionally identical to one without the treatment.

Under certain conditions, both of the components of equation (2) can be estimated in principle [unlike equation (1), which is conceptually impossible to observe]. For example, we can draw a random sample of N observations out of the population of interest, randomly assign half of this sample to be exposed to the treatment, record their value for y, and then average over the $n = N/2$ observations to estimate the first term of equation (2):

$$\hat{E}\left[y|T=1\right] = \frac{1}{n}\sum_{i=1}^{n} y_i\left(T=1,X=X_i\right) \tag{3}$$

If we average y for the n observations randomly assigned *not* to be exposed to the treatment, we get an estimate of the second term of equation (2):

$$\hat{E}\left[y|T=0\right] = \frac{1}{n}\sum_{i=1}^{n} y_i\left(T=0,X=X_i\right) \tag{4}$$

This is the venerable logic of experimental design.[14]

When will the difference between (3) and (4) be equal to the ATE? We require two assumptions. First, we must make the stable unit treatment value assumption (SUTVA):

> SUTVA is simply the a priori assumption that the value of y for unit i when exposed to treatment T will be the same no matter what mechanism is used to assign treatment T to unit i and no matter what treatments the other units receive, and this holds for all $i = 1, ..., N$ and all $T = 1, ..., T_k$.[15]

This assumption makes clear that the underlying estimand—equation (2)—exists and is not subject to influences from other units. Without this assumption, y_i could be a function not just of T and X but also of the other units' treatment assignments, T_{-i}. Thus our expectation $E[y|T = k]$ would have to be taken not only over i but also over all possible combinations of other units' treatment assignments, in order to accurately reflect the ATE. This requirement would make most experiments prohibitively complex and data intensive.

The second assumption we require is that assignment to the treatment is "strongly ignorable,"[16] which is defined by two conditions:

$$\{y(T = 1, X), y(T = 0, X)\} \perp T|X$$

$$\Pr(T = 1|X) \in (0, 1)$$

This assumption tells us that a unit's assignment to a treatment condition is not a function of that unit's potential outcomes; it rules out, for example, the possibility that certain people are selected into a treatment because a particular outcome is expected.[17]

An integral property of the experimental environment ensures strong ignorability: random assignment to the treatment.[18] It also allows us to assume that the empirical distribution of X in the treatment cases matches the empirical distribution of X in the control cases, and furthermore that both of these empirical distributions match the distribution of X in the population from which the sample was drawn. In an experiment, equations (3) and (4) are estimators of $E[y(T = k)]$ for the treatment and control groups, respectively.[19]

The assumption of strong ignorability is most transparently met under experimental conditions. Subjects in an experiment are selected randomly out of a population of interest and then randomly assigned to the treatment or control condition. Any external influences on subjects are held constant by the carefully regulated environment of the laboratory. Consequently, the only difference (on average) between the subjects in the treatment and control conditions is the presence or absence of the treatment itself. Any observed difference in outcome between these two groups must therefore be attributable to the treatment. Furthermore, because the subjects are selected randomly out of the population of interest, the ATE we calculate from the experiment can be inferred to apply to that population.[20]

Non-experimental Data

Outside the laboratory, where treatment conditions are generally not randomly assigned, we usually cannot directly compare the average outcomes of treated and untreated units in order to calculate an ATE. Very often even the fact of choosing to be treated is itself an important influence on outcomes. Returning to the example of high school education, it is plausible that students who stand to gain the most from a high school education are the students most likely to choose to attain it. It is therefore problematic to simply compare the expected earnings y for high school graduates to the expected earnings of non-graduates when estimating the effect of a high school education on income.

If we designate T as the treatment of receiving a high school education ($= 1$) or not ($= 0$) and S as being selected (or choosing oneself) to finish high school ($= 1$) or not ($= 0$), then this simple comparison of expected values[21] works out to

$$E[y|T = 1, S = 1] - E[y|T = 0, S = 0] \tag{5}$$

but the average treatment effect[22] (presuming no other confounding influences) is

$$\begin{aligned} \text{ATE} = p\big(E[y|T = 1, S = 1] - E[y|T = 0, S = 1]\big) \\ + (1 - p)\big(E[y|T = 1, S = 0] - E[y|T = 0, S = 0]\big) \end{aligned} \tag{6}$$

where p is the fraction of the population selecting into the treatment condition. If assignment to receive a high school education is random, as in an experiment, then equations (5) and (6) are equivalent because $E[y|T = 1, S = 1] = E[y|T = 1, S = 0]$ and $E[y|T = 0, S = 1] = E[y|T = 1, S = 0]$; this is why the ATE is so easy to calculate in an experimental setting. But it is rare that assignment is truly random outside the laboratory, and in this case, $E[y|T = 1, S = 1] \neq E[y|T = 1, S = 0]$ and $E[y|T = 0, S = 1] \neq E[y|T = 0, S = 0]$. That is, we expect the effect of the treatment on the sample selected to receive it to differ systematically from the treatment effect on the sample selected not to receive it.[23]

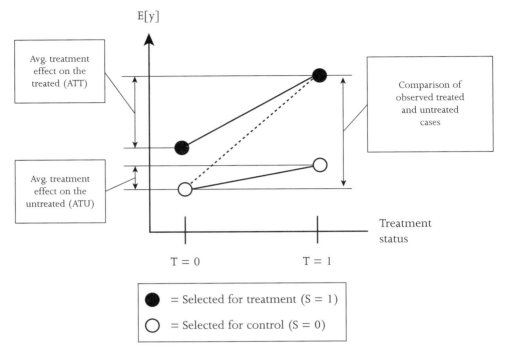

Figure 2.1. An example of biased causal inference caused by simple comparison of treated and untreated cases

The problem is illustrated in figure 2.1, which depicts two cases: observations assigned to the treatment ($S = 1$, shown as solid circles) and observations assigned to the control ($S = 0$, shown as open circles). Each circle shows the expected value of y for each type of case when the treatment is present ($T = 1$) and absent ($T = 0$). The effect of the treatment on the $S = 1$ cases is shown by the line connecting the solid circles; this effect is larger than the treatment effect on the $S = 0$ cases, which is shown by the line connecting the open circles. The simple comparison of equation (5) is equivalent to the dashed line connecting observed untreated cases ($T = 0, S = 0$) to observed treated cases ($T = 1, S = 1$) cases. Note that this dashed line is not equal to the treatment effect for cases selected into the treatment ($S = 1$), cases selected into the control ($S = 0$), or the average between the two.

This problem leads us to differentiate between estimating the treatment effect on units selected to receive the treatment and estimating the treatment effect on units selected to receive the control. The average treatment effect on the treated population, or ATT,[24] is

$$ATT = E[y|T = 1, S = 1] - E[y|T = 0, S = 1]$$

This is the degree to which a treatment affects those who are selected to receive that treatment in a natural setting (the difference between the two solid circles in figure 2.1). To continue our education example, we might assume that the ATT of a high school education on income would be larger than the average treatment effect on the untreated, or ATU:

$$ATU = E[y|T = 1, S = 0] - E[y|T = 0, S = 0]$$

which corresponds to the difference between the two open circles in figure 2.1. We might expect that ATT > ATU in this case because rational, self-interested people are more likely to incur the effort and opportunity costs of an education when they expect to receive larger benefits from that education.

The distinction among ATT, ATU, and ATE is important for those interested in estimating the effect of a policy intervention. It is likely that any policy change will have heterogeneous effects on the population to which it is applied; some will be more greatly affected, others less so. The change in outcomes that we observe from any policy initiative will be a complex function of who receives the treatment that wasn't receiving it before, and how large an effect that the treatment has on that group.

In the example of high school education, suppose that the government chose to make it legally compulsory to complete high school (removing the option for older students to drop out). We might expect this change to have an impact on students' life outcomes. However, the observed change would likely be much closer to the ATU than to the ATE or ATT. Prior to the policy change, those who self-select into receiving a high school education are probably the people who most strongly benefit from that education.[25] These people received a high school education before the policy intervention, and they will continue to receive it afterward. It is those who do not already self-select into receiving an education who will be most affected by the policy.

A Word on Endogeneity

It is possible that increased education causes increased income, but that increases in one's income also cause better access to education even net of the effects of other variables (e.g., individual ability level or parental household income). That is, one may argue that education and income are *endogenous*, such that the two variables are simultaneously determined. Endogenously related variables are well known to social scientists; to take a famous example, every student of microeconomics learns that the price and quantity of a good are simultaneously determined by the intersection of a supply and demand function. A simple regression predicting the quantity of a good using its price in a functioning market will not necessarily uncover the law of demand $[d(\text{quantity})/d(\text{price}) < 0]$ because the countervailing law of supply $[d(\text{quantity})/d(\text{price}) > 0]$ is simultaneously in operation.

The Rubin causal model does not explicitly contemplate simultaneous relationships of this type. This fact is evident from the definition of a causal effect embodied in equation (1), which writes y_i as a function of T and X. When y and T are endogenously related, their levels are *jointly* determined by the solution of a set of simultaneous equations. We can also see this in the assumption of strong ignorability, which presumes that potential outcomes are independent of the value of the treatment conditional on observable covariates. When y and T are endogenously related, the value of T is a direct function of the value of y.

To operate inside of the framework of the Rubin causal model, we must be able to recast any apparent simultaneity between y and T as the product of an external factor X which determines y and T, thus restoring the assumption of strong ignorability. In the case of education and income, an apparent endogeneity between education levels and one's own income *might* be explainable as the product of innate ability, which determines both. But if y and T really are simultaneously determined and we wish to isolate the causal impact of T on y, we will have to take a different approach; a structural interpretation of instrumental variables models can serve this function.[26]

APPLIED CAUSAL INFERENCE: STATISTICAL PROCEDURES

The Rubin causal model provides an epistemological and ontological framework for drawing a causal inference. But actually drawing such an inference outside the laboratory requires us to specify how we will estimate a particular treatment effect in practice. I describe three approaches to observational data in this section: matching methods, regression, and instrumental variables models.

Regression with Matched Data

Recognizing the ATT and ATU as distinct estimands suggests a solution for estimating causal effects in a non-experimental setting. When estimating the ATT, for example, we might compare a unit that was selected to receive the treatment and did $(T = 1, S = 1)$ to a unit that was selected to receive the treatment but didn't $(T = 0, S = 1)$. If we match every selected and treated case in our sample to a selected but untreated case, we might be able to get an estimate of the sample ATT.[27]

Indeed, as demonstrated by Rosenbaum and Rubin,[28] a treatment effect can still be estimated on observational data as long as (1) SUTVA holds, (2) the treatment is strongly ignorable conditional on observable covariates X, and (3) observations can be compared according to their similarity on X or on a measure of the propensity to be assigned to the treatment $\Pr(S = 1)$ (which is typically a function of X).

In describing how to use regression with matching methods, I follow recent methodological literature in focusing on estimation of the sample ATT.[29] Methods to estimate the ATU and ATE using matching are extensions of these ideas; a variety of sources give helpful details on how to implement these procedures.[30]

Setting Up a Matching Procedure to Estimate a Sample ATT

When estimating the sample ATT, all matching methods aim to pair cases in the treated group with cases in the untreated group that are the same in every observable respect *except* for the fact that they are untreated. Once this is done, the result is assessed for *balance*, the degree to which the observable characteristics of the treated sample match those of the newly constructed control sample; some procedures aim to achieve balance automatically without extensive post-matching assessment.[31]

There are many possible ways to set up a matching procedure,[32] but this chapter is too short to give a thorough description of these choices or analyze the trade-offs embedded in them. I opt instead to describe one approach in detail: coarsened exact matching (CEM) as developed by Iacus, King, and Porro.[33]

Coarsened exact matching approaches the matching problem by "coarsening" multivalued covariates into a small number of discrete bins (or strata) that cover a range of values for each covariate; these ranges can be automatically determined by the program or defined by the user. Observations are matched when they fall into a stratum containing a non-zero number of treated and control cases, meaning that these cases have close to the same value (inside the stratum range) for all covariates; other observations are discarded. Inside of each stratum, treatment and control cases are weighted so that each receives equal weight inside the stratum.

The within-stratum weights are

$$
\omega_i^s = \begin{cases} 1 & \text{if} \quad T_i = 1 \\ \dfrac{m_{T=1}^s}{m_{T=0}^s} & \text{if} \quad T_i = 0 \end{cases}
$$

where i indexes observations inside stratum s, T_i gives the treatment status of observation i, and $m_{T=k}^s$ is the number of matched observations in stratum s with treatment status k. Let $m_{T=k}$ be the total number of matched observations in the dataset with treatment status k. Using these within-stratum weights, $\sum_{i \in \mathbb{S}_{T=1}} \omega_i^s = m_{T=1}$ (as appropriate) but $\sum_{i \in \mathbb{S}_{T=0}} \omega_i^s$ also equals $m_{T=1}$, which means that the sum of these weights would not equal the total matched sample size.[34] Therefore, every observation i in the matched dataset is instead assigned a normalized weight equal to

$$
\omega_i = \begin{cases} 1 & \text{if} \quad i \in \mathbb{S}_{T=1} \\ \dfrac{m_{T=1}^s/m_{T=1}}{m_{T=0}^s/m_{T=0}} & \text{if} \quad i \in \mathbb{S}_{T=0} \end{cases} \tag{7}
$$

which correspond to the weights given by Iacus, King, and Porro.[35]

If there are observations in a stratum that does not include both treatment and control cases, then these cases are dropped from the analysis. Dropping these cases means that our causal estimand is the *local sample ATT*, "the treatment effect averaged over only the subset of treated units for which good matches exist among available controls."[36]

Analysis of the Matched Data

After matching has been performed, the matched sample can be used to estimate a quantity of interest. If we are aiming to estimate the sample ATT, the matched sample ideally includes all treatment cases paired with appropriately selected and weighted control cases. We might then simply compare the average value of the outcome variable y between the two groups to estimate the sample ATT; this is equivalent to specifying the following regression model on the matched and weighted sample:

$$y_i = \beta_T * T_i + \beta_C * (1 - T_i) + \varepsilon_i$$

where i indexes observations in the matched sample, $T \in \{0, 1\}$ is a binary indicator of being exposed to the treatment, and the β_T and β_C coefficients correspond to estimates of the predicted value of y for the treatment and control cases, respectively. The sample ATT is $\beta_T - \beta_C$, and its regression estimate is $\hat{\beta}_T - \hat{\beta}_C$.[37] More simply, we can estimate

$$y_i = \beta_0 + \beta_{TE} * T_i + \varepsilon_i$$

The estimated coefficient $\hat{\beta}_{TE}$ is an estimator of the sample ATT.[38]

Alternatively, one might include the K many elements of X that were previously used to create the matched sample as control variables in the regression:

$$y_i = \beta_T * T_i + \beta_C * (1 - T_i) + \sum_{k=1}^{K} \beta_k X_{ik} + \varepsilon_i \qquad (8)$$

An estimate of the sample ATT is $\frac{1}{n} \sum_{i \in S_{T=1}} [y_i - \hat{y}_i(T_i = 0, X_i)]$ from this modified regression for the set of n treated cases in the sample $S_{T=1}$.[39] The y_i cases are simply the observed outcomes for the treated cases, while the $\hat{y}_i$ are constructed by computing the regression prediction for these same cases for $T = 0$ (and with all other covariates X left the same) using equation (8). The sample ATT can also be estimated[40] using $\hat{\beta}_{TE}$ in the regression:

$$y_i = \beta_0 + \beta_{TE} * T_i + \sum_{k=1}^{K} \beta_k X_{ik} + \varepsilon_i \qquad (9)$$

These procedures have the advantage of being "doubly robust" in that they will yield a correct estimate of the sample ATT if either the matching procedure achieves appropriate balance or the regression model in equations (8) and (9) is a mathematically accurate description of the true functional relationship among y, T, and X.[41]

Regression Analysis of Unmatched Data

We can also run the regression in equation (9) *without* performing a matching procedure first; this is certainly a common practice in the social scientific literature.

In this case, $\hat{\beta}_{\text{TE}}$ will have a causal interpretation[42] in the event that the regression estimates are unbiased. It is sufficient that the following hold:

1. The model is correctly specified; that is, equation (9) accurately describes the data-generating process.
2. The ε noise term is uncorrelated with the regressors T and X.
3. The matrix of all covariates, including the treatment indicators, has full rank (i.e., the number of observations exceeds the number of covariates).

These assumptions are standard in the econometric literature for unbiased estimation of regression coefficients.[43]

Under these conditions, $\hat{\beta}_{\text{TE}}$ is an estimate of the ATT, ATU, and ATE of the treatment. We see this via the derivative of equation (9) with respect to T:

$$\frac{dy_i}{dT} = \beta_{\text{TE}}$$

Under the assumption of correct specification, this relationship is constant for all treated and control cases, and thus ATT = ATU = ATE.

The cost of this greatly simplified procedure lies in the stronger assumptions we must make about the data-generating process in order to derive a causal inference in the sense of the Rubin causal model. The Gauss-Markov theorem tells us that the regression-only approach will be the most efficient linear unbiased estimate of causal estimands possible, meaning that the uncertainty around our answers will be smaller than any other (linear) unbiased estimator—but only when additional assumptions hold.[44]

Instrumental Variables

Instrumental variables (IV) techniques provide a third avenue for drawing causal inferences. The procedure attempts to replace the random assignment to a treatment that takes place in a laboratory with a model for treatment assignment that is known to be unrelated to the outcome of interest except through its effect on $\Pr(T = 1)$, the probability of receiving the treatment. The idea hinges upon being able to find a set of eponymous *instrumental variables*: variables that are correlated with $\Pr(T = 1)$ but not correlated with *y* except through $\Pr(T = 1)$. We thus substitute the controlled assignment to treatment in a laboratory for assignment to treatment by random observable factors.

If we find a binary instrumental variable (call it z), with $z \in \{0, 1\}$, then the Wald IV estimator[45] for the relationship between T and y in a set of observations $i \in 1, ..., N$ is

$$\hat{\rho}_w = \frac{\hat{E}[y_i|z_i = 1] - \hat{E}[y_i|z_i = 0]}{\hat{E}[T_i|z_i = 1] - \hat{E}[T_i|z_i = 0]} \tag{10}$$

More generally, we can estimate the impact of treatments T on an outcome y using instruments Z with instrumental variables regression:[46]

$$\hat{\beta}_{IV} = (X'P_V X)^{-1} X'P_V y$$

where P_V is the projection matrix onto the space defined by V:

$$P_V = V(V'V)^{-1}V'$$

where V is an $\{N \times L\}$ matrix of the N observations in the rows and the K control variables and $L - K$ instruments in the columns. X is the $\{N \times (K + 1)\}$ matrix of the treatment variable and the controls; thus, $V = [Z \ X_{-T}]$, where X_{-T} is the X matrix with the column corresponding to the treatment variable deleted. The relationship between T and y, β_T, is estimated by the element of the $\hat{\beta}_{IV}$ vector corresponding to the treatment variable T. Control variables need not be included, but can be in order to improve the efficiency of results; T can be continuous or binary.

A Causal Interpretation for IV: The Local Average Treatment Effect

Under some assumptions, $\hat{\rho}_w$ and $\hat{\beta}_T$ have a causal interpretation under the Rubin causal model. Consider the Wald IV estimator first; I follow the presentation of Angrist, Imbens, and Rubin.[47] Distinguish between T_i and z_i, unit i's value for the treatment and instrument, respectively, and **T** and **z**, the $N \times 1$ vectors of treatment and instrument values for the entire set of units. Define the following terms:

- $T_i(\mathbf{z})$ is unit i's treatment status contingent on the configuration of all units' instrument value **z**.
- $y_i(T_i(\mathbf{z}), \mathbf{z})$ is unit i's outcome value contingent on the unit's own treatment status $T_i(\mathbf{z})$ and all units' instrument vector **z**.
- $y_i(\mathbf{T}, \mathbf{z})$ is unit i's outcome value contingent on all units' treatment status and instrument value.
- $\mathbf{y}(\mathbf{T}, \mathbf{z})$ is the vector of all units' outcome values contingent on all units' treatment status and instrument value.

A causal interpretation of ρ_w requires the following:

1. The stable unit treatment value assumption (SUTVA) as defined earlier, which can now be formally stated as
   (a) $z_i = z_i' \rightarrow T_i(\mathbf{z}) = T_i(\mathbf{z}')$
   (b) $z_i = z_i'$ and $T_i = T_i' \rightarrow y_i(\mathbf{T}, \mathbf{z}) = y_i(\mathbf{T}', \mathbf{z}')$
2. Random assignment[48] of the instrument: $\Pr(\mathbf{z} = \mathbf{c}) = \Pr(\mathbf{z} = \mathbf{c}')$ for any two $N \times 1$ instrument vectors $\mathbf{c}$ and $\mathbf{c}'$
3. The *exclusion restriction*: z affects y only through its effect on $\Pr(T = 1)$, or $\mathbf{y}(\mathbf{T}, \mathbf{z}) = \mathbf{y}(\mathbf{T}, \mathbf{z}')$ for all values of $\mathbf{z}$, $\mathbf{z}'$, and $\mathbf{T}$
4. *Strong monotonicity*: the instrumental variable moves the probability of assignment to treatment in one direction, or $T_i(z_i = 1) \geq T_i(z_i = 0)$ for all $i \in 1, ..., N$ and $\exists j : T_j(z_j = 1) > T_j(z_j = 0)$

Under these conditions, proposition 1 in Angrist, Imbens, and Rubin[49] shows that $\hat{\rho}_w$ is an estimate of the local average treatment effect (LATE):

$$\text{LATE} = \frac{E[y_i(T_i(z_i = 1), z_i = 1) - y_i(T_i(z_i = 0), z_i = 0)]}{E[T_i(z_i = 1) - T_i(z_i = 0)]} \tag{11}$$

Given our earlier assumptions, the LATE has an interesting interpretation: it is the effect of the treatment on the outcome for that subgroup of people who would take the treatment when exposed to the instrument $[T_i(z_i = 1) = 1]$ but would *not* take the treatment when not exposed to the instrument $[T_i(z_i = 0) = 0]$. Consider table 2.1, a duplication of table 1 in Angrist, Imbens, and Rubin.[50] The table shows that there are four types of observations in the $z = 1$ and $z = 0$ pools: never-takers, always-takers, defiers, and compliers. The never-takers and always-takers have the same treatment status regardless of z, compliers take the treatment when $z = 1$ and do not when $z = 0$, and defiers take the treatment when $z = 0$ but do not when $z = 1$. The existence of defiers is ruled out by the strong monotonicity assumption. The exclusion restriction tells us that the never- and always-takers have the same value for y regardless of z because their treatment status does not change. Thus, the only difference in the treated and untreated samples is the response of compliers.

Ergo, $\hat{E}[y_i | z_i = 1] - \hat{E}[y_i | z_i = 0]$ is a weighted average of the effect of the treatment on compliers and a zero effect (for the never- and always-takers).[51] Once we multiply by the estimated inverse proportion of compliers in the population, $\hat{E}[T_i | z_i = 1] - \hat{E}[T_i | z_i = 0]$, we obtain an estimate of the treatment effect on compliers (the LATE).

Table 2.1. Unit types and treatment assignments

		$T_i(0)$	
		0	1
$T_i(1)$	0	Never-takers	Defiers
	1	Compliers	Always-takers

Source: Joshua D. Angrist, Guido W. Imbens, and Donald B. Rubin, "Identification of Causal Effects Using Instrumental Variables," *Journal of the American Statistical Association* 91, no. 434 (1996), table 1.

When two-stage least squares (2SLS) regression is used to estimate β_T, the resulting estimand is still a local average treatment effect, albeit averaged over some characteristic of the sample.

> 2SLS with multiple instruments produces a causal effect that averages IV estimands using the instruments one at a time; 2SLS with covariates produces an average of covariate-specific LATEs; 2SLS with variable or continuous treatment intensity produces a weighted average derivative along the length of a possible non-linear causal response function. These results provide a simple causal interpretation for 2SLS in most empirically relevant settings.[52]

The LATE and Its Connection to Policy Scholarship

The LATE is of particular interest to those studying policy because of the close conceptual connection between instruments and policy interventions. As the preceding exposition indicates, an instrument is an influence that has an isolated impact on exposure to the treatment; that is, it affects receipt of the treatment without affecting (or being affected by) anything else. Under ideal circumstances, the instrument is actually randomly assigned just as a treatment would be in an experiment. But the instrument is not the treatment itself.

Similarly, most policy interventions are not identical to the treatment. Policy interventions are instruments that we hope will change behavior, which, in turn, changes an outcome of interest. The change in behavior is the actual treatment. Scholars of policy are thus intrinsically interested in the causal impact of a behavioral change on outcomes through the mechanism of instruments.

Furthermore, not everyone who is exposed to the instrument will receive the treatment, and not everyone who is not exposed to the instrument will not receive the treatment. This is analogous to the effect of a policy intervention. For example, imposing cigarette taxes (the instrument) will cause some people to stop smoking (the treatment), but some people will smoke whether the tax exists or not, while others will remain non-smokers regardless of the tax. The relevant information for a policy maker is how much the change in taxes will change outcomes (such as life expectancy or health care costs) through its impact on the behavior of those who do respond to the instrument. This is precisely the definition of the LATE.[53]

Returning to our example of education, an IV estimator can be used to tell us the effect of attaining a high school education (the treatment) on income (the outcome of interest) for the subset of people whose school attendance choices are actually changed by a policy initiative. An ideal instrument would be created by a government initiative to randomly select a subset of 1,000 students in a particular cohort and guarantee to pay them a cash bounty for completing high school. The instrument is ideal because (a) we strongly expect the instrument to be correlated with the decision to complete high school, and (b) we do not expect weekly earning potential to be affected by the receipt of a one-time cash bounty except through its effect on whether the student completes high school. Furthermore, we know the instrument is not spuriously correlated with other influences on income (e.g., through individual ability or parental education levels) because it has been randomly assigned: participants cannot preferentially select themselves into participation in the program.

Inside of the group, some set of "always-takers" will complete high school with or without the bounty; another set of "never-takers" will not complete a high school education even with the bounty. However, some set of individuals will complete high school with the bounty when they would not have done so without it; this set of "compliers" has their behavior changed by the program. By comparing the expected earnings of the set of people in the program to the set of people not in the program using equation (10), we can calculate the impact of high school completion on this compliant population.

Note, however, that any particular estimated LATE is not necessarily a measure of the impact of an arbitrary policy change.[54] It is not, for example, when "compliers" with an instrument are not the same as the "compliers" with a policy change.

> If the instrumental variable we use is exactly the policy we want to evaluate, then the IV estimand and the policy relevant parameter coincide. But whenever that is not the case, the IV estimand does not identify the effect of the policy when returns vary among people and they make choices of treatment based on those returns. For example, if the policy we want to consider is a tuition subsidy directed toward the very poor within the pool [of people who would not ordinarily attend schooling], then an instrumental variable estimate based on compulsory schooling will not be the relevant return to estimate the policy.[55]

APPLICATION: THE EFFECT OF HIGH SCHOOL EDUCATION ON EARNINGS

To illustrate the application of causal inference techniques to an important policy problem, I reanalyze data collected by Angrist and Krueger[56] using standard regression techniques, regression with coarsened exact matching, and two-stage least squares regression using an instrumental variable. Angrist and Krueger originally used the public use file of the 1970 U.S. Census to study the relationship between income and total years of education received. I will use their replication data to estimate the causal impact of receiving a high school education on income; the original article briefly discusses this relationship but does not directly study it.[57]

Regression with Control Variables

The easiest and most straightforward approach to estimating the causal effect of a high school education on income is to simply regress one on the other in a large observational dataset of individual respondents and control for likely sources of spurious correlation. The Angrist and Krueger dataset is derived from the public sample of the 1970 U.S. Census; I analyze the cohort of respondents born between 1920 and 1929.[58] It contains the following variables:

- **log weekly earnings**
- **Education** completed in years
- **Race** (1 = black, 0 = white)
- **Married** (1 = yes, 0 = no)
- **SMSA** (1 = respondent lives in the central city of a metropolitan statistical area)
- Census **region** indicators (9 binary dummy variables)
- **Year of birth** (10 binary dummy variables)

I recode the years of education variable to a high school completion variable (= 1 if the respondent has 12 or more years of education, and = 0 otherwise); this is the treatment variable, T.

I use these data to estimate the following regression model:

$$y_i = \beta_0 + \beta_{TE} * T_i + \sum_{k=1}^{K} \beta_k X_{ik} + \varepsilon_i \tag{12}$$

The control variables of race, marriage status, SMSA, census region, and year of birth are included as elements $k \in 1, ..., K$. The results are shown in column 2 of table 2.2.

Table 2.2. How much does completing high school change future income?

Variable	Regression	CEM with regression	IV 2SLS
At least 12 years of schooling	0.346***	0.339***	0.388**
(1 = yes)	(139.39)	(140.94)	(3.21)
Race (1 = black)	−0.367***	−0.357***	−0.355***
	(−82.02)	(−61.49)	(−10.73)
Married (1 = yes)	0.306***	0.305***	0.304***
	(78.84)	(76.21)	(45.64)
Metro area (1 = center city)	−0.156***	−0.143***	−0.153***
	(−58.65)	(−53.57)	(−20.50)
N	247,199	247,090	247,199

Notes: t-statistics are given in parentheses. The dependent variable, log weekly wage, is given in dollars. Data are from the 1920–1929 Cohort of the 1970 U.S. Census. All models also include year of birth dummy variables, region dummies, and a constant. $^*p < 0.05$, $^{**}p < 0.01$, $^{***}p < 0.001$.

The regression coefficient for attaining a high school education is 0.346, indicating that high school graduates earn approximately 35 percent more than non-graduates, on average. If equation (12) is an accurate specification of the data-generating process, then, on average, receipt of a high school education causes a 35 percent increase in weekly wages for both the populations who received the treatment (high school graduates) and those who did not (non-graduates).

Regression with Coarsened Exact Matching

One weakness of the regression procedure is that it relies on an accurate specification of the data-generating process. By contrast, matching procedures do not require this condition. We still, however, require SUTVA and strong ignorability of $Pr(T = 1)$ contingent on our set of control variables. Thus, the validity of the procedure requires (among other things) that we use a complete set of confounding variables in the matching process.

As noted previously, there are many possible choices that one can make as a part of a matching procedure. For this demonstration, I elect to use CEM as developed by Iacus, King, and Porro[59] and implemented in Stata by Blackwell et al.[60]

I use the cem command in Stata to match the Angrist and Krueger data on all control covariates (including year of birth and region of residence dummy variables); the process discards 89 control and 20 treatment cases that fall into a stratum with no matching observations and assigns the rest weights given by equation (7). I then repeat the regression of equation (12) on the matched and weighted data; the principle of "double robustness" ensures an accurate estimate of the local sample ATT if either the matching procedure is adequate or the regression is accurately specified.

The matching procedure is successful at improving balance between the observable characteristics of the treated and control samples. Balance is calculated in the cem software using the $\mathcal{L}_1$ statistic:

$$\mathcal{L}_1(f, g) = \frac{1}{2} \sum_{\ell_1 \dots \ell_K} |f_{\ell_1 \dots \ell_K} - g_{\ell_1 \dots \ell_K}|$$

where K indexes the number of (coarsened) independent variables, $\ell_1 \dots \ell_K$ is the coordinate of a matching stratum, $f_{\ell_1 \dots \ell_K}$ is the frequency of treated cases in the stratum, and $g_{\ell_1 \dots \ell_K}$ is the frequency of control cases in the stratum. Perfect balance is indicated by an $\mathcal{L}_1 = 0$.[61] Before performing matching on the Angrist and Krueger dataset, $\mathcal{L}_1 = 0.159$; after matching, $\mathcal{L}_1 = 2.29 * 10^{-14}$.

The results are shown in column 3 of table 2.2. The coefficient for the attainment of a high school education is 0.339, indicating that earning a high school diploma causes a 33.9 percent increase in weekly wages for those in the sample who received the treatment (i.e., this is the local sample ATT). This is very similar to the estimate of a 34.6 percent increase that we achieved with a regression analysis alone.

Instrumental Variables Models

Finally, we consider the possibility of using the 2SLS IV procedure to determine the causal effect of high school education on earnings. The first and most important question is: What instrumental variable is correlated with the decision to complete high school but not correlated with weekly income except through its effect on high school completion?

Angrist and Krueger argue that an individual's quarter of birth (i.e., the quarter of the year in which a student was born) is a good choice of instrument. Their reasoning is that compulsory school attendance laws in the United States (which require students to achieve a certain age before they may discontinue their education) create a link between educational attainment and quarter of birth.

Students who are born early in the calendar year are typically older when they enter school than children born late in the year. . . . Because children born in the first quarter of the year enter school at an older age, they attain the legal dropout age after having attended school for a shorter period of time than those born near the end of the year. Hence, if a fixed fraction of students is constrained by the compulsory attendance law, those born in the beginning of the year will have less schooling, on average, than those born near the end of the year.[62]

2SLS Estimates

In their original article, Angrist and Krueger interact three separate dummies for quarter of birth (one for each quarter, omitting the fourth as a base category) with 10 years of birth dummies (one for each year between 1920 and 1929) for a total of 30 instruments. We can use this larger set of instruments, along with the full set of control variables, to create a 2SLS IV estimate of the effect of completing high school on log weekly earnings. The F-test of a regression of all instruments on high school completion rejects the null that the full set of instruments is not related to completing high school ($F_{(30,247,148)} = 3.48$, $p < 0.001$). The R^2 of this regression is 0.0465, which is relatively weak.

The presence of multiple instruments allows us to perform a Sargan test for overidentifying restrictions in the set of instruments.[63] The Sargan test checks a key assumption of the IV procedure:

$$E[Z'\varepsilon] = 0$$

That is, the $N \times (L - K)$ matrix of instrumental variables Z should be uncorrelated with the second-stage 2SLS errors. In the context of the 2SLS model, this is a restatement of the exclusion restriction: $\mathbf{y}(\mathbf{T}, \mathbf{Z}) = \mathbf{y}(\mathbf{T}, \mathbf{Z}')$ for all values of $\mathbf{Z}$, $\mathbf{Z}'$, and $\mathbf{T}$. When the 2SLS model of equation (11) is just identified (one instrument with a single treatment condition), we cannot perform this test. The abundance of instruments allows us to implicitly compare the results of single-instrument models to one another; if the instruments are valid, "the estimates should differ only as a result of sampling error."[64] The test is equivalent to regressing the fitted error terms of the 2SLS regression $\hat{\varepsilon}$ on the set of instruments Z; under the null hypothesis that all instruments are valid, N times the R^2 from this regression is distributed $\chi^2_{L-(K+1)}$.[65]

For the quarter of birth $\times$ year of birth dummy instruments, the Sargan test yields a p-value of 0.0885. This is a marginal result, close to rejecting the validity of the instruments but not quite doing so at the 0.05 level. Thus, we cautiously proceed to interpret the 2SLS estimates of the relationship between high school education and log weekly earnings as a measurement of the LATE.

The 2SLS results are shown in column 4 of table 2.2. The coefficient of 0.388 indicates a LATE of a 38.8 percent increase in weekly earnings associated with attainment of a high school education. Thus, the model indicates that a high school graduate who completed high school as a result of birth timing (when she would not have otherwise) receives 38.8 percent more weekly earnings as a result of completing high school. The uncertainty associated with these results is somewhat higher than in the other models due to the addition of the second stage of the 2SLS estimator and the comparative weakness of the instruments; this is reflected in smaller t-statistics. However, the magnitude and direction of the 2SLS results are extremely similar to those for our plain regression and regression-with-matching estimates.

CONCLUSION: WHAT CAN POLICY MAKERS AND SCHOLARS LEARN FROM THE CAUSAL INFERENCE MOVEMENT?

As I hope this chapter has shown, it is challenging to use observational data from outside the laboratory to draw a causal inference. Observing an association between the value of a treatment T and an outcome y is not sufficient to conclude that a change in the treatment will cause a change in expected outcome $E[y]$. At a minimum, we must rule out the possibility that confounding factors could be simultaneously causing y and T; confounding can create an observed association between y and T where no causal association exists.

Even if changes in T *do* cause changes in y, the strength of the observed association is unlikely to correspond to the magnitude of the causal impact of a change in T initiated by a policy intervention. In observational data, people choose whether to be exposed to a treatment, and thus those who stand to derive the greatest benefit from a treatment are often the most likely to choose to receive the treatment. Thus, simply comparing the outcomes of treated and untreated units from observational data is likely to give a highly misleading indication of how much outcomes would change if a change in treatment status was *imposed* by an external event, such as a legal mandate.

In my judgment, the most important lesson that policy makers and scholars can draw from the causal inference literature is that describing (let alone predicting) the practical impact of a policy change using observational data is complicated. Scholarship on causal inference alerts us to the practical problem of confounding, but, perhaps even more important, it reminds us that causal relationships are heterogeneous and that policy interventions will not cause uniform changes across a target population.

Consider the results of our inquiry into the causal impact of high school completion on income. Which, if any, of the results in table 2.2 is most informative about the potential increase in earnings that would result if we legally compelled all students to complete high school? Our matching estimator of the sample ATT is probably not the right estimand; this is the effect of high school completion on those who already receive it, not on the population of those with less education whose behavior would be changed.

The 2SLS IV estimator of the LATE is perhaps more informative; this, at least, tells us the response of people whose status was changed as a result of an accident of birth. But there is still a substantial set of "never-compliers" whose decision to drop out of high school was not changed by time of birth, and these non-compliers would be a significant subset of the group affected by the policy change. Our LATE estimate is not guaranteed to describe the change in earnings for this subset.[66]

Moreover, there is the possibility that our 2SLS estimates are subject to "coarsening bias."[67] Increased years of schooling have an impact on weekly earnings even if high school is not completed, and the quarter-of-birth instrument affects years of schooling aside from increasing the chance of completing high school; this creates a pathway between the instrument and the dependent variable that does not pass through the treatment (high school completion). Because high school completion necessarily entails attaining more years of schooling, it may be challenging to causally separate these effects with an instrumental variable.

All of these approaches depend directly on the stable unit treatment value assumption (SUTVA), and there is a strong reason to believe that SUTVA would not hold in the presence of our proposed policy change. Weekly earnings are determined in part by the market forces of supply and demand, and increasing the supply of high school graduates via the proposed policy without changing demand is likely to drive down the wage for a person with a high school diploma. In terms of SUTVA, the relationship between treatment and outcome for person i depends on the treatment status of person j; a high school diploma is more valuable if fewer people have one. This is particularly true if education serves as a signal of underlying quality for employers rather than as a source of practical skills.[68] Thus, we have reason to doubt that any of our results in table 2.2 are truly reflective of the probable impact of our policy intervention on income.[69]

None of this is to say that it is impossible to derive a causal inference from observational data, or that quantitative tools cannot determine the causal impact of a policy intervention. Instead, it is important to precisely determine the desired causal estimand before performing an empirical analysis, ensure that our empirical design gives us the best chance of obtaining an accurate estimate, and be aware of the sensitivity of any causal inference we draw to the assumptions we had to make in order to justify that inference. For example, the estimates in table 2.2 are more defensible as estimates of the causal impact of a smaller-scale policy intervention to increase high school graduation that is unlikely to influence the market as a whole; this is true because such a program is unlikely to entail a violation of SUTVA. The causal inference framework is well suited to reminding us of these limitations and preventing us from drawing inferences beyond the support of our evidence.

NOTES

I thank Katie Dessi, Carolina Tchintian, Matt Blackwell, and Ahra Wu for helpful comments and corrections.

1. Jasjeet S. Sekhon, "The Neyman-Rubin Model of Causal Inference and Estimation via Matching Methods," in *The Oxford Handbook of Political Methodology*, ed. Janet M. Box-Steffensmeier, Henry E. Brady, and David Collier (New York: Oxford University Press, 2008), 271–299.

2. Joshua D. Angrist and Jörn-Steffen Pischke, "The Credibility Revolution in Empirical Economics: How Better Research Design Is Taking the Con Out of Econometrics," *Journal of Economic Perspectives* 24, no. 2 (2010): 3–30.

3. Donald B. Rubin, "Estimating Causal Effects of Treatments in Randomized and Nonrandomized Studies," *Journal of Educational Psychology* 66, no. 5 (1974): 688–701; and Paul W. Holland, "Statistics and Causal Inference," *Journal of the American Statistical Association* 81, no. 396 (1986): 945–960.

4. Judea Pearl, *Causality: Models, Reasoning and Inference* (Cambridge: Cambridge University Press, 2000).

5. Joshua D. Angrist and David Card, "Empirical Strategies in Labor Economics," in *Handbook of Labor Economics*, ed. Orley Ashenfelter and David Card (Amsterdam: Elsevier, 1999) 3: 1277–1366, 1284; and Angrist and Pischke, "Credibility Revolution in Empirical Economics," 16–17.

6. Angrist and Card, "Empirical Strategies in Labor Economics," 1282–1283.

7. There are other such summaries that share similar themes and structures but are somewhat different in their emphases and depth of topical coverage. See, for example, Angrist and Card, "Empirical Strategies in Labor Economics"; Sekhon, "Neyman-Rubin Model"; and Elizabeth A. Stuart, "Matching Methods for Causal Inference: A Review and a Look Forward," *Statistical Science* 25, no. 1 (2010): 1–21.

8. For a review of ideas and findings from relevant literature, see Robert J. Willis, "Wage Determinants: A Survey and Reinterpretation of Human Capital Earnings Functions," in *Handbook of Labor Economics*, ed. Orley Ashenfelter and Richard Layard (Amsterdam: Elsevier, 1986), 1: 525–602.

9. Joshua D. Angrist and Alan B. Krueger, "Does Compulsory School Attendance Affect Schooling and Earnings?," *Quarterly Journal of Economics* 106, no. 4 (1991): 979–1014.

10. Rubin, "Estimating Causal Effects"; and Holland, "Statistics and Causal Inference."

11. This section loosely follows the presentation of Holland, "Statistics and Causal Inference."

12. Ibid., 947.

13. The following illustration is given in Rocio Titiunik, "ATE, ATT and Potential Outcomes" (2007), http://goo.gl/ZKprMS, esp. p. 8.

14. See the section titled "Independence" in Holland, "Statistics and Causal Inference," 948–949; see also Sekhon, "Neyman-Rubin Model," 272–275.

15. Donald B. Rubin, "Comment: Which Ifs Have Causal Answers," *Journal of the American Statistical Association* 81, no. 396 (1986): 961. Note that I have changed Rubin's notation in this quote to match the notation used in the rest of this chapter.

16. Paul R. Rosenbaum and Donald B. Rubin, "The Central Role of the Propensity Score in Observational Studies for Causal Effects," *Biometrika* 70, no. 1 (1983): 43.

17. Guido W. Imbens, "Nonparametric Estimation of Average Treatment Effects Under Exogeneity: A Review," *Review of Economics and Statistics* 86, no. 1 (2004): 4–29, calls these two conditions "unconfoundedness" and "overlap," respectively (pp. 7–8).

18. Holland, "Statistics and Causal Inference," 948.

19. Imbens, "Nonparametric Estimation of Average Treatment Effects," 8.

20. Holland, "Statistics and Causal Inference," 948–949.

21. The notation and basic ideas of this section are similar to those presented in Stephen L. Morgan and Christopher Winship, *Counterfactuals and Causal Inference: Methods and Principles for Social Research* (New York: Cambridge University Press, 2007), sec. 2.2 and chap. 4.

22. Ibid., 103.

23. See Morgan and Winship, *Counterfactuals and Causal Inference*, 46–48; and Holland, "Statistics and Causal Inference," 948. I assume that there is no possibility for those selected to receive the treatment not to receive it ($T = 0$; $S = 1$) or for those not selected to receive the treatment to receive it ($T = 1$; $S = 0$). The possibility of the former leads to estimation of an intention-to-treat effect (ITT), $\text{ITT} = E[y|S = 1] - E[y|S = 0] = q(E[y|T = 1, S = 1]) + (1 - q)E[y|T = 0, S = 1] - E[y|T = 0, S = 0]$, which averages the results of all those selected to receive the treatment, where $(1 - q)$ is the proportion of "non-compliers" who do not take the treatment. For more information on the ITT, see Joshua D. Angrist, Guido W. Imbens, and Donald B. Rubin, "Identification of Causal Effects Using Instrumental Variables," *Journal of the American Statistical Association* 91, no. 434 (1996): 444–455; and Joshua D. Angrist and Jörn-Steffen Pischke, *Mostly Harmless Econometrics: An Empiricist's Companion* (Princeton, NJ: Princeton University Press, 2009), 163–164.

24. See Morgan and Winship, *Counterfactuals and Causal Inference*, 42.

25. See Willis, "Wage Determinants," 534–535. Evidence for this phenomenon in the context of college education is given by Pedro Carneiro, James J. Heckman, and Edward J. Vytlacil, "Estimating Marginal Returns to Education," *American Economic Review* 101 (2011): 2754–2781.

26. Russell Davidson and James G. MacKinnon, *Econometric Theory and Methods* (New York: Oxford University Press, 2003), chap. 8.

27. These ideas are covered in Morgan and Winship, *Counterfactuals and Causal Inference*, chap. 4.

28. Rosenbaum and Rubin, "Central Role of the Propensity Score," esp. p. 46, theorem 4.

29. See, for example, Morgan and Winship, *Counterfactuals and Causal Inference*, 105–116; Daniel E. Ho, Kosuke Imai, Gary King, and Elizabeth Stuart, "Matching as Nonparametric Preprocessing for Reducing Model Dependence in Parametric Causal Inference," *Political Analysis* 15, no. 3 (2007): 199–236; Stefano M. Iacus, Gary King, and Giuseppe Porro, "Causal Inference Without Balance Checking: Coarsened Exact Matching," *Political Analysis* 20, no. 1 (2012): 1–24; Sekhon, "Neyman-Rubin Model," 275–276; and Matthew Blackwell, Stefano Iacus, Gary King, and Giuseppe Porro, "cem: Coarsened Exact Matching in Stata," *Stata Journal* 9, no. 4 (2009): 524–546.

30. See, for example, Imbens, "Nonparametric Estimation of Average Treatment Effects"; and Morgan and Winship, *Counterfactuals and Causal Inference*, 98–105.

31. Iacus, King, and Porro, "Causal Inference Without Balance Checking."
32. To see these choices laid out in detail, consider the options available in the MatchIt package for using matching methods in the R statistical environment of Daniel Ho, Kosuke Imai, Gary King, and Elizabeth Stuart, "MatchIt: Nonparametric Preprocessing for Parametric Causal Inference," *Journal of Statistical Software* 42, no. 8 (2011): 1–28. See also Morgan and Winship, *Counterfactuals and Causal Inference*, 107–109.
33. Iacus, King, and Porro, "Causal Inference Without Balance Checking."
34. Gary King, Richard Nielsen, Carter Coberley, James E. Pope, and Aaron Wells, "Comparative Effectiveness of Matching Methods for Causal Inference" (2011), http://gking.harvard.edu/files/psparadox.pdf, p. 4.
35. Iacus, King, and Porro, "Causal Inference Without Balance Checking," 8.
36. Ibid., 5.
37. The estimated sample ATT can be assessed for statistical significance using the relevant t-statistic for the estimated quantities:

$$t = \frac{\hat{\beta}_T - \hat{\beta}_C}{\hat{se}_{dif}}$$

$$\hat{se}_{dif} = \sqrt{\text{Var}(\hat{\beta}_T) + \text{Var}(\hat{\beta}_C) - 2\text{Cov}(\hat{\beta}_T, \hat{\beta}_C)}$$

The variances can be obtained from the variance-covariance matrix normally produced in a regression analysis, and will be appropriate in the case that we treat the matching procedure as non-stochastic and the usual Gauss-Markov assumptions for ordinary least squares are met in this case; see Ho et al., "Matching as Nonparametric Preprocessing," 207–208, 223–224.
38. See Blackwell et al., "cem: Coarsened Exact Matching in Stata," 537; see also Imbens, "Nonparametric Estimation of Average Treatment Effects," 19, for a procedure with slightly different weights applied to estimating an ATE.
39. See Donald B. Rubin, "The Use of Matched Sampling and Regression Adjustment to Remove Bias in Observational Studies," *Biometrics* 29 (1973): 185–203; Donald B. Rubin, "Using Multivariate Matched Sampling and Regression Adjustment to Control Bias in Observational Studies," *Journal of the American Statistical Association* 74, no. 366 (1979): 318–328; Imbens, "Nonparametric Estimation of Average Treatment Effects," 12–13, 19; and Ho et al., "Matching as Nonparametric Preprocessing," 207–208, 223–224.
40. See Blackwell et al., "cem: Coarsened Exact Matching in Stata," 537–538.
41. Ho et al., "Matching as Nonparametric Preprocessing," 215.
42. See Angrist and Card, "Empirical Strategies in Labor Economics," 1284–1293; and Morgan and Winship, *Counterfactuals and Causal Inference*, chap. 5, for an in-depth examination of causally interpreting regression estimates.
43. See, for example, Davidson and MacKinnon, *Econometric Theory and Methods*, chaps. 1–3, esp. sec. 3.2.
44. Ibid., 106.
45. Angrist and Pischke, *Mostly Harmless Econometrics*, 127–128.
46. Davidson and MacKinnon, *Econometric Theory and Methods*, 321, eq. 8.29.
47. Angrist, Imbens, and Rubin, "Identification of Causal Effects," 446–447; see also Angrist and Pischke, *Mostly Harmless Econometrics*, secs. 4.4–4.5.

48. It is also sufficient to assume that assignment to z is strongly ignorable; see Angrist, Imbens, and Rubin, "Identification of Causal Effects," 446. I follow their original proof in assuming the stronger condition of random assignment.

49. Ibid., 448.

50. Ibid.

51. A related point is made in Angrist and Pischke, *Mostly Harmless Econometrics*, 163–165.

52. Ibid., 173; see also pp. 174–186.

53. For a more thorough explanation of the policy relevance of the LATE, see Angrist and Card, "Empirical Strategies in Labor Economics," 1320–1326.

54. Carneiro, Heckman, and Vytlacil, "Estimating Marginal Returns to Education."

55. Pedro Carneiro, James J. Heckman, and Edward Vytlacil, "Understanding What Instrumental Variables Estimate: Estimating Marginal and Average Returns to Education" (July 2003), http://goo.gl/PWQMcA, p. 16.

56. Angrist and Krueger, "Does Compulsory School Attendance Affect Schooling and Earnings?"

57. Ibid., 1004–1005.

58. Quoting from ibid., 1010–1011:

> Our extract [of the 1970 Census Data] combines data from three separate public-use files: the State, County group, and Neighborhood files. Each file contains a self-weighting, mutually exclusive sample of 1 percent of the population (as of April 1, 1970), yielding a total sample of 3 percent of the population. The data sets we use are based on the questionnaire that was administered to 15 percent of the population. The sample consists of white and black men born between 1920–1929 in the United States. Birth year was derived from reported age and quarter of birth. In addition, we excluded any man whose age, sex, race, veteran status, weeks worked, highest grade completed or salary was allocated by the Census Bureau. Finally, the sample is limited to men with positive wage and salary earnings and positive weeks worked in 1969.

59. Iacus, King, and Porro, "Causal Inference Without Balance Checking."

60. Blackwell et al., "cem: Coarsened Exact Matching in Stata."

61. Ibid., 530; and Iacus, King, and Porro, "Causal Inference Without Balance Checking," 7.

62. Angrist and Krueger, "Does Compulsory School Attendance Affect Schooling and Earnings?," 982.

63. Jeffrey M. Wooldridge, *Econometric Analysis of Cross Section and Panel Data* (Cambridge, MA: MIT Press, 2002), 122–123, refers to this as a Hausman test after Jerry A. Hausman, "Specification Tests in Econometrics," *Econometrica* 46, no. 6 (1978): 1251–1271, but a standard reference (e.g., in the Stata 13 help file for the test) is J. D. Sargan, "The Estimation of Economic Relationships Using Instrumental Variables," *Econometrica* 26, no. 3 (1958): 393–415.

64. Wooldridge, *Econometric Analysis of Cross Section and Panel Data*, 123.

65. Ibid.

66. Carneiro, Heckman, and Vytlacil, "Estimating Marginal Returns to Education."

67. John Marshall, "Coarsening Bias: How Instrumenting for Coarsening Treatments Upwardly Biases Instrumental Variable Estimates" (2014), http://goo.gl/YA5Sjo.

68. Michael Spence, "Job Market Signaling," *Quarterly Journal of Economics* 87, no. 3 (1973): 355–374.

69. A similar argument, applied to the effectiveness of Catholic schools and job training programs, is made by Morgan and Winship, *Counterfactuals and Causal Inference*, 38–40.

CHAPTER THREE

Causal Inference with Experimental Data

David W. Nickerson

IN THIS CHAPTER

This chapter explains how randomized experiments can help solve the fundamental problem of causal inference and provides basic guidelines about the design and analysis of experiments. The running example throughout the text will be voter mobilization field experiments, but the lessons found in the text are broadly applicable beyond this narrow question. While the internal validity of experiments is unparalleled, the chapter concludes by exploring limitations regarding the external validity of experimental findings—even when research is carried out in the field. Despite these limitations, randomized experiments offer unparalleled ability to identify the causal effect of policy interventions and are an essential arrow in the policy analysis quiver.

WHY EXPERIMENTS?

One of the most fundamental questions that researchers and policy makers can ask about a public policy is "What is the effect of this policy?" This seemingly simple question is actually very hard to answer because of the complicated web of causal effects that shape the real world. Estimating the effect of a policy intervention using observational data requires many assumptions about the data generation process. The validity of these assumptions depends on the setting, but the researcher can never be certain that all possible confounding factors are accounted for. In contrast, randomly assigning the intervention of interest can eliminate most of the barriers to causal inference. The ease of inference is the reason why randomized experiments are the gold standard in fields so disparate as medicine, economics, ecology, clinical psychology, and public policy. By creating a valid baseline for comparison, experiments allow the researcher to estimate the average effect of an intervention.

The goal of program evaluation is to understand the effect of a program, T, on an outcome or set of outcomes, Y. For the sake of expositional clarity, assume that our policy is either implemented, $T = 1$, or not implemented, $T = 0$. While there are many possible definitions of effect, one of the most straightforward quantities that can be estimated is the average difference between the outcome of interest when the program is implemented, $E(Y \mid T = 1)$, and when the program is not implemented, $E(Y \mid T = 0)$. Once this difference, $\beta = E(Y|T = 1) - E(Y|T = 0)$, is known, then policy makers can begin to perform cost-benefit analyses and make informed decisions on whether the policy should be implemented.

To provide a concrete example, suppose a political campaign wants to know the cost effectiveness of having volunteers call eligible voters. The campaign can assign registered voters to be called, $T = 1$, or not, $T = 0$. There are many possible outcomes, Y, that a campaign may be interested in such as willingness to volunteer with the campaign, likelihood of voting for the candidate, or turning out to vote. That the outcome can be measured using identical processes for people targeted or ignored by volunteers is the only restriction. We'll focus on voter turnout as the outcome of interest as we develop this concrete example.

While our definition of the effect of the policy involves simple subtraction, it is not adequate to compare the average outcomes for experimental units (e.g., people or areas) where the policy was successfully implemented to the experimental units where the policy was not implemented. The units where the policy was implemented may be very different from the units where the policy was not implemented. If these differences are correlated with the outcome of interest, then the researcher will not be able to determine whether differences in the outcomes across areas is due to the policy being studied or underlying differences.

Returning to the concrete example of phone calls from campaigns encouraging voter turnout, comparing the voting behavior of people successfully called by the campaign to people not called by the campaign is likely to yield very biased inferences. For starters, the campaign can only call people for whom they have phone numbers. Since having a listed phone number is closely associated with age and income, which are two correlates of voter turnout, people the campaign is able to call will vote at higher rates than the people they cannot call regardless of how effective the phone call is at increasing voter turnout. Similarly, campaigns typically target supporters for voter mobilization rather than people with weak or unknown partisan attachments. Again, partisan attachment is associated with interest in politics and past turnout behavior, which correlate strongly with voter turnout, so the people targeted by the campaign for mobilization calls have a higher baseline rate of voting independent of the calls' efficacy. Thus, directly comparing rates of voter turnout across people called by the campaign to people not called could lead a researcher to conclude that phone calls are immensely successful even if a single phone call is never made. The reason is the baseline rates of expected turnout for the two groups are not comparable.

A common approach of policy analysts facing imbalance of this type is to add control variables, X, that could confound the analysis. When the analyst knows the data-generating function, accounting for confounding factors can yield better estimates of the effect of the policy, β. While the specific technique used to account for these measured confounding factors varies (e.g., linear regression, matching, data mining), the central logic remains the same across techniques. By adding control variables, the analyst assumes that the only difference in the outcome is due to the policy of interest once specific variables are controlled for. That is,

$$\beta = E(Y|T = 1, X) - E(Y|T = 0, X) \tag{1}$$

With a little algebra, equation (1) can be transformed into the canonical ordinary least squares model presented in introductory econometrics textbooks:

$$Y = \alpha + \beta T + \delta X + \varepsilon \tag{2}$$

where α is a constant, δ is a vector of coefficients, and ε represents all the unmeasured causes of Y (or, random residual error, depending on your epistemological interpretation of linear models). The connection between the linear model presented in equation (2) and the definition of the average treatment effect, β, presented in equation (1) can be seen by decomposing equation (2) into separate equations for the treatment, $T = 1$, and control, $T = 0$, groups:

$$\begin{aligned} \text{Treatment } (T = 1): \ & Y_T = \alpha_T + \beta + \delta X_T + \varepsilon_T \\ \text{Control } (T = 0): \ & Y_C = \alpha_C + \delta X_C + \varepsilon_C \end{aligned} \tag{3}$$

Solving equation (3) for β, we get

$$\beta = Y_T - Y_C + (\alpha_T - \alpha_C) + \delta(X_T - X_C) + (\varepsilon_T - \varepsilon_C)$$

which is clearly the difference in Ys for the treatment and control groups conditional on the control variables, X.

Many assumptions need to hold for equation (2) to yield unbiased estimates of the average treatment effect, β, but a key assumption is that the treatment variable, T, be uncorrelated with the error term, ε. That is, $\text{cov}(T, \varepsilon|X) = 0$. When using observational data, this assumption is impossible to verify, and the analyst must make theoretical arguments as to why the assumption holds. Demonstrating balance on observable characteristics across treatment and control conditions is a good step, but hardly definitive. There may be characteristics that are hard to measure but undoubtedly important causes of both the outcome, Y, and the policy variable of interest, T. While many datasets contain information on education, income, age, gender, occupation, and health, important predictors of outcomes such as motivation, self-control, family obligations, and agreeableness are often unmeasured and may be correlated with uptake or exposure to the policy intervention.

The voter mobilization campaign via phone calls provides a nice illustration of this dynamic. Most voter files contain a wealth of information, X, that allows an analyst to accurately predict voter turnout, Y. Many voter files contain information on age, race, party registration (a proxy for political interest and engagement), address (which can be used to append census data to estimate socioeconomic status), and—the best predictor of voter turnout—whether the person voted in past elections. Furthermore, campaigns know the criteria they used to target people, so they can account for those factors by including them as covariates or limiting the sample analyzed to people contacted. These rich data form the backbone of campaign analytics and make voter turnout an excellent candidate for satisfying the assumptions required for unbiased estimates of the effect of campaign contact [i.e., $\text{cov}(T, \varepsilon|X) = 0$].[1]

Despite this wealth of information, it is highly likely that people successfully contacted over the phone by campaigns have different baseline rates of voting than people who are not contacted. Even limiting the sample to only those people with phone numbers targeted by the campaign, answering the phone reveals information about the targeted person that is positively correlated with voter turnout. The mere act of answering the phone means that the target has not disconnected the phone, moved to another city, or died—all three of which are negatively correlated with voter turnout. Similarly, people screen calls, hang up, and otherwise avoid contact with campaigns, which may indicate that they are less engaged and interested in the election and therefore also less likely to vote. For reasons such as these, people who answer phone calls from campaigns are more likely to vote than people who do not answer the phone whether or not the phone call has any effect on turnout. In terms of equation (2), it is far from certain that being contacted by a campaign phone call is uncorrelated with unobserved causes of voter turnout and $\text{cov}(T, \varepsilon|X) = 0$. In terms of equation (3), while we can hold the Xs constant (i.e., $X_T - X_C = 0$), it is unlikely that the baseline rates of turnout are the same in the contacted and uncontacted groups ($\alpha_T - \alpha_C \neq 0$). Thus, observational techniques cannot guarantee unbiased estimates of the effect of campaign phone calls, β.[2]

Randomized, controlled experiments solve the problem of comparability by directly manipulating the policy of interest. Rather than let nature assign which observations receive the policy, experiments randomly assign observations to the policy. The archetypical experiment involves randomly assigning people via a coin flip to either a treatment group that receives the intervention (heads) or a control group that receives no intervention (tails). On average, the people assigned to the treatment and control groups should be equally tall, smart, motivated, good looking, old, religious, and suspicious of researchers flipping coins. That is, because the coin flip is designed to be completely exogenous to all possible factors of the outcome variables, assignment to the treatment and control groups tells the researcher nothing about the subject and only indicates the state of the coin when it was flipped. By creating the theoretically perfect distribution of treatment assignment, the researcher knows that, in the language of equation (2), $\text{cov}(T, \varepsilon) = 0$, and, in the language of equation (3), $E(\alpha_T - \alpha_C) = E(X_T - X_C) = E(\varepsilon_T - \varepsilon_C) = 0$. The only systematic difference between the two groups is the assignment to the treatment condition. Thus, in a randomized experiment, we can estimate the effect of assigning a subject to the treatment group as

$$\beta_{ITT} = \overline{Y}_T - \overline{Y}_C \tag{4}$$

In words, by subtracting the average outcome of the control group, $\overline{Y}_C$, from the average outcome of the treatment group, $\overline{Y}_T$, the researcher receives an unbiased estimate of the effect of assignment to the treatment condition. Because this estimate relies only on the assignment to the treatment condition, which is randomly determined, and not on actual receipt of the treatment, which is determined by many factors, this estimand is frequently called the "intent-to-treat effect," or ITT.

Returning to our running example of estimating the effect of phone calls on voter turnout, let's consider the field experiment conducted by the Youth Vote Coalition during the 2002 congressional elections.[3] The Youth Vote Coalition was an organization dedicated to increasing voter turnout among people under the age of 27. To test the effectiveness of their paid professional mobilization calls, the Youth Vote Coalition randomly assigned 54,717 registered voters spread across 15 jurisdictions with phone numbers to either a treatment group to be called by the phone bank (N = 27,496) or a control group that received no call (N = 27,221). The calls were made during the month leading up to Election Day and were monitored by Youth Vote employees for quality. The turnout behavior of subjects was ascertained by referencing official voter turnout records maintained by the local jurisdictions for both the treatment and control groups. The consistency in the measurement across both treatment conditions ensures that any measurement error associated with the outcome variable (e.g., a poll worker crossing off the incorrect name) is uncorrelated with the phone call, so measurement error will not bias estimates of the intent-to-treat effect, β. Table 3.1 reports the results of the experiment.

One of the first things to check when analyzing an experiment is whether the treatment and control groups look balanced across available covariates. Such balance checks cannot prove the randomization was performed correctly (either it was random or it wasn't), but large imbalances can help to diagnose problems with the randomization procedure. The column in table 3.1 labeled "Turnout in 2000" reports the differences in turnout between the group targeted by the professional phone bank and the control group in the 2000 presidential election. Since the election took place nearly two years before the calls took place, there is no way that the calls could have affected this behavior and the treatment and control group should look very similar along this dimension. The difference in past voter turnout rates between the professional call group (40.9 percent) and the control group (40.8 percent) is a mere 0.1 percentage point; there is no evidence that the randomization was compromised in any way.[4] So we will attribute any differences in voter turnout between the treatment and control groups to being assigned a phone call.

Examining turnout in 2002, which is our dependent variable of interest, we observe that 31.4 percent of the group assigned the professional phone call vote

Table 3.1. Intent-to-treat effects from the 2002 Youth Vote Coalition professional phone call experiment

Assignment	N	Turnout in 2000	Turnout in 2002
Professional phone call	27,496	40.9%	31.4%
No-call group	27,221	40.8%	29.8%
Difference		0.1 pp	1.7 pp
		(0.4)	(0.4)
Probability		0.79	<0.001

Notes: Numbers in parentheses report standard errors. "pp" stands for percentage point(s).

compared to 29.8 percent of the control. This difference of 1.7 percentage points means that for every 1,000 people targeted by the phone bank, 17 votes are created. By randomizing the people targeted by the phone campaign, the Youth Vote Coalition could conclude that its professional phone bank was mobilizing voters as intended by simply comparing mean rates of turnout.

While the canonical experiment involves splitting subjects evenly across a single treatment and control group, the logic of the experiment does not impose any restrictions on the number of possible treatment conditions or the ratios assigned to particular groups. The only requirement is that each subject have an equal probability of being assigned to each treatment condition. Random assignment ensures that the subjects assigned to each treatment condition are comparable. For example, the 2002 Youth Vote Coalition phone experiment reported in table 3.1 involved two other treatment conditions not reported here: called by volunteers and called by both volunteers and the professional phone bank.[5] Similarly, there may be good programmatic reasons to deviate from a 50/50 split between treatment and control groups. Many organizations may have a desire to provide the treatment—presumed to be beneficial—to as many people as possible. For example, researchers conducting a voter mobilization experiment with the Michigan Democratic Party assigned 80 percent of the sample to the phone call treatment condition in order to maximize the number of votes created.[6] This flexibility in the number of possible treatment conditions and the percentage of subjects assigned to each condition allows experiments to accommodate a large range of research demands and programmatic requirements.

THE STABLE UNIT TREATMENT VALUE ASSUMPTION

By purposefully constructing a treatment variable uncorrelated with all possible causes of the outcome variable, experiments allow the researcher to sidestep the "ignorability" assumption that most observational research requires (i.e., that the treatment variable is uncorrelated with possible causes of Y conditional on X). However, experiments must still make what statistician Donald Rubin calls the "stable unit treatment value assumption" (SUTVA).[7] There are two primary components to this assumption. First, the researcher must assume that the treatment assignment of any subject does not affect the behavior of any other subject. This component is often called "non-interference." There are many ways in which this assumption could be violated. Returning to the example on voter mobilization, receiving the treatment may cause a subject to attempt to mobilize people their neighbors or a strong response to a treatment could create lines at polling stations that dissuade members of the control group from voting. Most of the time, problems with non-interference are unverifiable and dismissed by researchers. However, it is possible to design experiments isolating the units of analysis to avoid interference[8] or even detect non-interference, thereby making it a quantity of interest.[9]

The second component of Rubin's SUTVA is that the treatments for all units are comparable. This assumption is often thought to imply that the treatment provided must be a monolithic unchanging entity so that all subjects receive exactly the same treatment. Voter mobilization experiments in which subjects are sent identical postcards[10] or e-mails certainly satisfy this understanding.[11] However, such a narrow interpretation of the no variation in treatment assumption would disallow a huge number of experiments. For instance, the drugs prescribed in experimental pills may be perfectly consistent across all subjects, but experiments on all doctor-patient interactions would be nearly impossible.[12] While a researcher cannot manipulate and account for every nuance of doctor visits to ensure complete uniformity, it is possible to manipulate approaches such as patient-led medicine or the use of checklists or accountability language. Similarly, the Youth Vote Coalition's 2002 experiment described previously would violate this interpretation of the assumption because the precise nature of the phone call differed depending on the reactions of the subject. The whole point was to tailor the phone calls to the individual targeted. That said, you can manipulate broad attributes such as message tone and have a well-defined estimand.[13] SUTVA's call for consistency in treatment should be viewed as a requirement to precisely define the treatment. This does not necessitate that every word of the experimental interaction be identical in every instance. The treatment could be defined as using a particular psychological concept in a script,[14] being called by a volunteer,[15] or even being targeted by a political campaign by any means it desires.[16] A well-defined experimental treatment will be consistent across all subjects but does not require the treatment to be inflexible.

ACCOUNTING FOR COMPLIANCE WITH THE TREATMENT

In many instances, it is likely that experimental subjects assigned to the treatment may not comply with the protocol and accept it. Non-compliance can take active forms, such as opting out of an experiment or consciously seeking out an alternate to the prescribed treatment regime, or it can take passive forms like simply being unable to be reached by the experimenter. In the case of our voter mobilization via phone calls example, reasons for non-compliance could include disconnected phone numbers, not answering the phone, screening calls, and hanging up before the treatment can be administered. Regardless of the cause, non-compliance means that the intent-to-treat effect is averaging in people who were correctly treated with people who received the incorrect treatment. While this quantity may be of interest in many settings, there may be times when researchers want to know the effect of the treatment on the people actually taking the treatment. This treatment goes by many names, such as the treatment on the treated (TOT), average treatment on the treated (ATT), and the complier average treatment effect (CATE). We will use the ATT in this chapter.

Adjusting for the contact rate is straightforward as long as the researcher keeps in mind that the power of the experiment comes from the random assignment. As mentioned previously, the reasons that a subject cannot or will not receive the treatment are likely to be correlated with causes of the outcome of interest. For this reason, all estimates of treatment effects need to be based on the ITT, which relies solely on the assignment. To derive the average treatment on the treated estimator, let us incorporate the application rate, γ, into the basic model of the data generation process from equation (3). The treatment group is divided into people who can be treated and people who cannot be treated. The overall outcome variable is a weighted average of the behavior of both types of subjects. Subjects who can be treated have a baseline propensity of α_γ for the outcome and receive the average treatment effect on the treated, β_{ATT}, by definition. Similarly, subjects assigned to the treatment group but do not receive the treatment have a baseline propensity for the outcome of α_N and are assumed to be unaffected by the treatment. This relationship can be expressed as

$$\overline{Y}_\text{T} = \gamma(\alpha_\gamma + \beta_{\text{ATT}}) + (1 - \gamma)(\alpha_N) + \varepsilon_\text{T} \tag{5}$$

Recall that all observed and unobserved pre-treatment characteristics of the subjects are balanced in expectation across treatment assignments. This balance, ensured by randomization, includes the tendency of subjects to refuse treatment or be available to be treated. Thus, the application rate parameter, γ, may not be observed in the control group, but we can assume that the control group would have the same proportion successfully treated as the treatment group. Moreover, the type of people who could have been treated in the control will have the same baseline propensity for the outcome of interest as those successfully treated in the treatment group. That is, α_γ will be the same for the treatment and control groups. The same can be said for the baseline propensity among people who would not have been treated if given the opportunity, α_N. Thus, the data generation process in the control group can be expressed as a similar weighted average between the two types of subjects even though we can't place subjects into categories. As equation (6) makes clear, the only difference is that the subjects who could be treated do not receive the treatment, so β_{ATT} does not play a role.

$$\bar{Y}_C = \gamma(\alpha_\gamma) + (1 - \gamma)(\alpha_N) + \varepsilon_C \tag{6}$$

Subtracting equation (6) from equation (5), we can solve for β_{ATT}. The random assignment ensures that all the extraneous terms cancel, and β_{ATT} can be expressed as

$$\beta_{ATT} = \frac{\bar{Y}_T - \bar{Y}_C}{\gamma} = \frac{ITT}{\gamma} \tag{7}$$

That is, our estimate of the average treatment effect on the treated is simply the intent-to-treat effect divided by the application rate.[17] In instances where every subject is treated as assigned, $\gamma = 1$, the intent-to-treat effect and the average treatment effect on the treated estimators are identical.

To illustrate this calculation, let us return to the Youth Vote Coalition's 2002 voter mobilization experiment. While the professional phone bank may have targeted 27,496 registered young voters with phone numbers, they successfully completed their prepared "Get Out the Vote" script with only 39 percent of subjects in the treatment group. If we assume that simply dialing the phone number had no effect on turnout for members of the treatment group, the effect of the call on the people listening to the call must have been larger than the 1.7 percentage point intent-to-treat effect reported in table 3.1. In fact, the effect was 4.3 percentage points (1.7 / 39% = 4.3) with a standard error of 1.0 percentage points. That is, for every 1,000 people contacted by the professional phone bank employed by the Youth Vote Coalition, 43 young people voted who would have otherwise stayed home. Since the Youth Vote Coalition paid $1.25 for each contact made by the phone bank, each additional vote generated cost $29 ($1.25 * 100 / 4.3). The effect of the overall program (ITT) was to raise turnout by 1.7 percentage points, and this effect was generated because the people actually contacted (ATT) were 4.3 percentage points more likely to vote.

The assumption that the treatment assignment only affects the outcome variable through actual receipt of the treatment deserves special emphasis. This assumption that the exclusion restriction holds may be problematic in some instances or require careful definition of what compliance with the treatment entails. For instance, if callers left messages at households where no one answered the phone, it is theoretically possible that the treatment assignment had an effect via these phone messages rather than the full conversation. The same is true for partial conversations cut off by the subjects before the conversations were completed. If either causal pathway is true, then an estimate of the ATT using completed phone conversations as the application rate would overstate the true effect of successfully completed phone conversations. If the list of people assigned to the treatment group were posted publicly, then subjects' reactions to the list or outside groups deciding to target the control group could also serve as pathways to altering turnout behavior outside of the phone calls.[18] Thus, the researcher needs to carefully define what constitutes compliance with a treatment regime when estimating the average treatment effect on the treated.

The assumption that the assignment only affects the outcome through receipt of the treatment also makes it clear to whom the average treatment effect on the treated will generalize. Namely, such experiments are completely silent with regard to what the effect of the treatment would be on subjects who did not comply with the protocol. This limitation is entirely intuitive; the experiment cannot speak to the effect of the treatment on non-compliant people because they were non-compliant in the experiment. This inferential problem can be a major limitation when the policy being studied would be implemented in a manner that compels compliance. For instance, a field experiment evaluating voter registration drives may accurately capture the effect of registration drives on turnout among those who register to vote as a response to the drive, but it cannot directly estimate the effect of voter registration through other means or the impact of universal voter registration.[19] Extrapolating would require theoretically informed arguments and cannot be derived from the data alone.

CALCULATING THE DEGREE OF UNCERTAINTY

Just as the margin of error in a poll taken from a random sample of a population can be calculated, estimated treatment effects also have standard errors. In fact, we can think of the experiment as a comparison of two random samples: the treatment group and the control group. Deriving the standard error is therefore a straightforward application of variance arithmetic with numerous possible approaches yielding equivalent formulas.[20] If we assume equal variance in outcomes for treatment and control groups (which is often approximately the case) and the covariance between a person's outcome value under treatment and control conditions is 0 (generally a conservative estimate), we can express the standard error for our average treatment effect on the treated estimate as

$$\text{SE}_{\text{ATT}} = \sqrt{\frac{\sigma_{Y|X}^2}{\gamma^2 NT(1-T)}} \tag{8}$$

where $\sigma_{Y|X}^2$ is the unexplained variance of the outcome measure for the entire sample, γ is the rate of compliance, N is the total number of subjects in the experiment, and T is the percentage of subjects assigned to the treatment group. Each term in the formula presented in equation (8) provides guidance as to how to maximize the power of an experiment.

N: Since the number of subjects in the experiment appears in the denominator, adding subjects to the experiment will decrease the standard error associated with our estimated treatment effect. A survey with 1,000 respondents has more precision than a survey with only 300 respondents, and the exact same logic applies to experiments. Since we take the square root of the entire term, the gains from adding sample decline exponentially, and increasing our sample size from 200 to 300 yields larger efficiency gains than increasing our sample size from 3,000 to 3,100. So researchers should include as many subjects in an experiment as time and resources allow, but the returns diminish quickly.

T: The percentage of subjects assigned to the treatment group and the percentage of subjects assigned to the control group, $(1 - T)$, can range between 0 and 1.[21] Jointly, their product, $T(1 - T)$, is maximized when subjects are split evenly between the treatment and control groups, $T = 0.5$, which makes intuitive sense. If we were to shift subjects from the treatment group to the control group, we would have a more precise estimate of the control group, but a less precise estimate of the treatment group. Since the point is to compare the two populations, our overall estimate of the difference is actually worse than if they were evenly divided. While there may be programmatic and logistical reasons to deviate from even splits, statistically even divides are the most powerful designs.

γ^2: Since the compliance rate is in the denominator, we know that the higher the compliance rate the more precise our estimates of the treatment effect will be. Intuitively, an experiment where only 15 percent of the sample receives the treatment *should* be less powerful than one where 85 percent receives the correct treatment because more subjects are being treated as assigned. Problems with low compliance rates are compounded because the term is squared. Thus, falling compliance rates cause standard errors to grow quickly, and most quality (i.e., high compliance rate) versus quantity (i.e., N) trade-offs favor keeping the compliance rate high at the expense of sample size.[22] It should also be noted that in cases where $\gamma = 1$, the standard error for the ATE and ITT are identical.

$\sigma^2_{Y|X}$: The unexplained variance in the outcome variable sits in the numerator of equation (8), which implies that average treatment effects with low-variance outcomes will have smaller standard errors. In one sense, there is not much the researcher can do about this factor. The question asked by the researcher largely dictates the outcome to be measured, so the variance of the outcome is baked into the research agenda. However, there are two tactics researchers can employ to increase the precision of the experimental estimator.

First, predictors of the outcome variable can be collected and included in the analysis.[23] By reducing the unexplained variance in Y, modest reductions in the size of the standard error can sometimes be obtained. Returning to our ongoing example, including dummy variables for turnout in 2000 and each of the 15 jurisdictions in the Youth Vote Coalition's 2002 mobilization experiment only reduces the estimated standard error from 1.01 percentage points for the ATT to 0.97 percentage points. That is, despite the fact that dummy variables explain considerable variance (e.g., the R^2 jumps from 0.01 to 0.10), the gain in statistical efficiency is negligible.

The second way in which researchers reduce the unexplained variance in the outcome variable is stratified randomization. Stratified randomization involves placing subjects into groups based on pre-treatment predictors of the outcome variable. Within these groups, subjects are randomly assigned to treatment and control groups. The analysis then adds a dummy variable for each one of the blocks or strata created.[24] In essence, the research is running a separate experiment for each block/stratum and pooling the result of these small experiments together. The variance of Y within each block should be limited, but the technique allows the researcher to generalize across a wide range of the sample.[25] Again, gains in precision may be modest, but blocking on irrelevant regressors does not bias estimates and there is no downside to the practice.

The fact that the researcher generated data in which the key policy intervention is uncorrelated with other causes of the outcome of interest allows for estimates of the precision of treatment effect estimates that are less reliant on assumptions about the data generation process. The clarity of the calculation allows for researchers to calculate the statistical power of experimental designs in advance and proceed with confidence.

DESIGNING EXPERIMENTS TO ROBUSTLY MEASURE THE QUANTITY OF INTEREST

The power of experiments comes from the fact that the researcher has the ability to manipulate and assign the policy intervention of interest randomly rather than rely on the assignment nature provides. This active role in the data generation process allows the researcher to sidestep hurdles to inferences such as ignorability and endogeneity. Unsurprisingly, imposing additional control over the data affords the researcher some additional advantages—albeit more marginal than the random assignment of the treatment. This section presents three experimental designs that improve on simple random sampling and the canonical assignment into dichotomous treatment and control groups.

The preceding section extolled the virtues of placing subjects into blocks (also known as strata) before randomization to improve statistical efficiency. Stratified randomization has two additional benefits that are worth noting. First, stratified randomization ensures nearly perfect balance on the covariates included in the stratification. As mentioned previously when random assignment was introduced, simple random assignment ensures that all characteristics of the subjects and the environment are identical across the treatment and control groups *in expectation*. That is, if the experiment were conducted thousands of times, individual trials may exhibit differences in important covariates, but there would be no difference between the two groups on average across those replications. However, researchers rarely have the opportunity to conduct the same experiment thousands of times. If the researcher gets an unlucky draw and the two treatment groups appear unbalanced, then the ability to interpret the findings of that particular trial may be compromised.

For instance, suppose the random assignment in the 2002 Youth Vote Coalition resulted in a 1.2 point difference in voter turnout in the 2000 election rather than the 0.1 point difference presented in table 3.1. Such an imbalance would occur only about 5 times in every 1,000 trials, so it is unlikely but not impossible; nothing necessarily went wrong with the randomization procedure. The observed difference of 1.7 percentage points in 2002 is now less impressive because it is only 0.5 percentage points bigger than what is observed in 2000, which is akin to a failed placebo test. The textbook response to this situation is to simply include the 2000 vote history as a covariate to adjust for the observed imbalance. In expectation, the residual error term, ε, will be uncorrelated with the treatment variable once the imbalance is accounted for. However, we already know that our assignment is an outlier, and it is possible that the imbalance also occurs in unobserved causes of the turnout and the imbalance in 2000 turnout is a symptom of a deeper imbalance. In such a situation, our process for generating and analyzing the data remains unbiased, but the specific point estimate for $\hat{\beta}$ may be above the true parameter value, β. Thus, the interpretation of the results from that particular trial will be more complicated.

Since researchers often only get to run randomized trials a handful of times at best, it would be a best practice to limit the likelihood of observing an unbalanced assignment. Stratified random assignment can accomplish this goal by guaranteeing that the treatment and control groups are balanced on the variables taken into account during the stratification. Assuming these covariates are correlated with other causes of the outcome variable, the samples are more likely to be balanced across observed and unobserved causes of Y. Thus, stratified random sampling can minimize the probability of obtaining an unlucky random assignment that makes interpreting the estimated treatment effect difficult.

A second benefit to blocked randomization is that it allows the researcher to pare down the experiment in the face of a resource shortfall and preserve statistical precision. The best laid plans of lab mice and men occasionally go awry and experiments become more expensive than anticipated. The randomization blocks/strata provide the researcher a principled way to trim the experiment and cut costs because each stratum constitutes its own experiment. When the reason for non-compliance is unrelated to the potential outcomes of the subjects or the nature of the treatment, excising entire strata allows the researcher to preserve statistical power without biasing estimates of the treatment effect.[26]

An alternative to stratified/blocked randomization is a "rolling" procedure that places subjects in a random order and assigns them to the treatment group as the treatment becomes available. To illustrate the protocol, suppose there are 120 school districts and the state government has the capacity to provide textbooks and software for a new science curriculum to 40 schools each year. The rolling protocol would suggest placing the school districts in a random order and giving the first 40 districts the materials for the new curriculum the first year, the next 40 schools the curriculum in the second year, and the final 40 schools the curriculum in the final year. Since the order of the schools is random, the schools farther down on the list could serve as a control group for the schools higher up on the list that receive the new curriculum, which could allow for a rigorous evaluation of the new curriculum. There are two reasons this rolling procedure is advantageous in settings where the treatment will be allocated over a long time period or the quantity of the treatment available is unclear.

First, the procedure does not deny subjects assigned to the control group a beneficial treatment unnecessarily. Accurately measuring the effectiveness of treatments thought to be beneficial is a valuable activity because it can verify the presupposition that the treatment is helpful and it can help policy makers understand the cost effectiveness of the treatment compared to other policy alternatives. Conducting randomized trials sometimes necessitates people being denied the experimental treatment in the name of science, which can potentially be a short-term detriment to the individual. In instances where the treatment is scarce, not every person can receive the experimental treatment. The rolling experiment protocol turns this shortfall into an opportunity to learn about the effectiveness of the treatment, and it also solves a normative problem by creating a lottery for receiving the scarce resource.

Second, the rolling protocol maximizes statistical power in the face of uncertain resource availability.[27] If subjects were assigned to treatment and control groups in a predetermined manner, then an unexpected shortfall would mean subjects assigned to the treatment condition would not receive the treatment and surprise surpluses would entail subjects assigned to the control being treated. Both lower the compliance rate, γ, for the experiment and inflate standard errors. In contrast, by placing subjects in a random order, the rolling protocol is sufficiently flexible to let the assignment exactly match the availability of the treatment. In this way, the rolling protocol is strictly more efficient than the canonical assignments to set treatment and control groups.[28]

A Youth Vote Coalition phone voter mobilization experiment from 2001 in Boston provides a nice example of this design principle. The names and phone numbers of 7,055 registered voters were obtained and randomly divided into even-sized treatment and control groups. The treatment group was then placed in a random order. The plan was to call all the targeted individuals, but roughly 30 percent of the committed volunteers failed to show up. As a result, the campaign could only make its way through one-third of the list of the subjects assigned to the treatment and contacted 55 percent of the subjects actually attempted. Table 3.2 compares the precision of the experiment using the rolling protocol to the precision that would result if the original treatment and control assignments had been kept [using

Table 3.2. Comparison of rolling and traditional protocols in the 2001 Youth Vote Coalition experiment in Boston

Protocol	Rolling	Traditional
Percentage assigned to treatment	17.1%	50.7%
Application rate	55.4%	18.7%
Control group voting rate	54.5%	54.4%
Treatment group voting rate	56.1%	55.1%
Intent-to-treat effect	1.6 pp	0.7 pp
Estimated effect on the treated	2.9 pp	3.5 pp
Standard error of estimated effect	**2.8 pp**	**6.3 pp**

Note: The number of subjects in the experiment was 7,055.

equation (8) to calculate standard errors]. As expected, the precise point estimates are indistinguishable from each other using the two protocols (neither technique should be biased), but the standard errors on the estimate of the ATT effect in the rolling protocol is half the size of the standard error using the traditional protocol. Thus, the rolling protocol can offer substantial gains in precision when resources are highly volatile.

The final design principle explained here concerns placebo treatments and the ability to precisely isolate the quantity of interest. A problem with the canonical dichotomous treatment and control group framework is that treatments often have multiple facets and the researcher may only be interested in one of those facets. Demonstrating that such a compound treatment differs from the control group may be useful for establishing that a suite of policies can have the desired outcome, but it cannot isolate the effectiveness of each component. To isolate a single component, the researcher should create multiple treatment arms that differ in only one narrow regard. For instance, one of the objectives of a social accountability mail experiment in Michigan was to measure the effect of mailing people the turnout behavior of neighbors on a target's own turnout.[29] To nail down the effect of mailing a neighbor's turnout rather than simply raising awareness that voter turnout is a public record or that they were part of a study or simply receiving a piece of Get Out the Vote mail, researchers added treatment conditions to estimate each component separately. Table 3.3 presents the resulting cascade of treatment conditions and results.

Table 3.3. Design and results from Gerber, Green, and Larimer social accountability experiment

Condition	Treatment effect compared to control	Standard error
Simple Get Out the Vote (GOTV) mail	1.8 pp	0.3
Simple GOTV mail + you are part of a study and voter turnout is a public record	2.5 pp	0.3
Simple GOTV mail + you are part of a study and voter turnout is a public record + here is your voter turnout record	4.8 pp	0.3
Simple GOTV mail + you are part of a study and voter turnout is a public record + here is your neighbors' voter turnout record	8.1 pp	0.3

Simply comparing the mail reporting a person's own voter turnout to the control group, readers would know that the tactic boosts turnout a lot (4.8 percentage points) but not the effect of sending a person's own turnout rather than threatening to look up a person's turnout or simply sending a letter reminding the person to vote. Adding the "Hawthorne effect" treatment allows the researcher to conclude that the personal turnout information adds 2.3 percentage points to the effectiveness of the treatment on top of the effect of sending a letter explaining that voter turnout is a public record and they are part of a study. Carefully layering the treatments allows the researcher to measure the effect of isolated mechanisms.

CONCLUSION AND LIMITATIONS

Randomized experiments offer unique insight into the causal effects of policies implemented because the construction of the data ensures that assignment to receive the experimental policy is uncorrelated with all possible causes of the outcome of interest. Internal validity is the chief strength of randomized experiments, but concerns about external validity often limit the ability of experiments to draw generalizable conclusions.

External validity is sometimes viewed as a concern primarily for experiments conducted in a laboratory rather than in the field. Such sentiments simultaneously sell laboratory studies short and oversell the virtues of field experiments. By and large, whether a laboratory or field experiment is preferable depends on the question being asked by the researcher. Any topic requiring careful or detailed measurement is likely to be better answered in a laboratory. Adequately answering a question such as "What is a person's initial emotional reaction to a particular campaign ad?" is probably beyond the capacity of a field experiment where researchers have difficulty simply contacting subjects much less conducting a survey at a very precise time. "Do tragic news stories cause physiological changes in people?" is a question in which monitoring hormone levels, heart rates, and brain activity might be in order and all of those activities are impractical to perform in the field. While subjects may be exposed to the experimental stimuli in an environment that differs from their natural surroundings, it is not immediately obvious that split-second responses will differ markedly in the admittedly artificial confines of the laboratory. People too often dismiss laboratory research on external validity grounds without considering whether the laboratory may be the best possible setting in which to study a phenomenon.

That said, many laboratory studies make claims outside of immediate reactions and want to generalize their findings to real-world, long-run behaviors. While it is possible that watching argumentative political shows reduces people's faith in the democratic process, it is not clear such laboratory findings would apply in settings where the subject has other choices of viewing, is distracted by competing messages, or has time to have the treatment wash out as the chaos of daily life washes over the subject.[30] For example, the results of a small experiment ($N = 60$) conducted on undergraduate students reveal that the simple act of predicting whether you registered and voted increased turnout by 25 points compared to a control group. An attempt to replicate the finding with 1,160 randomly selected registered voters in a Connecticut town failed to find any hint of a mobilization effect from predicting one's behavior.[31] Several years later, another experiment failed to find any support for the self-prophesy effect on a sample of 287,228 registered voters in Pennsylvania.[32] Why did the self-prophesy effect not work well in the field? Was the initial study a small-sample fluke? Was it because it involved college students? Was the treatment more immediately proximate to Election Day? The self-prophesy theory was plausible and intriguing; it just didn't work out in the larger "real world" setting for some reason.

Of course, field experiments have also had trouble being replicated in larger samples. There is a strong negative correlation between reported treatment effect size in voter mobilization studies and sample size.[33] That is, big studies report small effects, and small studies report big effects. Publication bias does not have to account for the observed relationship either. There are times where situations change. I worked with a group of progressive civic engagement organizations from 2006 to 2008 in congressional, local, and presidential elections measuring the effectiveness of their outreach strategy. In 2006, most of the organizations were successful in mobilizing voters and increased turnout among the people contacted by 4 to 6 percentage points. In the off-year local elections, the average treatment effect was on the order of 8 to 15 percentage points. How did the organizations perform in 2008? I discovered airtight evidence that the organizations increased turnout by a statistically significant 0.1 to 0.2 percentage points. Clearly, the strong performance in local and congressional elections did not transfer to the presidential race. Despite well-crafted program evaluations and operating on well-established best practices, the civic organizations could not replicate their findings from just the year prior. Perhaps these grassroots mobilization strategies don't work when many organizations are targeting a similar set of people for mobilization. Maybe a different set of individuals was mobilizable in different settings. Strategies may lose their effectiveness when they are no longer notable and stand out from the crowd. Converging on the same set of strategies may change the efficacy of those findings.

Thus, despite their claim to internal validity, experiments suffer some concerns about external validity that must be addressed. The challenge and opportunity is that the best way to assess the external validity of a finding is to test it in multiple circumstances. Not only will such agendas keep researchers employed, but making sense of the disparate findings will lead to other puzzles to solve.

NOTES

1. David W. Nickerson and Todd Rogers, "Political Campaigns and Big Data," *Journal of Economic Perspectives* 28, no. 2 (2014): 58–71.
2. For an elegant demonstration of this claim, see Kevin T. Arceneaux, Alan S. Gerber, and Donald P. Green, "Comparing Experimental and Matching Methods Using a Large-Scale Field Experiment on Voter Mobilization," *Political Analysis* 14, no. 1 (2006): 37–62.
3. For a full description, see David W. Nickerson, "Quality Is Job One: Volunteer and Professional Phone Calls," *American Journal of Political Science* 51, no. 2 (2007): 269–282.
4. Similarly, the average age in both the treatment and control groups was 22.7 years of age.

5. The volunteer phone calls were noticeably less effective than the professional calls in this experiment.

6. David W. Nickerson, Ryan F. Friedrichs, and David C. King, "Partisan Mobilization Experiments in the Field: Results from a Statewide Turnout Experiment in Michigan," *Political Research Quarterly* 34, no. 1 (2006): 271–292.

7. Donald B. Rubin, "Formal Modes of Statistical Inference for Causal Effects," *Journal of Statistical Planning and Inference* 25, no. 3 (1990): 279–292.

8. Susan D. Hyde, "Experimenting in Democracy Promotion: International Observers and the 2004 Presidential Elections in Indonesia," *Perspectives on Politics* 8, no. 2 (2010): 511–527.

9. David W. Nickerson, "Is Voting Contagious? Evidence from Two Field Experiments," *American Political Science Review* 102, no. 1 (2008): 49–57; and Betsy Sinclair, Margaret McConnell, and Donald P. Green, "Detecting Spillover Effects: Design and Analysis of Multilevel Experiments," *American Journal of Political Science* 56, no. 4 (2012): 1055–1069.

10. Alan S. Gerber and Donald P. Green, "The Effects of Canvassing, Direct Mail, and Telephone Contact on Voter Turnout: A Field Experiment," *American Political Science Review* 94, no. 3 (2000): 653–663.

11. David W. Nickerson, "Does Email Boost Turnout?," *Quarterly Journal of Political Science* 2, no. 4 (2007): 369–379; and Neil Malhotra, Melissa R. Michelson, and Ali Adam Valenzuela, "Emails from Official Sources Can Increase Turnout," *Quarterly Journal of Political Science* 7, no. 3 (2012): 321–332.

12. Sherrie H. Kaplan, Sheldon Greenfield, and John E. Ware, "Assessing the Effects of Physician-Patient Interactions on the Outcomes of Chronic Disease," *Medical Care* 27, no. 3 (1989): S110–S127.

13. Kevin Arceneaux and David W. Nickerson, "Negative and Positive Campaign Messages: Evidence from Two Field Experiments," *American Politics Research* 38, no. 1 (2010): 54–83.

14. David W. Nickerson and Todd Rogers, "Do You Have a Voting Plan? Implementation Intentions, Voter Turnout, and Organic Plan Making," *Psychological Science* 21, no. 2 (2010): 194–199.

15. David W. Nickerson, "Volunteer Phone Calls Can Increase Turnout," *American Politics Research* 34, no. 3 (2006): 271–292.

16. R. Michael Alvarez, Asa Hopkins, and Betsy Sinclair, "Mobilizing Pasadena Democrats: Measuring the Effects of Partisan Campaign Contacts," *Journal of Politics* 72, no. 1 (2010): 31–44.

17. It is also possible to think of the adjustment in terms of two-stage least squares where the assignment, T, serves as an instrument for the experimental policy of interest, P. Treatment assignment actually serves as the nearly perfect instrument since it affects the outcome, Y, but only through the application of the policy so the typically problematic exclusion restriction holds. For more on two-stage least squares estimation, see Joshua D. Angrist, Guido W. Imbens, and Donald B. Rubin, "Identification of Causal Effects Using Instrumental Variables," *Journal of the American Statistical Association* 91, no. 434 (1996): 444–455.

18. Costas Panagopoulos, "Affect, Social Pressure and Prosocial Motivation: Field Experimental Evidence of the Mobilizing Effects of Pride, Shame and Publicizing Voting Behavior," *Political Behavior* 32, no. 3 (2010): 369–386.

19. David W. Nickerson, "Do Voter Registration Drives Increase Participation? For Whom and When?," *Journal of Politics* 77, no. 1 (2015): 88–101.

20. Readers wanting to read clear derivations of the formula are referred to David Freedman, Robert Pisani, and Roger Purves, *Statistics*, 3rd ed. (New York: Norton, 1998), A32–A34.

21. This range is non-inclusive of the endpoints. If all the subjects are placed into either the treatment or the control group, then there is no baseline for comparison and no experiment.

22. See David W. Nickerson, "Scalable Protocols Offer Efficient Design for Field Experiments," *Political Analysis* 13, no. 3 (2005): 233–252.

23. Researchers should be extremely disciplined in their use of covariates. While adding covariates to experimental analysis does not bias estimates, it creates space for researcher discretion that can bias estimates toward statistically significant point estimates. See Alan S. Gerber and Neil Malhotra, "Do Statistical Reporting Standards Affect What Is Published? Publication Bias in Two Leading Political Science Journals," *Quarterly Journal of Political Science* 3, no. 3 (2008): 313–326.

    Pre-registering the analysis plan can force researchers to be more transparent in the analysis and allow the reader to better gauge how sample dependent the results may be. See Macartan Humphreys, Raul Sanchez de la Sierra, and Peter van der Windt, "Fishing, Commitment, and Communication: A Proposal for Comprehensive Nonbinding Research Registration," *Political Analysis* 21, no. 1 (2013): 1–20.

24. Block randomization often places subjects into equal-sized groups prior to randomization. Stratified randomization refers to the practice of creating blocks based on covariates related to the outcome of interest and then randomizing within each block. While block randomization does not necessitate stratified random sampling, in practice the two techniques are synonymous.

25. For a detailed explanation of the advantages of blocking, see Ryan T. Moore, "Multivariate Continuous Blocking to Improve Political Science Experiments," *Political Analysis* 20, no. 4 (2012): 460–479.

26. Nickerson, "Scalable Protocols."

27. Ibid.

28. See Nickerson, "Scalable Protocols," prop. 3, for a proof.

29. Alan S. Gerber, Donald P. Green, and Christopher W. Larimer, "Social Pressure and Voter Turnout: Evidence from a Large-Scale Field Experiment," *American Political Science Review* 102, no. 1 (2008): 33–48.

30. Kevin Arceneaux and Martin Johnson, *Changing Minds or Changing Channels?* (Chicago: University of Chicago Press, 2013).

31. Jennifer K. Smith, Alan S. Gerber, and Anton Orlich, "Self-Prophesy Effects and Voter Turnout: An Experimental Replication," *Political Psychology* 24, no. 3 (2003): 593–604.

32. Nickerson and Rogers, "Do You Have a Voting Plan?"

33. Alan S. Gerber, Donald P. Green, and David Nickerson, "Testing for Publication Bias in Political Science," *Political Analysis* 9, no. 4 (2001): 385–392.

II EMERGING DATA SOURCES AND TECHNIQUES

CHAPTER FOUR

Descriptive Network Analysis

Interest Group Lobbying Dynamics Around
Immigration Policy

Alexander Furnas and Lee Drutman

IN THIS CHAPTER

This chapter provides an introduction to the use of network methods for descriptive and exploratory political analysis.[1] We offer a general introduction to the kinds of data that can be represented and interrogated with network tools and then provide some introductory guidance on effectively using those tools. We also walk through an example of using these network methods on real-world political data by presenting an analysis of lobbying on immigration issues.

INTRODUCTION TO NETWORKS

"Network analysis" is a term used to encompass a range of techniques for exploring, analyzing, and visualizing relationships between entities. For example, in political science, networks could be used to understand the relationships between interest groups as they form advocacy coalitions, international actors engaged in multipartite trade agreements, or members of the legislature who cosponsor bills with each other (we will return to this example in simplified form later). Network analysis is founded upon graph theory, the branch of mathematics concerned with studying and modeling relationships between objects. Network-based methods are used to model relational phenomena in a broad variety of disciplines, ranging from epidemiology to physics to sociology. Networks (or graphs, more formally) are composed of objects that are related to each other in pairwise fashion. For example, in a friendship network, each person would be connected to every other person who was her friend. Because network analysis has an interdisciplinary history, there are multiple terms for the objects and relations represented in a network. The objects are called either "nodes" or "vertices," and the relationships between them are called "links," "arcs," "ties," or "edges." We call each pairwise connection between two nodes a "dyad." For the sake of clarity, we will confine ourselves to using "node" to refer to an object in a graph and "edge" to refer to a dyad between two nodes. This might take the form of two people (nodes) connected by virtue of their friendship (edge). When visualized, the nodes are typically represented as circles, and edges are shown as lines connecting those circles.

Scholars in the social sciences have used networks extensively to examine the structure of social groups. In this context, we might imagine a social network graph in which each node is a person in a social group, and the links signify friendship. One might use such a network to examine the different cliques or groups of friends that appear in the network. This type of network could be used to model how information might diffuse from one person in the network to others throughout the graph.

Nodes can be any type of actor, and we can define a link as any type of relationship. For example, in political science, we might be interested in the bill-sponsoring behavior of members of the U.S. House of Representatives. We might represent sponsorship activity as a network by considering every member of the House of Representatives as a node. There would be an edge between any two nodes if there were mutual cosponsorship.

For illustrative purposes, we have created a fictitious sample cosponsorship dataset comprising 10 legislators (five Republicans and five Democrats) who may have sponsored any of six bills. These sample data can be found in part D of the online companion to this chapter. Figure 4.1 displays the cosponsorship network of these 10 hypothetical representatives.

For example, in the network in figure 4.1, Congressperson Wexler and Congressperson Johnson sponsored at least one bill together, so the network contains a link between the nodes that represent them. A real-world network of this kind could be used to find clusters of congresspeople who tend to sponsor bills together. It could also be used to empirically observe the behavior of existing caucuses as shown in the work of Fowler and Zhang et al.[2]

In the network in figure 4.1, all relationships are necessarily reciprocal. If it is true that Beyers sponsored a bill with Brown, then it follows that Brown also sponsored a bill with Beyers. In other applications, however, relationships are not always entirely reciprocal. For example, two congresspeople could be connected because one chairs a committee and has the power to appoint people to the committee. This kind of relationship can be represented in a network as a dyad that flows in one direction, called a "directed edge." Edges can have a variety of characteristics that are analytically useful. An edge can be either directed or undirected. As another example, edges in a scholarly citation network are directed because it is possible for author A to cite author B without author B having also cited author A. Each directed edge is said to have a source, the node from which it originates, and a target, the node at which

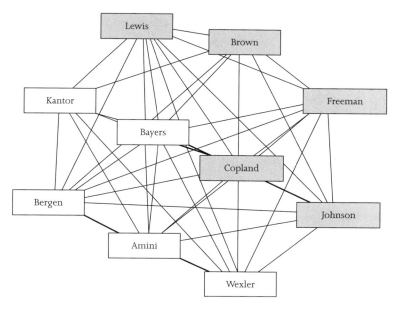

Figure 4.1. Hypothetical cosponsorship network

the edge is directed. For our citation example, if scholar A cited scholar B, scholar A would be the source node and scholar B would be the target node of the edge connecting them.

In online social networks, for instance, Facebook is composed of undirected edges—all friendships are mutual—while Twitter is a network of directed edges because one person can follow another without being followed by that person in turn.

This first network visualization (figure 4.1) represents the simplest possible way we could model our cosponsorship data as a network. Each edge merely answers the question: Did these two congresspeople ever cosponsor a bill? As a result of this simplicity, figure 4.1 is not particularly informative. It just looks like everybody is connected to everybody else. However, when we choose to represent data as a network and analyze them using network tools, we are confronted with an array of design choices. A critical component of descriptive network analysis is understanding the manner in which these choices over how to encode relevant data into your network structure can enable you to draw meaningful and noteworthy conclusions about actors and groups of actors within your network.

The first set of choices involves evaluating the value of different relationships. Not all relationships are of equal importance. In our bill cosponsorship network example, almost all of the legislators were connected because they had sponsored at least one bill together. However, only one cosponsored bill may signal a limited relationship. If we care about the strength of the relationships, we could represent the strength as a simple count of the number of bills that two congresspeople had sponsored together. This operationalizes the assumption that working together on more bills signifies a stronger relationship. In networks, this is the weight of an edge, a numeric value we assign to an edge based on observed data to signify the edge's importance. Figure 4.2 shows our sample cosponsorship network with the edges now weighted by the number of times the legislators have cosponsored bills together. In this visualization, as is standard, higher-weight edges are shown as thicker lines.

Notice that the position of the nodes in figure 4.2 differs notably from their position in figure 4.1. While both of these networks contain the same set of ties between nodes, the edges in figure 4.2 are weighted as we have described. The

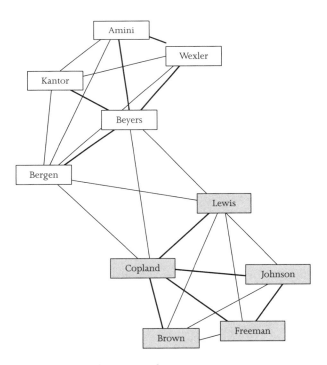

Figure 4.2. Weighted cosponsorship network

layout algorithm we have used to create these visualizations, Force Atlas 2 in the open-source Gephi software package, incorporates the weight of the edges into its function for positioning nodes, so the position of the nodes has changed.[3] Subsequent figures use this same algorithm with the same parameterization. We will discuss layout algorithms in slightly more detail later in this chapter.

When relationships are represented in a network, it is possible to see patterns that go beyond the individual connections. To analyze these larger-level structures within a graph, we typically examine sets of subgraphs within the larger graph. A graph, G, is defined by a set of nodes and edges between them. A subgraph of G is any graph whose sets of nodes and edges are subsets of the node and edge sets of G. In the most minimal form, each dyad within the graph (e.g., Amini and Wexler) is its own subgraph. Often we will be interested in larger subgraphs like triads (sets of three nodes) or cliques. A clique is a subgraph of any size, in which every dyad within that subgraph is connected. In the cosponsorship example, the Democratic congresspeople (represented by white) are a distinct clique, because they have all sponsored bills with each other, as are the Republican congresspeople. If the full graph is a clique—that is, if every node in the graph is connected to every other node in the graph—it is called a "complete graph." In complete graphs, all possible edges we could construct exist. If you were to raise your glasses in a celebratory toast and if everyone clinked glasses with everyone else, you would have made a complete graph with your clinking.

To have a complete graph in our congressional cosponsorship example, all of the congresspeople would have cosponsored bills with all of the other congresspeople—this was almost true, but there were two unconnected dyads. While we would usually not expect complete graphs, we can expect different degrees of connectivity. For example, the rate at which we expect congresspeople to be cosponsoring bills with other congresspeople would likely differ from the rate at which we would expect congresspeople to go on vacation together. The degree to which they are interconnected is called the "density of the graph." The density of a graph, G, is defined as the number of edges that exist in G divided by the number of edges that would exist in a hypothetical complete-graph version of G where all nodes were connected to all other nodes. The density of G is the percentage of all possible edges among a set of nodes that are actually observed in G. A denser graph is said to be more "tight knit," although we may also be interested in how tightly knit various subgraphs of G are. Figure 4.3 displays three graphs with progressively decreasing density; from top to bottom, they are as follows: 1 (a complete graph), 0.5, and 0.2.

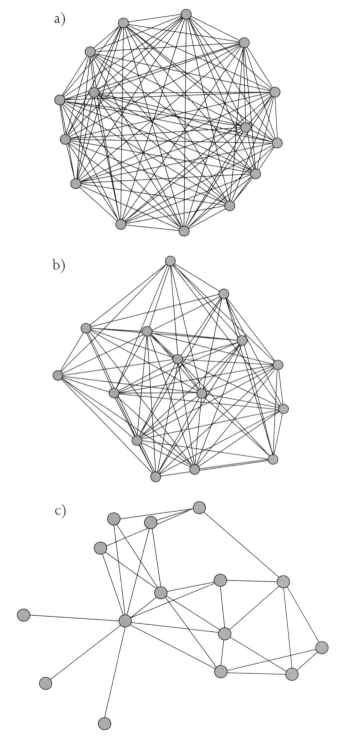

Figure 4.3. Networks with varying densities

Representing a set of objects as nodes in a network allows us to explore how these objects relate to each other. When we work with complicated relationships, we often want to understand who the critical players are and how they are related to each other. If you want to get a bill passed, you might care about who has connections with the most important legislators, or who serves as an important bridge connecting many disparate actors, or who would be effective at informally spreading information most efficiently. These important relationships are represented in networks by the connections of nodes with edges.

One way we commonly talk about which actors are important is to ask the following question: What actors are in the center of a network? However, even a question as simple on its face as this can have many different answers depending on how we choose to think about the meaning of centrality. Social network researchers have developed a set of common measures of centrality based on differing ways of defining "central." The three simplest and most common are degree centrality, closeness centrality, and betweenness centrality.[4]

Degree centrality (often referred to simply as that node's "degree") is the count of how many edges are connected to that given node, or the number of other nodes that node is connected to. The simplest notion of degree centrality assumes that all edges are undirected; that is, we count each edge once and weight them all equally. A weighted degree of a node, n, would be the sum of the weights of all edges incident upon node n. In a directed graph, each node has both an in-degree and an out-degree. The in-degree of a given node, n, is the number of edges for which n is the target node; that is, how many other nodes link to node n? The out-degree of a given node, n, is the number of edges for which n is the source node; that is, how many other nodes does node n link to? As was true for degree centrality in undirected graphs, both in- and out-degree centrality can be measured to account for edge weight by summing the weights of the relevant edges.

Closeness centrality is a way to measure how close a node is to the rest of the graph. A congressperson may not have cosponsored bills with everyone, but she could still have a relatively high closeness centrality by being connected through her connections. More formally, the distance between any two nodes is understood as the number of edges in the shortest path that connects those two nodes. This is also sometimes called the "geodesic distance" (or simply "geodesic") between two nodes. The closeness centrality of a node, n, is the mean geodesic distances between node n and all other nodes in the graph. Put another way, a node's closeness centrality score is the expected value of the length between that node and a randomly chosen other node in the graph. People often use the reciprocal of this value as the "closeness centrality" so that nodes with a higher value are those that are more central in this sense, but this is simply a transformation for the sake of clarity when ranking nodes. A node that is more central in this sense will tend to be fewer steps away from a randomly selected node than a less central node.[5]

Betweenness centrality measures how instrumental a particular person (node) is in connecting others in the network. It is measured as a count of how many of the shortest paths between nodes a given node lies upon. To find the betweenness centrality of node n, we take the full set of geodesic paths used for calculating the closeness centrality between all nodes (i.e., every shortest path between every two sets of nodes) and then count the number of these paths that flow through node n.[6] A node is understood to be more central if more of these paths go through that node. One way of thinking about this metric is to imagine what would happen if a given node were removed from the graph. Removing a node, n_1, with a high betweenness centrality from graph G would disrupt many of the shortest paths between other nodes and have a larger effect on the mean geodesic distance between nodes in the resulting subgraph of G than would removing a node, n_2, with a low betweenness centrality.

As we found when we looked at our sample cosponsorship data originally, almost everyone had sponsored at least one bill with each other. This was because all but two of the congresspeople had sponsored the Must Pass Appropriations Act (the sample cosponsorship data we have used are available in the online companion to this chapter). However, if we remove all edges with a weight of 1, we are left with a subgraph based on cosponsorship of the other five bills. Filtering of this kind can be a useful tool. The resulting graph (figure 4.4) highlights the partisan cliques more clearly than the previous unfiltered graph. The nodes in figure 4.4 are sized by their betweenness centrality. Because all paths between the Republican and Democratic cliques must pass through them, Bergen, Beyers, Copland, and Lewis are the most central nodes in terms of betweenness.

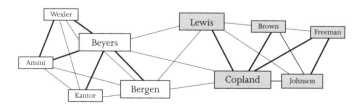

Figure 4.4. Filtered network

It is worth noting that these measures of centrality are applications of graph mathematics that were originally operationalized in large part by sociologists to explore conditions and patterns of information diffusion and flow in social networks. As a result, these different measures make different assumptions about the significant features of a node's network position. Borgatti and Everett provide a two-dimensional typology for understanding the theoretical assumptions upon which common centrality measures are based, which may be useful for students interested in learning more about which centrality measure may be right for their specific application.[7]

In addition to analyzing the characteristics of individual nodes as they relate to other nodes at the micro level, networks can help us to see how relationships cluster and form communities. For example, in Washington, DC, lobbyists and legislators travel in circles of mutual influence that are compartmentalized around special interests, ideologies, and financial incentives. Network methods can help us detect noteworthy patterns at this level, by focusing on the structure of communities or groups within the graph. In an excellent survey of community detection literature, Porter, Onnela, and Mucha note that while a rigorous universal definition of a network community has remained elusive, the formation and behavior of groups of actors has been a central focus of sociologists and network scientists for decades.[8] In more recent years, computational and algorithmic methods of community detection have been a rich topic of research. Researchers from a diverse set of disciplinary backgrounds have developed a wide range of techniques for estimating network modularity, cliquishness, and community patterns. Although a detailed exegesis of these various technical methods is beyond the scope of this chapter, the work of Porter, Onnela, and Mucha referenced earlier provides a thorough introduction to the history, development, and application of these methods.

Community detection and clustering methods are concerned with partitioning networks into groups of nodes, which are more connected to each other than they are to the rest of the graph. This is implicitly related to the notion of subgraph density: network communities are subgraphs that are comparatively dense internally but more sparsely connected to the rest of the graph. A related subgraph is the clique, defined as a subgraph in which every two nodes are connected by an edge. It may be useful to think of a clique as a smaller complete graph embedded within the full graph. For example, in our congresspeople network, congresspeople who cosponsor bills create two cliques, one Democratic and one Republican. However, a clique is a very specific type of subgraph (a fully connected one), while a community is a more general term referring to a comparatively dense subgraph within a larger graph. Exactly how "community" is operationalized may vary greatly, but this general intuitive definition of more densely connected internally than to the rest of the graph tends to hold true. Some common general approaches for community detection use iterative hierarchical processes, either "agglomerative" if they join together nodes into groups based on similarity, or "divisive" if they partition the network into ever-smaller subgroups based on dissimilarity.[9] Fortunato discusses a variety of commonly used community detection approaches in extensive detail, for those students interested in learning more.[10] Because the partisan communities in our example network are in fact fully connected cliques, it is unlikely that any major community detection methods would disagree when classifying these nodes. However, in larger real-world networks, there is often disagreement in boundary cases.

So far we have discussed networks in which all nodes are of the same type (e.g., congresspeople), and it is possible to have edges from one node to any other node. Sometimes, though, we are interested in networks in which there are different types of nodes. This is called a "multi-mode network." The most common form of multi-mode network is the two-mode network, or bipartite graph. If a graph, G_B, is bipartite, every node, n_i, is a member of one of two types (or modes), say mode U and mode V. Every edge in G_B will connect a node from mode U to a node from mode V or vice versa. In a bipartite graph (or any multipartite graph), edges never connect nodes of the same type. A generic bipartite graph, with node types U and V, is shown in figure 4.5.

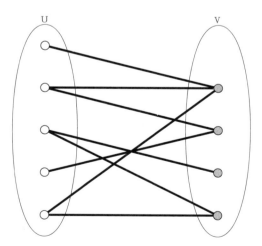

Figure 4.5. Bipartite graph

Bipartite graphs are also sometimes called "affiliation networks" in the context of linking a set of people to a set of groups or organizations of which they are members. In such a graph, we have two types of nodes and thus two modes: people (U) and groups (V). In this case, a given edge$_{uv}$, from person u to group v signifies that a person u is a member of group v. Affiliation networks are frequently useful for social science questions beyond typical person-to-person relationships in standard social network analysis.[11] For example, Cho and Fowler use an affiliation network (based on bill sponsorship) to evaluate Congress as a network with small-world properties.[12]

Some of the centrality or community detection measures discussed previously have generalized forms that have been adapted for use in bipartite or multipartite graph contexts, but often it is useful to project a multi-mode network onto a one-mode network for analytic purposes.[13] In fact, in our previous congressional bill cosponsorship example, we already did this implicitly. Formally, we could have described the congressional bill sponsorship network as an affiliation (or bipartite/two-mode) graph that related congresspeople on the one hand to bills they had sponsored on the other.

We can project this bipartite graph onto a unipartite graph by considering congressperson nodes as connected if they share a tie to a bill node. Thus, shared affiliation between two nodes of one type to nodes of the other type becomes the measure for connection in the one-mode projection. In our example, this is mutual sponsorship of the same bill. An edge in a one-mode projection is typically weighted by the count of shared affiliations between the nodes it connects or, in the case of our example, the number of shared bills that two legislators have cosponsored. The one-mode unweighted projection of the graph in figure 4.6 would yield the graph we saw in figure 4.1. We saw the weighted version in figure 4.2. Our sample data contained two bipartisan bills sponsored by most of the 10 members: the Must Pass Appropriations Act and the Military Intervention Authorization Act. As figure 4.6 makes clear, there were also several clearly partisan bills. The cosponsorship behavior of legislators with respect to these hypothetical partisan bills resulted in the partisan clustering we saw in the one-mode projection earlier in this chapter.

Just as a graph may have multiple types of nodes, we can also construct a graph with multiple types of edges. Such a graph is said to be "multiplex." A multiplex network can also be understood as multiple overlapping networks that share nodes in common, but with different link structures between those nodes. For example,

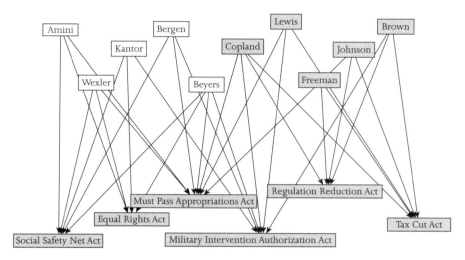

Figure 4.6. Unipartite graph

we might imagine a communication network among a group of friends in which edges based on interactions on different media platforms are each represented at a different network layer. While uses of multiplex graph representations may vary, multiplexity adds an additional dimension which can allow us to model more complex relational phenomena. Depending on the context, connections between two nodes at multiple layers of a multiplex network may serve as an indicator of a particularly strong relationship between those nodes, or analysis of when and why actors tend to be connected at one level and not at another can provide insight into the strategic behavior of actors. For example, Michael Heaney conceptualizes interest groups within a multiplex network.[14] Rather than assume that interest groups are defined by one characteristic that they share (e.g., a common issue), he examines the strength of connections in three overlapping networks. These networks are based on communication between members, common issues, and shared coalition memberships.

Figure 4.7 summarizes the aspects of relationships that can be represented in network analysis. Nodes and edges can represent one or more things, and the strengths and organizations of their relationships can be visualized and explored.

Looking at data relationally allows us to ask different types of questions and to consider agents within their particular (networked, structural) contexts.

Nodes

One type → One mode

OR

Multiple types → Multi-mode

Edges

All ties are reciprocal → Undirected edges

OR

Ties not necessarily reciprocal → Directed

Tie state is binary (e.g., connection is yes/no) → Unweighted edges

OR

Tie strength varies along some important numerical dimension → Weighted edges

All edges measure the same thing → One type of edge

OR

Different types of edges between same sets of nodes → Multiplex graph

Figure 4.7. Relationships represented in a network analysis

USING NETWORK METHODS TO STUDY LOBBYING

There is an old saying in Washington, DC: "If you are not at the table, you are probably on the menu." This saying is about the interrelatedness of the modern policy-making process. Interests and coalitions exist in relation to each other, competing to set the agenda or attach a provision to a critical bill. Essentially, lobbying is about creating and maintaining relationships among people, constituencies, issues, and campaigns. Lobbying is about relative position and competing interests.

Understanding and analyzing lobbying quantitatively requires that we use tools that are capable of dealing with the complexity and interconnection inherent in how lobbying is practiced. If gains can be made by shifting coalitions or relationships, we need tools that will help us see and understand those relational patterns. If policy on an issue is subject to countervailing pressures of multiple competing interests, each juggling their relationships with one another, we need tools that will help us understand that issue embedded within that context. Network analysis offers us a set of tools to measure, represent, explore, and hopefully explain these complex and contingent relational structures. In this section, will explore the use of some of these tools in the context of studying lobbying.

The example presented here is based on a specific analysis that we originally published on the Sunlight Foundation's blog in the spring of 2013, at a time when Congress was gearing up for a major debate over immigration reform. It used network analysis to better understand which sectors cared about which pieces of immigration reform, and to measure the relative intensity of those preferences.

We began by trying to solve a specific problem. Lobbying reports filed under the Lobbying Disclosure Act (LDA) rarely offer the granularity necessary to know what specific provisions of the bill an organization might actually be lobbying on, let alone that organization's position. This presents a serious challenge to those who might be interested in measuring the influence of a particular organization's lobbying efforts. In the work we show here, we attempted to mine historic lobbying reports to speak to lobbying interests and coalitions on large-scale comprehensive or omnibus legislation.

We begin from the premise that to understand lobbying, we can't look merely at lobbying in the direct lead-up to a piece of legislation. We need to look at lobbying over a several-year window. Very rarely does policy appear out of nowhere. More typically, it is the result of a multi-year lobbying process, involving many players hashing out agreements or re-hashing conflicts over a long time before an actual "policy window" opens and legislation moves.[15]

Immigration is a good example of this. While the previous attempt at comprehensive immigration reform died on the Senate floor in 2007, the arrayed interests with a stake in immigration policy did not simply pack up their bags and go home. Even if the policy window to do immigration reform closed for the time being, the immigration system was enough of a problem that few could argue that a policy window would not open eventually. In the meantime, the arrayed interests could continue to try to work out compromises, build consensus, or discredit opponents' arguments in preparation for that moment.

For this reason, we thought it valuable to analyze the lobbying that takes place in preparation for a major political battle. While lobbying reports can never match interviews for details, they can provide a more comprehensive and systematic understanding of the interests, coalitions, and intensity of lobbying. One of the advantages of lobbying reports during closed policy windows is that they are better measures of narrow interests. When comprehensive legislation passes, many groups pile onto a large bill. A specific issue mention of "comprehensive immigration reform" is not informative. But when there is no comprehensive legislation, groups advance more narrowly targeted legislation to address the particular problem that they care about. On immigration, tech companies wishing to expand their high-skill labor force advance legislation expanding the number of high-skill visas. Agricultural producers lobby on bills expanding the number of H-2A visas so they can hire more seasonal farmworkers from abroad. Hotels lobby on bills to expand the number of H-2B visas so they can hire more seasonal housekeepers from abroad. But because these bills rarely make it out of committee, only those who care enough about the bills to be involved in their formulation are likely to lobby on them. Thus, registered lobbying is a pretty good indicator of an intensity of preference, and the coalitions that form around these bills are good indicators of the true coalition of support. Here we use this fact at scale to determine which industries, sectors, or groups care about which issues under the broader umbrella of immigration, and introduce a methodology for getting more out of the coarse data provided by the LD-2 activity reports that lobbyists are required to file.

Methodology

To reveal the underlying structure of the previously opaque mass of lobbying activity, we developed a multi-method computational approach using both topical and network-based clustering. We used a natural language processing approach to group similar bills together. Then we used a network-based approach to reveal interest group coalitions. We will focus on the network analysis piece here. Working through this example of the use of some network methods provides an opportunity to explore decision making in network analysis and provides some insight into how one might apply some of the network basics detailed at the beginning of this chapter.

Dataset

The LDA regulates what data lobbying organizations are required to reveal about their activities on Capitol Hill. Since the 109th Congress, the primary means of disclosure mandated under the LDA has been quarterly reporting of activities by registrants, filed by organizations and lobbying firms engaged in lobbying activity. For each client, lobbying firms disclose the issues on which they lobbied by selecting a three-letter "general issue code" (e.g., TAX, IMM, and EDU, for taxes, immigration, and education, respectively) from a list of 79 possibilities provided by the Clerk of the U.S. House of Representatives. For each general issue that a group lobbied on for a client, they also include the specific lobbying issues, the House(s) of Congress and federal agencies contacted, and the names and covered positions of the specific lobbyists involved. For the purpose of this analysis, the relevant data fields were client (or registrant for in-house lobbying by companies), general issue code, and specific lobbying issue.

However, there are considerable problems in practice with the data, which substantially limit the use of disclosed information for research and oversight purposes. Unlike the general issue disclosure, the specific lobbying issue is disclosed as an unstructured text field. In practice, "description of the specific section(s) of interest" is often left out and, when disclosed, tends to be vague and uninformative. Largely, researchers must rely on general issue codes, manual inspection, and qualitative work to provide some sense of lobbying activity. As a result, usable LDA data are coarse, rather than fine grained, which presents significant challenges to meaningful detailed analysis.

These data are cleaned and structured by the Center for Responsive Politics (CRP) and made available in bulk form at the Sunlight Foundation. One key extension of the data that CRP makes is classifying politically active organizations at three levels of specificity. The hierarchy of CRP classification is as follows: at the top level are 13 "sectors," which are broken down into a total of approximately 100 "industries" at the midlevel, and, finally, more than 400 total "categories" at the most detailed level. Each organization is classified as belonging to one group at each level of specificity. For the purpose of this analysis, we use the most detailed CRP codes—those at the "category" level. Hereafter, though, we will refer to each of these some 400 categories as a "sector."

To test our approach, we chose a single general issue code, IMM (immigration). Immigration was selected because of the timeliness of the issue to current policy debates. We looked at only lobbying reports filed for activity during the 109th–112th Congresses (2005–2012) in which the registrant lobbied under the general issue code for immigration. This left us with a set of 7,814 lobbying reports. This allowed us to capture activity both related to and following the 2007 push for comprehensive immigration reform.

Each LD-2 report, then, can be thought of as an observation. For each observation, we used the following data:

- Client name
- CRP organization "category" classification of the client, the most specific of the three levels in CRP's organization ontology
- All bills mentioned as specific lobbying issues in the LD-2

For each bill, we gathered additional data from GovTrack.us:

- Bill name
- Bill number
- Congress in which a bill was introduced
- Congressional Research Service (CRS) summary of the bill

Since the purpose of this analysis was to reveal which sectors (industries, interest groups, unions, etc.) care about and are engaged in influencing policy on which specific immigration provisions, we sought to exclude omnibus bills. We removed the top 2 percent (20) most heavily lobbied on bills from the dataset. We also excluded any bills for which we could not find a valid match from GovTrack or for which there was no available CRS summary. Finally, we excluded the activity of clients classified by CRP as "other single issue or ideological groups," because this catchall category is not cohesive enough to warrant the sector-level aggregation we later conduct.

The complete dataset, built from the nearly 8,000 lobbying reports, included 678 lobbying clients in 170 different CRP sectors and 987 different bills.

Lobbying Network Construction and Visualization

Network analysis is a natural choice for exploring these lobbying data because they are fundamentally relational. Every lobbying record captures a relationship between a client, who has initiated the lobbying, and a bill (or set of bills) that they have revealed are important to them. We can understand this as a bipartite graph, which you will remember is a network with two types of nodes, wherein nodes of the first type are connected exclusively with nodes of the second type (and vice versa). In this case, clients are connected to specific bills they mentioned in their lobbying reports.

Rather than focusing on individual client activity, we collapsed the 678 lobbying clients into nodes based on their sector. This resulted in a set of 170 sector nodes, each of which represents the total activity by all of the constituent organizations in that sector. In other words, a node representing a given sector is connected to all of the immigration bills that were lobbied on by all of the clients in that sector.

The result of this process was a bipartite graph with two modes: 170 sector nodes and the 987 specific bills on which they had reported lobbying (on reports mentioning immigration as an issue). A single report in which a client lobbied on a specific bill is coded as an edge between the CRP sector of which that client is part and that specific bill. Rather than simply encoding the network with binary edges signaling either the existence or lack of a connection between a sector and a particular bill, we chose to weight our edges to account for the varying intensity with which clients in a given sector lobbied on the bill. The edges are weighted by a simple count of the number of lobbying reports that reference that particular bill.

For example, an LD-2 form in which Harvard University had hired a lobbyist to support the Dream Act (H.R. 1751, 111th Congress) is represented as an edge between the Schools and Colleges node and the Dream Act node. This form would contribute a weight of 1 to the association between the Schools and Colleges node and the Dream Act node, to be added to all other lobbying activity on the Dream Act by various schools and colleges. Thus, the more that clients within a given CRP sector have lobbied on a specific bill, the more we can infer that organizations in that sector care about that bill, and the higher the edge is weighted.

As a single LD-2 form represents one-quarter of a year's activity, if a single organization lobbies on a particular bill for multiple successive quarters, that lobbying activity will show up in multiple successive LD-2 forms. Each instance is counted toward the total edge weight. As a result, the edge weight between a sector and a bill is based on both the number of organizations lobbying on the bill in that sector and the duration of that lobbying activity. Thus, weight captures both intensity and duration of a sector's lobbying engagement on a particular bill. The result of this process was a single affiliation graph with weighted undirected edges.

The Challenges of Visualization

At the beginning of this chapter, we discussed how various data can be modeled as a network and looked at some descriptive metrics of node position and network structure that an analyst may find informative. Network visuals can be exceedingly useful tools for exploratory and descriptive analysis, although their effectiveness can be limited by legibility constraints as the size of the network grows. However, the insights one can garner from descriptive network visualization work often depend on the choices the analyst uses in presenting the network. Each choice allows us to highlight different aspects of the network. For this reason, we spend some time on the visualization choices we made when building our immigration network visualization. Figure 4.8 takes us through the several stages of choices we made in representing our network graph.

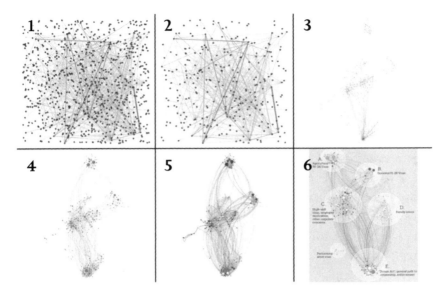

Figure 4.8. Stages of visualization

The purpose of the work we set out to do with our immigration lobbying network visualization was to provide a usable map to highlight the main communities of interest involved in the constituent sub-issues under the scope of immigration legislation. Given this, we adopted a judicious filtering approach that highlighted the most important nodes and strongest ties. Our goal here was to expose the backbone of the network for exploration.

Figure 4.8 shows the various stages of the filtering of this network to expose the main trends, while removing isolates and peripheral nodes not deeply embedded within the immigration lobbying structure. In subplot 1, we show the entire network with random assignment of node position. We then began by filtering the network to the subgraph with a k-core of 3, shown as subplot 2 of figure 4.8.[16] A k-core—where k can be any integer—is the maximal subgraph in which every node is connected to at least k other nodes in that subgraph. By employing k-core filtration, we limited the network we were to visualize to a cohesive subgraph containing only those nodes that were connected to at least three other nodes in the same subgraph. We chose a k of 3 after some trial and error in an attempt to strike a balance between inclusiveness and legibility. Essentially, we have removed extraneous and loosely connected nodes, leaving the more strongly connected backbone of sectors and bills: only those sectors lobbying on at least three bills which were themselves lobbied on by at least three sectors remain. Filtration of this kind can be useful for visualization, because larger networks can strain the bounds of legibility. However, it is worth noting that for many uses, such as investigating routes of information transfer, the distal nodes that k-core filtration excluded may be substantively important and k-core filtration would not be theoretically defensible.

We then turned to the question of how to display our filtered immigration lobbying bipartite graph. Graph layout algorithms are as varied as the clustering approaches we touched on earlier, and, as with clustering, there is no objectively correct layout for any particular situation. The layout procedure we employed here emphasized clustering within the network, as shown in subplot 3 of figure 4.8. We chose the OpenOrd modification of the Fruchterman-Reingold layout algorithm, which employs an edge cutting that ignores weaker links in favor of stronger ones.[17] Generally, increasing edge cutting in most algorithms will tend to highlight cliques or clustering, but in so doing may make these subgraph structures appear. See part B of the online companion to this chapter for more information on selecting a layout algorithm.

It is important to remember that the x, y position of a node in a visualization does not represent any sort of "ground truth" about that node; rather, it is a function of that node's position in the graph structure and, often just as significantly, the properties of the algorithm selected for layout. One must be careful not to overstate or over-interpret the significance of position in a network visualization, or understate the extent to which it is dependent on the layout algorithm and its assumptions.

Subplot 4, in figure 4.8, shows the network with the nodes sized according to their weighted in-degree, adjusted for the node type within the affiliation graph. We applied the two-mode degree normalization method suggested by Borgatti and Everett, which is a modification of Freeman's degree normalization.[18] For a given node A, this normalization process involves dividing the sum of the weights of A's edges by the number of nodes in the mode opposite A. This controls for the fact that sector nodes could potentially be connected to many more bills than a bill could be connected to sectors, simply because there are more total bills than sectors. See part A in the online companion for more details on this degree normalization.

Essentially, this shows, then, for a given bill, the average amount of lobbying activity directed at that bill by each sector. For sectors, the weighting shows the average amount of lobbying the sector directed at each bill. This weighted adjustment allows for nodes of both modes to be displayed on roughly the same scale, rather than the top sectors (which may lobby on hundreds of bills) dwarfing the top bills (which are constrained to a maximum of 170 sectors lobbying on them).

As noted previously, the general issue field is too broad to be analytically useful beyond simple filtering; it provides no help in discovering what sectors care about which specific policies. Conversely, the lack of standardization of the "specific lobbying issue," which provides meaningful, albeit inconsistent, information, doesn't provide a simple answer to that question either. We used a natural language processing approach to compare and then cluster bills to generate a taxonomy of specific sub-issues and policies within the broader set of immigration bills contained in our dataset. This approach seeks to move from the coarse to the granular, by providing sub-issue classification.[19] We used the output of this process to color nodes by their specific lobbying issue (bill similarity cluster), shown in subplot 5 of figure 4.8 (and the cleaner stylized version in subplot 6). This figure was originally produced for online publication and used a wide range of colors; it is reproduced in grayscale here. The association between particular bill sub-issue areas and network clusters is made clear upon exploration of the resulting graph. These associations are discussed in further detail next.

What the Network Tells Us

Figure 4.9 presents the big picture. Our final network connects lobbying interests with the specific immigration bills on which they've lobbied. The size of the circles represents the amount of lobbying activity. We've assigned a different color to each of 34 distinct sub-issues identified by a textual analysis of bill summaries, as described in our PolNet paper.[20]

We identified five main clusters of activity focused around different economic and industrial sectors with differing interests in the immigration space. We also included a small unconnected cluster, F. As color is an important component of this visualization, we have included a more detailed discussion of the visualization in the online companion. See part E of the online companion for an interactive version of this visualization and a look at individual issue clusters.

CONCLUSION

The example of descriptive network analysis research we presented in the previous section used network methods to try to understand the connection between immigration issues and specific lobbying sectors and groups. Preliminarily, our

Immigration Lobbying in Congress 2007–2012

This network is based on 6,712 quarterly lobbying reports filed by organizations in 170 sectors mentioning 987 unique bills, under the issue classification of immigration between 2007–2012. Here, we present the results of our classification and network analysis, which reveals multiple distinct clusters of different interests and sub-issues within the broader landscape of immigration lobbying.

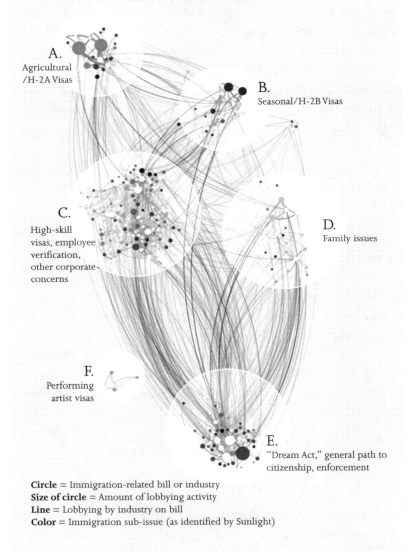

A.
Agricultural
/H-2A Visas

B.
Seasonal/H-2B Visas

C.
High-skill
visas, employee
verification,
other corporate
concerns

D.
Family issues

F.
Performing
artist visas

E.
"Dream Act," general path to
citizenship, enforcement

Circle = Immigration-related bill or industry
Size of circle = Amount of lobbying activity
Line = Lobbying by industry on bill
Color = Immigration sub-issue (as identified by Sunlight)

Figure 4.9. Interest group lobbying network

analysis suggests that we can learn a great deal about the interests of lobbying groups using this method. We can see who lobbies whom, and the relative strength and intensity of the ties.

It is important to keep in mind that as we constructed, filtered, clustered, and displayed our network, we made a series of conscious design choices. These choices balance the legibility and usefulness of our ultimate visualization against the real concern that in over-filtering our network or over-determining node membership and placement, we might visually convey false-positive messages about the structure of our graph. Given this balance, it is important to be aware of the limitations that these choices impose on the validity and generalizability of the conclusions that may be drawn from descriptive visualization work. There are several limitations on the reach of this project, which suggest avenues for further research. First, our analysis tells us nothing about which sectors support or oppose specific provisions, only the extent of their interest. The LDA data do not include information to that effect. It may, however, be possible to infer some degree of intention behind such lobbying activity. One approach might involve looking at bills on which only one industry or sector lobbied before the bill was tabled or died in committee. We might assume that such a bill was the brainchild of this sector and could glean information about what provisions those specific sectors support based on that. Those connections could, perhaps, serve as a training corpus for a machine learning approach to labeling sectors' positions on various other bills. If feasible and reliable enough, such a project would significantly add to the value of lobbying disclosure data.

Our analysis shows that the immigration debate is both structured and noisy. When we zoom out to view the entire network (figure 4.9), we can see five big clusters of activity on immigration. When we zoom in, we see much more messiness: lots of sectors, lots of bills, lots of interests, and many overlaps. However, the data-driven approach explored here provides a starting point for making sense of these connections and interests. This work demonstrates that some structure can be gleaned from the data buried in LD-2 forms. In doing so, it reveals some of the potential of network analysis. By using relationships and connections as the basic unit of analysis, we gain insights that mere summary statistics would miss.

In this chapter, we have explained the major features of using graph structures to represent relational data, and provided guidance on descriptive metrics and visualization techniques for learning things from the structure of these relationships. But the network analyst's toolkit is both broad and deep, and this chapter represents only the beginning of what can be done when using network structures for analytic purposes. For example, advanced network tools provide means for exploring contingent and interconnected relationships that can confound independence assumptions common in standard econometric practice. Networks allow us to model complex relationships and answer certain types of questions where it can be hard to gain purchase with traditional quantitative methods. Who is important within this community? Do similar individuals within a network tend to be connected to each other? How do subgroups within this larger group relate to each other and which actors serve important roles connecting these subgroups? How should we expect information to travel between a set of people or organizations? How robust is a community's capacity to communicate? Can the flow of information be disrupted by removing a few key actors? It is an exciting time to use network tools to address questions of politics and policy. The use of networks in political analysis is still relatively new, and there are significant areas worthy of investigation where there has been little research using network methods to date. Furthermore, easy-to-use computational tools for network analysis have never been more widely available, ranging from products with graphical user interfaces, such as Gephi and NodeXL, to popular packages in programming languages like R or Python. With the introduction provided in this chapter, these tools should now be conceptually accessible, and you can begin applying the techniques covered in this chapter to your own relational data.

FURTHER READING

In this chapter, we have provided an introduction to how to think about political data in network terms. While we have covered the basics of descriptive network analysis, this represents only the beginning of what can be done with network data. The basic concepts introduced here allow the motivated student to move on to more thorough, often mathematical, treatments of descriptive network analysis, as well advanced topics of statistical inference and hypothesis testing. Throughout this chapter, we have made an effort to reference texts that are particularly helpful for further reading. We would like to highlight some of those again here, as well as suggest some additional resources for continued study. Mark Newman's textbook *Networks: An Introduction* is widely used and excellent, and his survey article "The Structure and Function of Complex Networks" provides a concise but rich formal treatment of many of the topics we have covered in this chapter.[21] Porter, Onnela, and Mucha and Fortunato offer thorough accounts of various methods of community detection and layout.[22]

In the last five to ten years, the growth of computational resources has enabled a new wave of advanced network simulation and inference. Prominent among these various methods is exponential-family random graph modeling (ERGM), the results of which can be interpreted somewhat analogously to a logistic regression on the existence of ties between two nodes. However, in estimating the full network, ERGM uses Markov chain Monte Carlo maximum likelihood estimation to account for network structure and endogeneity that standard regression techniques cannot.[23] The book *Exponential Random Graph Models for Social Networks: Theory, Methods, and Applications*, edited by Dean Lusher, Johan Koskinen, and Garry Robins, is a great resource for learning about network analysis with ERGM. The statnet package is a popular implementation of this modeling approach in the statistical computing language R.[24] Others have taken stochastic actor-based approaches to modeling networks, for exploring change in networks over time.[25] RSiena, developed by Snijder and colleagues, is a popular R implementation of this framework for longitudinal network inference. Exciting recent work by Manuel Gomez-Rodriguez, Jure Leskovec, and others has presented an approach for inferring latent networks of transmission, infection, or diffusion and presented various packages (NETINF, NETRATE, INFOPATH) that implement their techniques. For political scientists, these tools may be useful for addressing questions of policy diffusion and political communication.[26]

NOTES

1. It is worth noting that many more advanced topics, especially statistical models of networks and inferential methods of networks, are well beyond the scope of this chapter. For advanced reading, we recommend Dean Lusher, Johan Koskinen, and Garry Robins, eds., *Exponential Random Graph Models for Social Networks: Theory, Methods, and Applications* (New York: Cambridge University Press, 2012); and Tom A. B. Snijders, Christian E. G. Steglich, and Gerhard G. van de Bunt, "Introduction to Actor-Based Models for Network Dynamics" (mimeo, 2008).

2. James H. Fowler, "Connecting the Congress: A Study of Cosponsorship Networks," *Political Analysis* 14, no. 4 (2006): 456–487; and Yan Zhang, A. J. Friend, Amanda L. Traud, Mason A. Porter, James H. Fowler, and Peter J. Mucha, "Community Structure in Congressional Cosponsorship Networks," *Physica A* 387 (2008): 1705–1712.

3. Mathieu Jacomy, Tommaso Venturini, Sebastien Heymann, and Mathieu Bastian, "ForceAtlas2, a Continuous Graph Layout Algorithm for Handy Network Visualization Designed for the Gephi Software," *PLOS ONE* 9, no. 6 (2014): e98679.

4. Alex Bavelas, "A Mathematical Model for Group Structures," *Human Organization* 7, no. 3 (1948): 16–30; Linton C. Freeman, "A Set of Measures of Centrality Based on Betweenness," *Sociometry* 40, no. 1 (1977): 35–41; Linton C. Freeman, "Centrality in Social Networks: Conceptual Clarification," *Social Networks* 1, no. 3 (1979): 215–239; and Phillip Bonacich, "Power and Centrality: A Family of Measures," *American Journal of Sociology* 92, no. 5 (1987): 1170–1182. There are many other types

of centrality beyond the primitives explained in this chapter. For example, modified betweenness centrality accounts for non-geodesics (flow betweenness). Also, eigenvector centrality and beta centrality are forms of iterative centrality that factor in the centrality of a node's neighbors into its own centrality score. See Mark E. J. Newman, "A Measure of Betweenness Centrality Based on Random Walks," *Social Networks* 27, no. 1 (2005): 39–54; Phillip Bonacich, "Factoring and Weighting Approaches to Status Scores and Clique Identification," *Journal of Mathematical Sociology* 2, no. 1 (1972): 113–120; and Bonacich, "Power and Centrality." For further reading on properties of these iterative centralities, see Phillip Bonacich, "Some Unique Properties of Eigenvector Centrality," *Social Networks* 29, no. 4 (2007): 555–564.

5. Bavelas, "A Mathematical Model for Group Structures."

6. Freeman, "A Set of Measures of Centrality"; and Newman, "A Measure of Betweenness Centrality."

7. Stephen P. Borgatti and Martin G. Everett, "A Graph-Theoretic Perspective on Centrality," *Social Networks* 28, no. 4 (2006): 466–484; see also Stephen P. Borgatti, "Centrality and Network Flow," *Social Networks* 27, no. 1 (2005): 55–71.

8. Mason A. Porter, Jukka-Pekka Onnela, and Peter J. Mucha, "Communities in Networks," *Notices of the AMS* 56, no. 9 (2009): 1082–1097. For the sociological origins of network communities, see Herbert A. Simon, *The Architecture of Complexity* (New York: Springer, 1962); and Robert S. Weiss and Eugene Jacobson, "A Method for the Analysis of the Structure of Complex Organizations," *American Sociological Review* 20 (1955): 661–668.

9. Michelle Girvan and Mark E. J. Newman, "Community Structure in Social and Biological Networks," *Proceedings of the National Academy of Sciences* 99, no. 12 (2002): 7821–7826; and Mark E. J. Newman and Michelle Girvan, "Finding and Evaluating Community Structure in Networks," *Physical Review E* 69, no. 2 (2004): 026113.

10. Santo Fortunato, "Community Detection in Graphs," *Physics Reports* 486, no. 3 (2010): 75–174.

11. Stephen P. Borgatti and Martin G. Everett, "Network Analysis of 2-Mode Data," *Social Networks* 19, no. 3 (1997): 243–269.

12. Wendy K. Tam Cho and James H. Fowler, "Legislative Success in a Small World: Social Network Analysis and the Dynamics of Congressional Legislation," *Journal of Politics* 72, no. 1 (2010): 124–135.

13. For details on these applications, see Katherine Faust, "Centrality in Affiliation Networks," *Social Networks* 19, no. 2 (1997): 157–191; Stephen P. Borgatti and Daniel S. Halgin, "Analyzing Affiliation Networks," in *The Sage Handbook of Social Network Analysis*, ed. John Scott and Peter J. Carrington (London: Sage, 2011), 417–433; Lei Tang, Huan Liu, Jianping Zhang, and Zohreh Nazeri, "Community Evolution in Dynamic Multi-mode Networks," in *Proceedings of the 14th ACM SIGKDD International Conference on Knowledge Discovery and Data Mining* (New York: ACM, 2008), 677–685; and Roger Guimerà, Marta Sales-Pardo, and Luís A. Nunes Amaral, "Module Identification in Bipartite and Directed Networks," *Physical Review E* 76, no. 3 (2007): 036102.

14. Michael T. Heaney, "Multiplex Networks and Interest Group Influence Reputation: An Exponential Random Graph Model," *Social Networks* 36 (2014): 66–81.

15. John W. Kingdon and James A. Thurber, *Agendas, Alternatives, and Public Policies*, vol. 45 (Boston: Little, Brown, 1984).

16. José Ignacio Alvarez-Hamlin, Luca Dall'Asta, Alain Barrat, and Alessandro Vespignani, "k-Core Decomposition: A Tool for the Visualization of Large Scale Networks" (arXiv preprint cs/0504107, 2005).

17. Shawn Martin, W. Michael Brown, Richard Klavans, and Kevin W. Boyack, "OpenOrd: An Open-Source Toolbox for Large Graph Layout," *Proceedings of SPIE* 7868 (2011): 786806; and Thomas M. J. Fruchterman and Edward M. Reingold, "Graph Drawing by Force-Directed Placement," *Software: Practice and Experience* 21, no. 11 (1991): 1129–1164.

18. Borgatti and Everett, "Network Analysis of 2-Mode Data"; and Freeman, "Centrality in Social Networks."

19. The details of this classification process are provided in Alexander C. Furnas and Lee Drutman, "Examining Networks of Influence: Using Semantic Similarity Clustering and Affiliation Network Analysis to Reveal Lobbying Dynamics" [paper prepared for the Sixth Annual Meeting of the Political Networks Section of the American Political Science Association (PolNet), June 28, 2013], http://papers.ssrn.com/sol3/papers.cfm?abstract id=2492568.

20. Ibid.

21. Mark Newman, *Networks: An Introduction* (Oxford: Oxford University Press, 2010); and Mark E. J. Newman, "The Structure and Function of Complex Networks," *SIAM Review* 45, no. 2 (2003): 167–256.

22. Porter, Onnela, and Mucha, "Communities in Networks"; and Fortunato, "Community Detection in Graphs."

23. Tom A. B. Snijders, "Markov Chain placeMonte Carlo Estimation of Exponential Random Graph Models," *Journal of Social Structure* 3, no. 2 (2002): 1–40; and Garry Robins, Pip Pattison, Yuval Kalish, and Dean Lusher, "An Introduction to Exponential Random Graph (*p**) Models for Social Networks," *Social Networks* 29, no. 2 (2007): 173–191.

24. Mark S. Handcock, David R. Hunter, Carter T. Butts, Steven M. Goodreau, and Martina Morris, "statnet: Software tools for the Statistical Modeling of Network Data," http://statnetproject.org.

25. Tom A. B. Snijders, Gerhard G. Van de Bunt, and Christian E. G. Steglich, "Introduction to Stochastic Actor-Based Models for Network Dynamics," *Social Networks* 32, no. 1 (2010): 44–60.

26. Manuel Gomez-Rodriguez, Jure Leskovec, and Bernhard Schölkopf, "Structure and Dynamics of Information Pathways in On-Line Media" (paper presented at the Sixth ACM International Conference on Web Search and Data Mining, Rome, February 6–8, 2013); Manuel Gomez-Rodriguez, David Balduzzi, and Bernhard Schölkopf, "Uncovering the Temporal Dynamics of Diffusion Networks" (paper presented at the 28th International Conference on Machine Learning, Bellevue, WA, June 28–July 2, 2011); Manuel Gomez-Rodriguez, Jure Leskovec, and Andreas Krause, "Inferring Networks of Diffusion and Influence," in *Proceedings of the 16th ACM SIGKDD International Conference on Knowledge Discovery and Data Mining* (New York: ACM, 2010); and Jure Leskovec, Lars Backstrom, and Jon Kleinberg, "Meme-Tracking and the Dynamics of the News Cycle," in *Proceedings of the 15th ACM SIGKDD International Conference on Knowledge Discovery and Data Mining* (New York: ACM, 2009).

CHAPTER FIVE Learning from Place in the Era of Geolocation

Ryan T. Moore and Andrew Reeves

IN THIS CHAPTER

In this chapter, we give an overview of the ways in which scholars and policy makers are currently using individual geolocation data. We also describe some new analytic and service-provision possibilities that geolocation data enable. We discuss several challenges inherent in obtaining geolocation data and making those data useful for social, political, and policy research and practice. We highlight the unique concerns over privacy that arise in this rich data environment and note some promising approaches for addressing them.

INTRODUCTION

For centuries, policy makers and social scientists have used geographic location data to improve services, solve vexing social problems, and learn more about how we affect and are affected by our environments. John Snow's investigation of the 19th-century London cholera epidemic, for example, relied on detailed knowledge of the locations of water suppliers, contaminants, and illness cases.[1] However, only recently has it become possible and inexpensive to collect fine, frequent, and automatic individual-level geolocation data for social and political research and practice.

The growth of smartphone adoption among Americans has expedited this new research possibility. The number of Americans with smartphones has grown rapidly in just the last few years. According to the Pew Research Center, in January 2014, 58 percent of American adults had a smartphone, up from 32 percent in May 2011.[2] With the widespread adoption of smartphones that include global positioning system (GPS) receivers, the collection of individuals' geolocation data is revolutionizing analysts' ability to understand how people interact with their social and physical environments.

In this chapter, we give an overview of the ways in which scholars and policy makers are currently using individual geolocation data, as well as the new analytic and service-provision possibilities that geolocation data enable. Researchers' ability to characterize and assess individuals' contexts of various sorts is vastly richer now than in the past, when "county of residence" was the state of the art in describing individuals' experiences. Similarly, governments' ability to diagnose and remedy problems and to evaluate how citizens use public spaces are fundamentally different now that feedback from constituents can be instant, accurate, and sometimes even automatic. We discuss several challenges inherent in obtaining and analyzing geolocation data, and we highlight concerns over privacy in this rich data environment.

APPLICATIONS OF GEOLOCATION DATA

Researchers, entrepreneurs, and governments have all taken advantage of rapid advancements in geolocation technology to achieve a number of ends. We highlight three broad areas to which analysts bring geolocation to bear. First, we discuss how scholars use these tools to understand the social milieus that individuals encounter in their daily lives. Geolocation data allow us to determine the social characteristics of the places that individuals actually experience, shedding new light on both social networks and contextual experiences. Second, we discuss how geolocation data and smartphone applications allow governments new insight and efficiencies in delivering public goods. By allowing individuals to more easily and quickly report public works needs, for example, local governments can better respond to breakdowns in public infrastructure. These tools often go hand in hand with improved reporting of public works project data to the public. Increased transparency, then, helps constituents hold government accountable. Third, geolocation tools assist in understanding how individuals interact with their natural and social environments. For urban planners and local governments, these data provide direction about maximizing investment in parks, bike trails, and running paths. For researchers in public health and health administration, these data provide insights that can be leveraged to promote preventive care, track disease contagion, and eliminate health insurance fraud.

Learning About Geographic Contexts

Scholars have long been interested in how geographically defined contexts shape social and political behaviors. Early work focused on racial concentrations and voter turnout.[3] More recent work has continued in a similar vein, focusing on the individual and social conditions under which contexts affect attitudes about racial and ethnic groups and racially targeted policies[4] and generalized trust.[5] Political scientist V. O. Key, in particular, used county-level estimates of the percent black—a sensible choice in an era when geographic mobility was significantly more restricted than it is today.[6] An individual's county of residence in the 1940s could circumscribe much of his or her life's experience. However, over the course of the 20th century, the average American went from a limited, slowly changing set of environments to traveling more than 13,000 miles per year, by car alone.[7]

Though scholars seek the characteristics of an individual's experience, they typically rely on the characteristics of a predetermined geographic container such as the state, county, or census tract in which the subject resides. Once the geographic unit of analysis is selected, its characteristics are assumed to be the experiences of the individual. The container may be small, like a census block group, or expansive, like a state. Small units of analysis arbitrarily assume individuals' experiences may be limited to a few city blocks, while large containers assume an individual experiences every corner of a state, for example. Despite the vast differences in these measures, studies may pick either container to try to capture the same individual's contextual experience.

The fact that results can depend on which level of geography an analyst chooses is known as the "modifiable areal unit problem" (MAUP). To explicate the degree to which higher levels of geography may misrepresent lower ones in the United States, we focus on a particular state. In figure 5.1, each county in Maryland is represented by a panel, and the density shows the distribution of the proportion of non-white residents within that county's census blocks. The counties are sorted by their overall proportion non-white (represented by each panel's vertical line). Since an individual in a census block encounters more people of a given demography when the census block is more populous, we weight the census blocks by population.

In some cases, the aggregate county measure represents most of the census blocks that comprise it. For example, in the upper left-hand corner, Garrett County has a small percentage of non-whites, and the same is true of its constituent census blocks. Similarly for Carroll County, where the overall fraction of non-whites is 9 percent, virtually all census blocks are between 0 and 25 percent non-white.

However, where there is variation in the census block measures within a county, the county mean may poorly summarize the distribution. For example, Baltimore County is about 37 percent non-white, but the modal block is significantly less diverse, only around 10 percent non-white. Many blocks (about 27 percent) in Baltimore County are more than half non-white, as well. Even worse, in Somerset

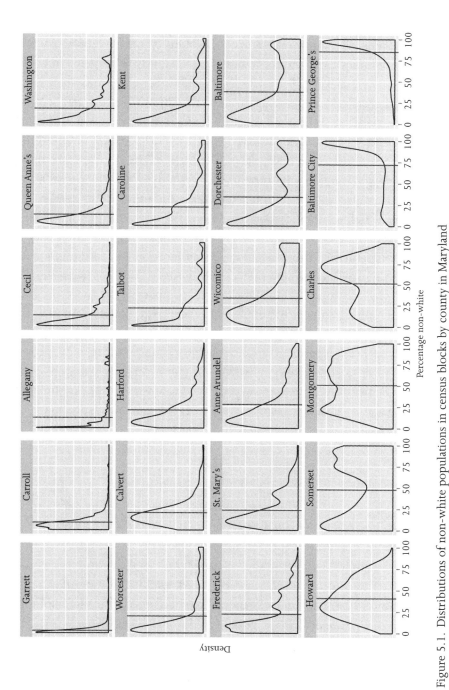

Figure 5.1. Distributions of non-white populations in census blocks by county in Maryland

Notes: Distributions are weighted by block population. County means are displayed as vertical lines. County means can describe block-level distributions well (e.g, Garrett County) or poorly (e.g., Somerset County).

County, blocks tend to be either extremely white, as represented by the mode to the left of the distribution, or highly non-white, as represented by the mode to the right. Though the average would summarize Somerset County as 50 percent non-white, this summary is not indicative of the concentration of relatively homogeneous blocks in the county.

Once the researchers select a geographic unit of analysis, they typically assume that individuals' experiences reflect only characteristics of that geographic container. Despite this assumption, an individual may spend a majority of her time in other geographies that are distinct from her place of residence. The standard practice is to measure context as a single location rather than as a dynamic experience across a number of locales over a period of time. However, we argue that this need not be the case in an era of rich geolocation data.

In other research, we seek to overcome these problems via geolocation data by introducing individual-level, automatically recorded location data that allow us to describe individuals' experiences more richly, more dynamically, and less constrained by single-geography measures.[8] This allows us to compare individuals' dynamic experiences to traditional scholarly proxies for those experiences. We estimate milieus for hundreds of individuals and show that these precise, dynamic measures reveal different contextual experiences than those based on the coarse, static proxies that scholars have, up to this point, relied on. In particular, our research shows that previous static measures overstate how extreme racial experiences are for most individuals. Ultimately, our new measures of contextual experience will allow us to understand how place shapes both attitudes and behaviors.

Understanding and Improving the Provision of Public Goods

One of the central roles of local government is to provide public goods in an efficient way that maximizes the benefit to residents. However, a local government may lack information about areas most in need of resources or the exact locations of breakdowns in public infrastructure. Smartphone applications that record geolocation data are transforming the accuracy, speed, and quantity of information that local governments have access to as they make decisions about the allocation of scarce resources to support public goods. Additionally, the delivery of these goods are often publicly posted under open government initiatives, which allow citizens, journalists, and researchers to analyze successes and failures of service delivery.

For example, many local governments have developed smartphone applications to supplement 3-1-1 services, non-emergency telephone numbers whereby citizens may report public works issues or request municipal services. Cities such as Philadelphia, Boston, New York, and San Francisco supplement their 3-1-1 service with smartphone applications. These apps allow residents to report noise complaints, rat sightings, lost items in taxis, illegal parking, broken parking meters, poor apartment conditions, graffiti, streetlight repair, and potholes, among other issues. These apps often allow users to take photographs and automatically record the location of nuisances and then relay that information directly to authorities.

In one innovative example, the city of Boston has made reporting road conditions even easier with its Street Bump application, produced by the Mayor's Office of New Urban Mechanics. This app "collects data about the smoothness of the ride" passively, eliminating the requirement for constituents themselves to report a nuisance.[9] By at least some reports, this new technology is allowing the city to do a better job in filling potholes. The mayor of Boston has touted that the city filled 50 percent more potholes in 2014 than in 2013.[10] The data are also providing new insights into other road conditions and safety hazards that inconvenience drivers. One of the insights gleaned from the app was that manhole and other grate covers accounted for "about eight times as many bumps and divots in the road as plain old potholes"; this led the city of Boston to pressure utility companies to correct the misaligned covers.[11] Prior to this sort of technology, residents could call 3-1-1 and report these nuisances, but authorities would have to rely on residents having a phone nearby, accurately reporting the location of the nuisance, and describing it faithfully. Local government 3-1-1 apps make the reporting process quick, detailed, and accurate.

Complementing the work of governments, firms have capitalized on the same sort of automated reporting to provide users with real-time transit information. The smartphone application Waze records users' routes, locations, and times to their destinations to calculate traffic speeds and immediately report conditions to its user base.[12] Automatically recording, processing, and delivering vast amounts of geolocation data led to Waze being acquired by Google in 2003 for over $1 billion.

Other firms have innovated by developing new methods to analyze geolocation data to improve understanding of traffic, commerce, and other human interactions. For instance, StreetLight Data purchases anonymized cell phone data and, based on its analyses, advises companies where to locate stores,[13] state departments of transportation where to build roads,[14] and local communities how to woo businesses to build in underdeveloped but heavily traveled parts of their city.[15] As in many other contexts where big data are available, there are numerous challenges to analyzing the data to gain insights into the questions that local governments, businesses, and individuals are asking.

For governments, these services create opportunities to more efficiently deliver public resources to citizens. They also create vast new datasets that allow researchers to better understand the classic political questions of "who gets what, when, how."[16] Do politicians reward particular subsets of voters with distributive resources? Are they more likely to do so near election time? These are questions that scholars have examined by considering, for example, the distribution of federal resources across counties,[17] congressional districts,[18] and states.[19] In one such study, researchers found that county-level presidential incumbent vote share increases as a function of county-level federal spending.[20] As local governments collect more fine-grained data on the provision of public goods and especially the public demand for such goods, the findings of these studies stand to be subjected to new, rigorous tests.

Understanding Interactions with Social and Physical Environments

Related to understanding the provision of public goods, geolocation data also help us understand how individuals interact directly with their social and physical environments. Knowing how individuals interact with public green space, public transit, or bicycle paths can aid urban planners as they design cities that maximize public health and happiness while reducing congestion, air pollution, and other urban blights. In the health care sector, knowing how individuals tend to interact with others and with nearby providers can be used to detect disease outbreaks and insurance fraud and to encourage health system utilization at critical junctures such as childbirth.

For example, one study examines how economic characteristics within an urban area influence residents' patterns of exercise.[21] As a report from the National Park Service notes, "Parks and protected areas have long been recognized as important resources for public health."[22] This study uses freely available public data from MapMyRun.com, a smartphone application that records an individual's jogging speeds and location through GPS. By analyzing the factors associated with the use of public green space for running, jogging, and walking, this study aids public health researchers in understanding the relationship between socioeconomic context and the healthy use of urban space. At the same time, it provides information to such groups as the Open Space Council for the St. Louis Region, a non-profit conservation group and one of the funders of the study, in its mission to "maintain the integrity of land and waterways for practical purposes, recreation and their natural beauty."[23]

Another study examines whether being in nature improves levels of happiness.[24] In a sample of over 1.1 million responses from nearly 22,000 respondents, this study analyzed how the environment, including things like weather, land cover type, and whom the participants were with, influenced their subjective well-being in the moment. Using Mappiness, an iPhone app the researchers developed, they periodically surveyed respondents about their happiness and also recorded their geolocation and other observations about their environment. This study's data analysis lends credence to the assertion of the National Park Service's report described earlier: individuals reported being significantly happier when they were outdoors in nature. Previous studies had been limited to correlating green space around an individual's home with health factors.[25]

Governments and non-governmental organizations also use geolocation data in efforts to improve health and health systems. For example, to target areas for possible follow-up intervention, researchers dynamically geolocated concentrations of men seeking sex with other men through a social network mobile phone application.[26] They demonstrate how the profile features of app users (such as their HIV status) can be used to identify neighborhoods for recruitment into research studies or provision of treatment clinics. Where there are more users from HIV-positive or vulnerable populations, researchers and clinicians can better focus their resources. Similarly, to describe where particular health conditions are becoming of local interest, the U.S. Department of Health and Human Services provides heat maps of geolocated Twitter posts about 30 different conditions.[27] These maps can help identify where disease outbreaks may be occurring and thus where treatment and research resources are best allocated.

Static geographic container data can be used along the same lines when policy makers and researchers exploit dynamic relationships between fixed points. For example, knowing where providers' offices are located and where their patients live can help detect suspicious billing behavior. Comparing the distances between individuals and their health providers can suggest instances of fraud to policy makers. Researchers have developed a method for detecting Medicare fraud by identifying providers who derive an unusually large proportion of their earnings from patients who have traveled unusually far.[28]

Geolocation data can also be used to understand the scope and limits of programs to encourage vulnerable populations to use a health system. A study by ORB

International used survey enumerators' GPS information to determine the distance from respondent households to the nearest health facility. Women near program facilities were more likely to give birth in a facility, when compared to those near non-program facilities, but the difference disappeared after a distance of about 10 kilometers. Beyond this, women were unlikely to give birth in any type of facility.[29] These household-level geolocation data can be incorporated into policy makers' plans for new clinic sitings both inside and outside the program.

CHALLENGES IN GEOLOCATED DATA

Accompanying the wealth of opportunities that individual smartphone geolocations provide are significant challenges that must be faced and decisions that must be made before researchers can collect or use the data. In the following discussion, we focus on how to obtain geolocated data and how to make the data useful by linking them to other sources.

Collecting Geolocated Data

Prior to the explosion in the use of mobile smartphones, recording geolocations required technologies with more severe limitations. Time diaries, for example, require active, accurate participation of respondents, but respondent reports suffer from a variety of biases and inadequacies.[30] Now, even in "resource-poor" areas, a variety of relatively inexpensive commercially available GPS-logging devices weighing less than 100 grams can accurately record individual geolocations.[31] In more resource-abundant areas, geolocation data collection is even easier. With widespread adoption of mobile phones that include GPS antennas, researchers and policy makers can access data from inexpensive, lightweight devices that individuals naturally carry with them over the course of their daily lives.

These devices use a combination of sensors to locate users in space. Mobile phones can determine user locations with a mixture of direct location sensors (GPS antennas) and other functional sensors that can interact with bases that can be traced to specific locations. For example, cellular antennas connect to specific cell towers during a call, WiFi antennas connect to specific access points, and Bluetooth sensors can connect to beacons whose locations are known. Different applications use different mixtures of sensors and triggers for those sensors to collect and distribute geographic data. Strategies have been developed for efficiently combining these data collection modes in an application.[32]

At one extreme are applications that show the user on a map and provide turn-by-turn directions to the next destination. These applications rely on GPS antennas, and they update the user location in real time to provide instructions that are useful in a moment. These applications tax the device's battery heavily, resulting in less usable time between recharges. On the other hand, applications specific to retail outlets (such as the Apple Store app, the Safeway grocery store app, or the American Eagle clothing store app) can use Bluetooth low-energy signals to prompt only users who are in the store to visit certain aisles. Governments and public facilities can use these beacons to guide museum visitors to specific exhibits, to provide information when a visitor is in a certain part of a national park, or to make airports easier to navigate for the blind. Such applications preserve battery life, but only provide feedback or geolocated data for very specific places.

Between these two extremes are applications that are interested in locations beyond a single cultural site or retail outlet, but that want to preserve battery life to collect geolocations throughout the user's daily activities. Examples of such applications rely predominantly on cell tower networks to determine user location, but then engage the GPS antenna when the device detects "significant movement."

Once researchers or governments decide to adopt mobile technology to provide information to or get feedback from individuals, they must decide whether to pursue a *native* application or a *mobile web* application. Native smartphone applications are written in the language that the operating system requires; third-party native applications are downloaded to the phone by the user. Mobile web applications work directly in a web browser, so programmers can deploy the application to any phone with a browser without having to rewrite it for iOS, Android, Windows Phone, or other platforms. In a political science example, a web application has been used to encourage engagement in and collect feedback from candidate debates.[33]

Although native applications require more infrastructure in order to be available across operating systems, they "provide a richer, more compelling experience with a more responsive interface and superior interaction."[34] Native applications can run at native speeds and can access the full functionality of the smartphone, including the camera, the microphone, Bluetooth connectivity for a variety of external sensors, and the GPS antenna for geolocation.[35] Governments exploit these functionalities to find out, for example, exactly where a user-reported pothole is located and even what it looks like—users can send photographs of the nuisance directly to officials through native apps. Researchers have developed a typology and list of example strategies for the spectrum of automatic, manual, and hybrid data collection approaches in native applications.[36]

Although mobile web applications are easier to distribute than native ones, centralized online software application markets like the Apple App Store and Google Play Store make distribution of native apps relatively easy. At the federal level, native applications are more common than web applications. The federal government's mobile application registry lists more than 150 registered native federal iOS apps, but fewer than half that many mobile web apps.[37]

Linking Geolocations to Other Data

In social science and governance applications, researchers want to link individual geolocations to other data. Geolocations alone can provide a sense of how mobile individuals are, but many other interesting substantive questions will remain elusive. In particular, we see two significant linking challenges of interest to social scientists and policy makers: linking to aggregate geographic contextual data and linking to individual-level background data and survey responses.

First, researchers will often want to link geolocations to aggregate geographic contextual data, such as measures of neighborhood racial and ethnic composition from the census. For each observation of a single individual (usually a latitude, longitude, and time triple), this process starts by taking the geographic coordinates and determining which census block that point is in. This can involve first reading in census block shapefiles, then locating the block code for each point. Next, the researcher retrieves the aggregate contextual measures for that block. This process can be computationally intensive, since the number of aggregate units and observations can both be large. In a moderately sized sample of about 450 individuals, for example, we observe about 2.6 million coordinate triples, each of which we then place within one of the roughly 8.2 million American census blocks. The process must be repeated for each geographic level of interest, since each geography will have its own shapefiles and, in some cases, files of aggregate measures.

Second, augmenting individual geolocations with individual-level data allows researchers to answer substantive questions such as "Do particular racial contexts affect individuals' attitudes about race?" and "Do men and women have different degrees of access to urban opportunities?" To examine these individual-level questions, we developed an original application that records both geolocations and responses to survey questions.[38] The survey questions are served directly within the application itself, and responses can themselves be geolocated. To enable future researchers to take advantage of this new platform, the infrastructure is quite general, and survey content can be determined by other interested researchers. Surveys can be administered to selected samples, including geographically determined ones. Smartphone geolocation data are an example of passive, automatic measurement of social quantities of interest. Instead of relying on respondent self-reports, passive, automatic measurement can better capture social behaviors. In a typical older approach, researchers tackled the question of gendered access to urban opportunities by pairing time diary reports with a demographic survey including gender, age, income, employment status, and automobile usage.[39]

Individual survey responses can also help validate approaches for estimating people's activities at the locations they inhabit each day. When an individual regularly spends a lot of time at geolocations near each other, clustering algorithms can identify his or her home and work locations quite accurately, for example. In one such study, algorithmically discovered locations are validated by asking participants to label them by hand in a web application.[40]

PRIVACY AND ETHICS

Geolocated data pose special problems for privacy and raise new ethical concerns for researchers and policy makers alike.[41] One source of these privacy concerns is the ability of phones to detect location with a high degree of accuracy. For example, iOS application developers can configure their software to record geolocations to within 10 meters or so.[42] Of course, this accuracy is precisely what makes mobile phone geolocations valuable—if local government receives a report that there is a pothole within 1 kilometer of a site, this information is not likely to be useful. On the other hand, iOS guidelines recommend developers use "significant change" location services, which only respond when the user's position changes by 500 meters or so. Coupled with precise time stamps, extremely accurate geolocations could identify where individuals are in real time.

As developers and consumers of technologies that use geolocation data, it is important to consider best practices for preserving the privacy of individual users while providing the insights that local governments, researchers, or businesses desire. While de-identified geolocation data can be purchased directly from wireless carriers without the direct consent of the user,[43] many entities collect these data via mobile applications. In these cases, it is important that the developer of the app provide transparency as to the types of data that will be collected, how they will be used, and how the users can terminate their participation in the study. Developers who must seek approval from institutional review boards, such as researchers at universities, may receive guidance on these questions. But all too often, these entities are ill-equipped to deal with the new challenges of emerging technologies, and their oversight may do more harm than good.[44]

In addition to specifying the types of data that will be collected, developers should collect only the data they need and no more than that. As discussed previously, software protocols allow developers to define the precision of the GPS coordinates that are recorded, and developers should collect the data at the coarsest level possible for their research purposes. Unless users consent, geolocation data should not be paired with identifying information such as names, e-mail addresses, or phone numbers. For example, our Milieu app, which combines survey data with geolocation data, provides users with a randomly generated user ID. This ID links a single (anonymous) user to geolocation data and to answers to survey questions delivered through the app. While this strategy means that users of the app get a new ID and appear as a new user if they reinstall the app, it further (and desirably) limits the developers' ability to identify the user. A model resting on user accounts identified by e-mail addresses, for example, could ease direct identification of users.

Still, study after study shows that individuals are easily identified in ostensibly "de-identified" data with far less information than geolocation data. For instance, one study using the 1990 U.S. Census found that 87 percent of the United States could be uniquely identified based on their zip code, gender, and date of birth.[45] In an "anonymized" dataset of credit card transactions in 10,000 stores over 3 months, researchers identified 90 percent of the 1.1 million people in the dataset.[46] While we argue every effort should be made to not collect identifying information, identifying de-identified individuals is easy without geolocation data and somewhat easier with it. For this reason, we argue that transparency with the user is especially important. Additionally, other protections may be employed such as inducing random noise into the data at the time of collection or employing a third party to act as a firewall between researchers and the individual location records.

The regularities in human mobility can, however, further facilitate identifying where an individual is at a given moment. Roughly 90 percent of people in a Swiss study tended to visit two to four locations on an average day, and novel places tended to be visited in well-defined patterns—during meal times and on Saturdays, for example.[47] Further, researchers were able to label frequently visited locations with greater than 80 percent true-positive rates.

Perhaps just as relevant for user identification, though, extremely accurate time stamps and geolocations are not required to uniquely characterize individual travels through environments. Geolocated data are surprisingly unique, even when coarsened. Even when characterized by just a handful of latitude, longitude, and time coordinate triples, the paths users take through their environments tend not to be shared with others.[48] This finding, apparently inherent in human mobility, poses challenges to anonymity and de-identification of a different type than simple demographics, say. Indeed, some 30 percent of smartphone users recently reported that they have "turned off the location tracking feature on [their] cell phone[s] because [they] were worried about other people or companies being able to access that information."[49] Several intellectual initiatives have sprung up in response to recent data privacy concerns, including the American Statistical Association's Committee on Privacy and Confidentiality, the Data Privacy Lab at Harvard University's Institute for Quantitative Social Science, and the resources on geospatial confidentiality provided by the National Aeronautics and Space Administration's Socioeconomic Data and Applications Center.

The uniqueness of individual geolocation data runs counter to recent social science trends regarding data openness and replication. In particular, scholars highlight the value of registration to counteract fishing for statistically significant results,[50] including in observational studies.[51] Others highlight the value in replicating others' findings[52] and in sharing and archiving data.[53] We support these trends and actively provide our own materials in public archives. However, since one can uniquely characterize mobility patterns with relatively few, relatively coarse observations, one must take special precautions with publicly shared replication data with geolocations to avoid re-identification, especially if the data are adjoined to static demographic measures. Even fine geolocated data can be shared publicly, however, if proper precautions are taken.[54] For example, researchers can release several datasets in which the individuals' geographic positions are multiply imputed, rather than releasing the original values.[55] Such an approach can preserve correlations between all the measures, geographic and non-geographic, without requiring the release of any true geolocations.[56] In political science, one can find several applications of overwriting observed data with multiply imputed values.[57]

One model for the future of sensitive data such as geolocations seeks to eliminate redundancies and to put control in the hands of each user. In an "openPDS" (for "open personal data store") infrastructure model, each individual amasses his or her own data in a personal data storage site. The individual then controls who can access the data study by study. Separate researchers do not need to duplicate data collection; they simply need to ask the user's permission for access to a part of the data.[58]

OpenPaths, a geolocation project of the Research and Development Lab of the *New York Times*, represents one such data store. OpenPaths bills itself as a "secure data locker for personal location information."[59] This project allows individuals who store their geolocation data with OpenPaths to receive invitations to participate in artistic, academic, and commercial projects. The user decides on a case-by-case basis whether to allow the project access to his or her data. Projects do not need to re-collect the individual's geolocation data, creating a significant research efficiency. Each project must, however, have each user's explicit consent. Elsewhere, we employ OpenPaths geolocation data to redefine racial and ethnic geographic contexts.[60]

DISCUSSION

Governments at all levels have begun to embrace mobile computing. From local councils to federal agencies, governments have released mobile applications to facilitate two-way communication with constituents and visitors. On one hand, governments use smartphone applications to provide users with information, ranging from precinct-level, real-time election results to features of local tourist sites (in Jefferson Parish, Louisiana, and Sparks, Nevada, respectively). On the other hand, governments encourage users to provide immediate, geolocated, and often visual feedback on local infrastructure. Citizens can report rat sightings, potholes, and street sign repairs to local governments via the burgeoning category of 3-1-1 smartphone applications. These two primary functionalities are complemented by the suite of technical guides packaged as applications, such as the federal Terrestrial Mollusc Key app, "designed for federal, state and other agencies or organizations within the U.S. that are concerned with the detection and identification of molluscs of [quarantine] significance."[61]

Academic researchers have also begun to use these new tools to answer long-standing difficult questions in the social sciences. When researchers posit theoretical mechanisms that involve individuals' experiences rather than simply the location of their residences or workplaces, rich geolocation data can and should be brought to bear. We can better reflect the modern realities of human mobility by measuring social and political contexts in dynamic ways; we are no longer tied to "county of residence" to describe people's experiences.

Of course, geolocations collected by policy makers to improve service delivery can inform important social scientific questions about the distribution of resources and the impact of political conditions. Similarly, as social scientists pair geolocations with social survey data, we see significant opportunities to improve policy makers' responsiveness to constituents' needs and to further deepen campaigns' knowledge of whom to try to turn out or persuade in an election.

The realities of modern geolocated data suggest that de-identification and anonymization strategies that were appropriate for long, in-person interviews in people's homes may no longer suffice to ensure respondent privacy. New statistical and technical solutions can help, but preserving both scientific value and individual privacy will be an ongoing challenge.

NOTES

1. The case is described in detail in David A. Freedman, "Statistical Models and Shoe Leather," *Sociological Methodology* 21 (1991): 291–313.
2. For details, see http://www.pewinternet.org/fact-sheets/mobile-technology-fact-sheet/ and http://www.pewinternet.org/data-trend/mobile/device-ownership/.
3. Valdimer Orlando Key, *Southern Politics in State and Nation* (Knoxville: University of Tennessee Press, 1949).
4. Daniel J. Hopkins, "Politicized Places: Explaining Where and When Immigrants Provoke Local Opposition," *American Political Science Review* 104, no. 1 (2010): 40–60; and Eric J. Oliver and Tali Mendelberg, "Reconsidering the Environmental Determinants of White Racial Attitudes," *American Journal of Political Science* 44, no. 3 (July 2000): 574–589.
5. Dietlind Stolle, Stuart Soroka, and Richard Johnston, "When Does Diversity Erode Trust? Neighborhood Diversity, Interpersonal Trust and the Mediating Effect of Social Interactions," *Political Studies* 56, no. 1 (2008): 57–75.
6. Key, *Southern Politics in State and Nation.*
7. See http://www.fhwa.dot.gov/ohim/onh00/bar8.htm.
8. Ryan T. Moore and Andrew Reeves, "Defining Racial and Ethnic Context with Geolocation Data" (unpublished manuscript, 2015).
9. http://www.cityofboston.gov/DoIT/apps/streetbump.asp.
10. Andrew Ryan, "City Touts Pothole Numbers, but What Exactly Qualifies?" *Boston Globe*, April 13, 2005, https://www.bostonglobe.com/metro/2015/04/12/potholes-count-does-counting -them/eP0jqKHac7wz0lGIU0sgYM/story.html.
11. Eric Moskowitz, "App Shows Jarring Role of Cast-Metal Covers in Boston," *Boston Globe*, December 16, 2012, https://www.bostonglobe.com/metro/2012/12/16/pothole/ 2iNCJ05M15vmr4aGHACNgP/story.html.
12. See https://support.google.com/waze/answer/6078702?hl=en for details.
13. http://www.streetlightdata.com/case-studies/.
14. Max Smith, "Tracking Data Aims to Speed Commutes in Virginia," *WTOP.com*, May 21, 2015, http://wtop.com/virginia/2015/05/tracking-data-aims-to-speed-commutes-in-virginia/.

15. Alex Salkever, "How Big Data Reveals the Secret Life of Cities," *readwrite*, September 2, 2014, http://readwrite.com/2014/09/02/streetlight-data-laura-schewel-big-data-tracking-surveillance.

16. Harold D. Laswell, *Politics: Who Gets What, When, How* (New York: McGraw-Hill, 1936).

17. Douglas L. Kriner and Andrew Reeves, "Presidential Particularism and Divide-the-Dollar Politics," *American Political Science Review* 109, no. 1 (2015): 155–171; and John T. Gasper and Andrew Reeves, "Make It Rain? Retrospection and the Attentive Electorate in the Context of Natural Disasters," *American Journal of Political Science* 55, no. 2 (2011): 340–355.

18. Christopher R. Berry, Barry C. Burden, and William G. Howell, "The President and the Distribution of Federal Spending," *American Political Science Review* 104, no. 4 (2010): 783–799.

19. Andrew Reeves, "Political Disaster: Unilateral Powers, Electoral Incentives, and Presidential Disaster Declarations," *Journal of Politics* 73, no. 4 (2011): 1142–1151.

20. Douglas L. Kriner and Andrew Reeves, "The Influence of Federal Spending on Presidential Elections," *American Political Science Review* 106, no. 2 (2012): 348–366.

21. Deepti Adlakha, Elizabeth L. Budd, Rebecca Gernes, Sonia Sequeira, and James A. Hipp, "Use of Emerging Technologies to Assess Differences in Outdoor Physical Activity in St. Louis, Missouri," *Frontiers in Public Health* 2 (2014): 1–8.

22. http://www.nps.gov/public_health/hp/hphp/press/HPHP_Science%20Plan_accessible%20version.final.23.july.2013.pdf.

23. http://www.openspacestl.org/missionabout-us.

24. George MacKerron and Susana Mourato, "Happiness Is Greater in Natural Environments," *Global Environmental Change* 23, no. 5 (2013): 992–1000.

25. Jolanda Maas, Robert A. Verheij, Sjerp de Vries, Peter Spreeuwenberg, François G. Schellevis, and Peter P. Groenewegen, "Morbidity Is Related to a Green Living Environment," *Journal of Epidemiology and Community Health* 63 (2009): 967–973.

26. Kevin P. Delaney, Michael R. Kramer, Lance A. Waller, W. Dana Flanders, and Patrick S. Sullivan, "Using a Geolocation Social Networking Application to Calculate the Population Density of Sex-Seeking Gay Men for Research and Prevention Services," *Journal of Medical Internet Research* 16, no. 11 (2014): e249.

27. See http://nowtrending.hhs.gov/heatmap.

28. Rasim Muzaffer Musal, "Two Models to Investigate Medicare Fraud Within Unsupervised Databases," *Expert Systems with Applications* 37, no. 12 (2010): 8628–8633.

29. http://www.opinion.co.uk/article.php?s=using-gis-mapping-in-aid-evaluation.

30. Peter R. Stopher, Philip Bullock, and Frederic Horst, "Exploring the Use of Passive GPS Devices to Measure Travel," in *Applications of Advanced Technologies in Transportation*, ed. Kelvin C. P. Wang, Samer Madanat, Shashi Nambisan, and Gary Spring (Reston, VA: American Society of Civil Engineers, 2002), 959–967.

31. Gonzalo M. Vazquez-Prokopec, Steven T. Stoddard, Valerie Paz-Soldan, Amy C. Morrison, John P. Elder, Tadeusz J. Kochel, Thomas W. Scott, and Uriel Kitron, "Usefulness of Commercially Available GPS Data-Loggers for Tracking Human Movement and Exposure to Dengue Virus," *International Journal of Health Geographics* 8, no. 68 (2009): 1–11.

32. Raul Montoliu, Jan Blom, and Daniel Gatica-Perez, "Discovering Places of Interest in Everyday Life from Smartphone Data," *Multimedia Tools and Applications* 62, no. 1 (2013): 179–207.

33. Amber E. Boydstun, Jessica T. Feezell, Rebecca A. Glazier, Timothy P. Jurka, and Matthew T. Pietryka, "Colleague Crowdsourcing: A Method for Fostering National Student Engagement and Large-N Data Collection," *PS: Political Science and Politics* 47, no. 4 (2014): 829–834.

34. Nicolás Serrano, Josune Hernantes, and Gorka Gallardo, "MobileWeb Apps," *IEEE Software*, September 2013, 24.

35. Johannes Schobel, Marc Schickler, Rüdiger Pryss, Hans Nienhaus, and Manfred Reichert, "Using Vital Sensors in Mobile Healthcare Business Applications: Challenges, Examples, Lessons Learned," in *Proceedings of the International Conference on Web Information Systems and Technologies*, ed. Karl-Heinz Krempels and Alexander Stocker (Setúbal, Portugal: SCITEPRESS, 2013), 509–518, http://www.scitepress.org/DigitalLibrary/ProceedingsDetails.aspx?ID=WfGHBX/1jPI=&t=1.

36. Emmanuel Kuntsche and Florian Labhart, "Using Personal Cell Phones for Ecological Momentary Assessment: An Overview of Current Developments," *European Psychologist* 18, no. 1 (2013): 3–11.

37. See http://www.usa.gov/mobileapps.shtml.

38. Pedro Valdeolmillos, Ryan T. Moore, and Andrew Reeves, Milieu, Apple App Store, version 1.0, milieu.cc.

39. Mei-Po Kwan, "Gender and Individual Access to Urban Opportunities: A Study Using Space-Time Measures," *Professional Geographer* 51, no. 2 (1999): 210–227.

40. Montoliu, Blom, and Gatica-Perez, "Discovering Places of Interest in Everyday Life from Smartphone Data."

41. For an overview of the challenges to civil liberties posted by digital technology, see Neil Richards, *Intellectual Privacy: Rethinking Civil Liberties in the Digital Age* (New York: Oxford University Press, 2015).

42. For technical specifications, see http://j.mp/1dB3C5w.

43. Russell Brandom, "Can You Find Me Now? How Carriers Sell Your-Location and Get Away with It," *The Verge*, April 9, 2013, http://www.theverge.com/2013/4/9/4187654/how-carriers-sell-your-location-and-get-away-with-it.

44. Carl E. Schneider, *The Censor's Hand* (Cambridge, MA: MIT Press, 2015).

45. Latanya Sweeney, "Simple Demographics Often Identify People Uniquely" (Data Privacy Working Paper 3, Carnegie Mellon University, Pittsburgh, PA, 2000).

46. Yves-Alexandre de Montjoye, Laura Radaelli, Vivek Kumar Singh, and Alex "Sandy" Pentland, "Unique in the Shopping Mall: On the Reidentifiability of Credit Card Metadata," *Science* 347 (2015): 536–539.

47. Trinh Minh Tri Do and Daniel Gatica-Perez, "The Places of Our Lives: Visiting Patterns and Automatic Labeling from Longitudinal Smartphone Data," *IEEE Transactions on Mobile Computing* 13, no. 3 (2014): 638–648.

48. Yves-Alexandre de Montjoye, César A. Hidalgo, Michel Verleysen, and Vincent D. Blondel, "Unique in the Crowd: The Privacy Bounds of Human Mobility," *Scientific Reports* 3 (2013): 1–5.

49. Jan Lauren Boyles, Aaron Smith, and Mary Madden, *Privacy and Data Management on Mobile Devices* (Washington, DC: Pew Research Center, May 2012), 16, http://www.pewinternet.org/files/old-media//Files/Reports/2012/PIP_MobilePrivacyManagement.pdf.

50. Macartan Humphreys, Raul Sanchez de la Sierra, and Peter van der Windt, "Fishing, Commitment, and Communication: A Proposal for Comprehensive Nonbinding Research Registration," *Political Analysis* 21, no. 1 (2013): 1–20.

51. James E. Monogan, "A Case for Registering Studies of Political Outcomes: An Application in the 2010 House Elections," *Political Analysis* 21, no. 1 (2013): 21–37.

52. Gary King, "Replication, Replication," *PS: Political Science and Politics* 28, no. 3 (1995): 444–452.

53. Gary King, "An Introduction to the Dataverse Network as an Infrastructure for Data Sharing," *Sociological Methods and Research* 36, no. 2 (2007): 173–199.

54. Myron P. Gutmann and Paul C. Stern, eds., *Putting People on the Map: Protecting Confidentiality with Linked Social-Spatial Data* (Washington, DC: National Academies Press, 2007).

55. Hao Wang and Jerome P. Reiter, "Multiple Imputation for Sharing Precise Geographies in Public Use Data," *Annals of Applied Statistics* 6, no. 1 (2012): 229–252.

56. Roderick J. A. Little and Donald B. Rubin, *Statistical Analysis with Missing Data*, 2nd ed. (Hoboken, NJ: Wiley, 2002); and Joseph L. Schafer, *Analysis of Incomplete Multivariate Data* (New York: CRC Press, 1997).

57. Matthew Blackwell, James Honaker, and Gary King, "A Unified Approach to Measurement Error and Missing Data: Overview," *Sociological Methods and Research*, http://j.mp/1rEBs1J.

58. Brian Tarran, "A New Model for Data Sharing," *Significance* 11, no. 4 (2014): 15–16.

59. See https://openpaths.cc/about.

60. Moore and Reeves, "Defining Racial and Ethnic Context with Geolocation Data."

61. http://j.mp/1wvgobw.

CHAPTER SIX Text Analysis

Estimating Policy Preferences from Written and Spoken Words

Kenneth Benoit and Alexander Herzog

IN THIS CHAPTER

This chapter provides an introduction into the emerging field of quantitative text analysis. Almost every aspect of the policy-making process involves some form of verbal or written communication. This communication is increasingly made available in electronic format, which requires new tools and methods to analyze large amounts of textual data. We begin with a general discussion of the method and its place in public policy analysis, including a brief review of existing applications in political science. We then discuss typical challenges that readers encounter when working with political texts. This includes differences in file formats, the definition of "documents" for analytical purposes, word and feature selection, and the transformation of unstructured data into a document-feature matrix. We will also discuss typical pre-processing steps that are made when working with text. Finally, we demonstrate the application of text analysis to measure individual legislators' policy preferences from annual budget debates in Ireland.

TEXT ANALYSIS AS A TOOL FOR ANALYZING PUBLIC POLICY

Public policy in democratic systems is produced by numerous political actors with different preferences. These differences are especially pronounced between parties in governments and those in opposition, but also exist between parties. We know from a great deal of research in political science, furthermore, that political parties are not unitary actors, but rather collections of individuals with often very divergent preferences influenced by different, sometimes conflicting pressures. Governing coalitions in parliamentary systems often expend a great deal of energy managing these differences, at the risk of coming apart should they fail to do so.

Accurately measuring the policy preferences of individual political actors has therefore long formed a key part of efforts to model intra-party politics and the public policy outcomes that result. The bulk of this work has traditionally relied on measuring differences through scaling roll call votes[1] or using roll call votes to measure voting agreement.[2] Yet roll call votes in parliamentary systems suffer from a number of problems that prevent them from forming a reliable basis for estimating legislators' preferences for policy. In most settings, a large share of legislative votes are not recorded as roll calls, and the votes that are selected for roll calls may be so chosen for strategic political reasons.[3] Measures of policy preferences based on these selective votes produce selection bias in the resulting measures.[4] Another problem with measuring intra-party differences on policy from roll call votes is that in most parliamentary systems, voting is tightly controlled through party discipline. This means that legislators vote with their party possibly not because of their policy preferences but rather in spite of them.[5]

These problems with roll call votes has led to the rapid growth in recent years in political science and policy analysis of using text as data for measuring policy preferences. Researchers have developed and applied a variety of scaling methods for measuring policy preferences from the speeches and writings of political parties and their members. The conventional wisdom is that while party discipline may strongly constrain what legislators *do* (in terms of voting behavior), these constraints do apply less to what legislators *say*, as recorded in floor debates, committee hearings, campaign speeches, websites, social media, or press releases. To make use of this information, a growing subfield within political science has emerged to extract policy preferences using text as data.[6]

Grimmer and Stewart[7] provide an excellent review of current approaches, which they divide roughly into classification approaches and scaling approaches. Scaling approaches include the methods we have discussed for measuring preferences on policy and may be divided into supervised and unsupervised methods. The most common supervised method in political science is the "Wordscores" method developed by Laver, Benoit, and Garry.[8] With roots in both naive Bayes machine learning approaches as well as regression approaches, Wordscores involves a training step on documents of "known" positions to produce scores for each word. These scores can then be used to estimate the position on the input dimension of any out-of-sample texts. This method has been used successfully in dozens of applications.[9]

The most commonly used unsupervised method for scaling policy preferences is the latent variable model dubbed "Wordfish" by Slapin and Proksch,[10] which models word generation in a document as a Poisson process from which a latent variable representing the document position can be estimated. This approach has been successfully applied to measure party preferences in German elections,[11] European interest group statements,[12] the European Parliament,[13] and Irish budget speeches.[14]

Classification approaches use mainly unsupervised methods adapted from computer science for topic discovery and for estimating the content and fluctuations in the discussions over policy. Since the publication of a seminal paper by Blei, Ng, and Jordan[15] describing a latent Dirichlet allocation (LDA) model for estimating topics based on collections of unlabeled documents, topic modeling has seen many extensions to political science. These have involved methodological innovations by political scientists, including the dynamic multi-topic model[16] and the expressed agenda model.[17] Other innovations developed in political science include revising the standard LDA model to allow for the incorporation of additional information to better estimate topic distributions.[18]

Estimating preferences or topics from text as data, of course, requires that texts have been prepared and that a researcher is familiar with the tools for carrying out this preparation and for estimating the models we have described. It is to this topic that we turn attention in the next section.

PRACTICAL ISSUES IN WORKING WITH TEXT

One of the overwhelming advantages of working with text as data is its easy and nearly universal availability: there are almost no aspects of the policy-making process that do not involve the verbal or written use of language that is recorded and published. This also poses a challenge, however, since there are almost as many formats for disseminating these texts as there are sources of texts. To be converted into useful data, texts must be processed, sometimes heavily. In this section, we outline some of these challenges and discuss several common solutions.

Wrestling with Text File Formats

Sources of textual data are found almost everywhere, but typically require a good deal of preparation in order to be ready for analysis as data. Unlike most quantitative data, which usually comes in structured formats where rows constitute units of observation and columns represent variables, textual data is usually unstructured or minimally structured when published. In addition, text may be embedded in a wide variety of different publication formats, such as Hypertext Markup Language (HTML) (if published to a website), a relational database, a set of many files, or a single large file. Databases and files containing texts, furthermore, come in many possible formats, which require conversion.

Table 6.1 lists a number of common file formats in which text files are often distributed, as well as the most likely file name extensions associated with each type and where they are most likely to be found. The types are distinguished by whether they tend to contain one document per file, or whether a single file might contain numerous documents. Together, the documents will form a *corpus*, a collection of multiple documents to be treated as data. Some file formats usually contain one document per file, such as a collection of political party manifestos from a single national election, which might be distributed as a set of Portable Document Format (PDF) files, one per political party. In such a case, the document-level meta-data such as the political party name might be known only through the file name and may need to be added later. A set of texts distributed in a "dataset" format such as .csv or

Table 6.1. Common data formats for text

Format	File name extension	Where found
Single-document formats		
Plain text	.txt	Various
Microsoft Word	.doc, .docx	Websites, file archives
Hypertext Markup Language	.htm, .html	Websites
Extensible Markup Language	.xml	Various structured software
Portable Document Format (text)	.pdf	File archives, websites
Documents as images	.pdf, .png, .jpg	Scanned documents, photographs of documents
Multiple-document formats		
Comma-separated value	.csv	File archives, some distribution outlets
Tab-separated value	.csv	File archives, some distribution outlets
JSON (Javascript Open Notation)	.json	Text provider APIs
Microsoft Excel	.xls, .xlsx	File archives, some distribution outlets
SPSS	.sav	SPSS statistical software
Stata	.dta	Stata (13) statistical software
R	.RData, .rda	R statistical software format

Stata—which as of version 13 allows text variables of practically unlimited size—will already have one document per row and possibly additional variables about the texts embedded as additional columns.

Commonly known as "meta-data," extra-textual information associated with each text file provides additional information about the texts, their sources, and the circumstances of their production, beyond their textual content. A set of parliamentary speeches, for instance, may also have the name and party of the speaker as document-level meta-data, in addition to a date and time stamp, and possibly the title of the debate in which the member of parliament spoke. Managing this meta-data and ensuring that it is associated with the text files through each stage of processing is one of the challenges of working with textual data, and one of the key reasons why researchers tend to use specialist software for this purpose.

When files contain multiple documents, they may also be associated with additional document-level information, as additional "variables." Texts in the form of single files, on the other hand, only contain additional, non-textual information if this is somehow embedded in the original texts as tags or document meta-data. Nearly all documents contain some form of meta-data, although the standards for meta-data differ widely among different formats. In HTML or XML, for instance, there are DOCTYPE declarations, as well as tags for the HTML version, and additional metadata declared by <meta key="value"> tags. In figure 6.1, for instance, the author, content type, source, and character encoding are recorded as meta-data. While nothing prevents individual documents from using a key-value tag convention for extra-textual data, this must not only be added to the text by the researcher or data source, but also the text processing tools used for analysis must be capable of separating this information from textual data and recording it separately from the content of the texts.

For large collections of documents that have been maintained by official sources, such as parliamentary records, it is common for texts to be stored in relational

```
<!DOCTYPE html>
<html xmlns="http://www.w3.org/1999/xhtml">
<meta charset="utf-8">
<meta http-equiv="Content-Type" content="text/html; charset=utf-8" />
<meta name="generator" content="pandoc" />
<meta name="author" content="Ken Benoit" />
```

Figure 6.1. Document meta-data example for HTML format

databases. Websites and DVDs that publish large collections of textual data, for instance, often use a database back end to store texts and a web front end to query that database per the user request. Either way, this information must be extracted or "scraped" from the front end in order to be stored as a corpus that can be analyzed.

For example, "DPSI: Database of Parliamentary Speeches in Ireland"[19] contains the complete record of parliamentary speeches from Dáil Éireann, the lower house of the Irish Parliament, from 1919 to the current session. This dataset had to be extracted using automated tools (in this case, text scraping programs written in the Python programming language), tagged with identifying information, and stored into another database. To extract texts for analysis, this database was queried with the results saved as plain text documents and read into an R package for subsequent processing.

Other, more direct alternatives are "application programming interfaces" (APIs) defined by a textual data source, such as Twitter or Facebook, that can be called using a syntax specified by the creator of the data source. This usually requires authentication with an API key that must be obtained from the data provider. A query calling the API generally results in a JSON file returned as a set of key-value pairs, with one key representing the textual data and the other key defining document variables and meta-data. JSON is itself a text file, but its tags defining the key-value pairs need to be read by additional software capable of keeping track of the keys and values. To give an example, figure 6.2 shows the output of a query to Capitol Words' API that retrieves frequency counts for the word "tax" in congressional speeches during each month of 2014. Here, the key sets in each record are identical, but additional processing is needed to convert the keys into variables (columns) in a traditional, rectangular dataset format.

Sometimes, documents are scanned in an image format, meaning the document exists only as a binary image in a PDF or photo file format (such as JPEG). This poses a challenge for extracting the text, because instead of having text encoded digitally in a way that a computer recognizes, image format files contain only the encoding of the image of the text. To be usable as textual data, the image must first be converted into text encoding using optical character recognition (OCR) software. The quality of this conversion will depend a lot on the quality of both the image and the software. Such conversion frequently introduces errors, especially with low-resolution or poor-quality images; errors are also caused by common typographic features such as ligatures in variable-width fonts.

```
{
    "results": [
        {
            "count": 664,
            "percentage": 0.045457968494341715,
            "total": 1460690,
            "month": "201401"
        },
        {
            "count": 590,
            "percentage": 0.04291370998478382,
            "total": 1374852,
            "month": "201402"
        },

    . . .


        {
            "count": 221,
            "percentage": 0.06546770901528863,
            "total": 337571,
            "month": "201412"
        }
    ]
}
```

Figure 6.2. Example of JSON data output collected through Capitol Words' API for the frequency count of the word "tax" during 2014

To be useful for text processing, files containing text are invariably converted into "plain text" format, stripped of markup tags, application-specific formatting codes, and any additional binary information that might be part of a file format. Unfortunately, there are numerous, differing conventions for what constitutes "plain" text. Computers represent text digitally by mapping into numbers the glyphs that human readers recognize as letters, numbers, and additional symbols. Unfortunately, this processing of *text encoding* did not develop according to a single standard and has led to a proliferation of "code pages" mapping characters into numeric representations, a problem mainly affecting non-English languages (with accented characters or non-roman character sets), but also affecting typographic symbols such as dashes and quotation marks. Depending on the country, platform, and year when the text was digitally recorded, the same numbers might map to different characters, causing headaches for novice and expert users alike. This explains why accented characters that look fine on one computer appear as diamond-shaped question marks or small alien head symbols on another computer.

Tools are widely available for converting between encodings, but not all encodings are detected automatically. The best recommendation we can offer is to make sure that all texts are coded as UTF-8, an eight-bit variable-length encoding of the Unicode standard, a modern mapping of almost every character in existence to a unique code point. Most modern operating systems operate in UTF-8, and most new software tools also use this text encoding as standard.

Once texts have been converted into a usable format, two key issues remain before the data can be processed. Because the "document" will form the aggregate unit of analysis, this unit first needs to be defined from the corpus. Second, once documents are defined, decisions also need to be made as to what textual features to extract.

Defining Documents

A corpus is a collection of documents, but the manner in which that corpus is segmented into documents is up to the user. Segmentation is the process of separating the texts found in the corpus into units that make sense for a particular analysis. This segmentation may be quite natural and simple, but may also involve reorganizing the units depending on the research purpose.

Source texts are often organized in ways that naturally correspond to document units. The corpus of presidential inaugural addresses, for instance, consists of 57 separate speeches with a median length of about 2,100 words. For most purposes, each speech would define a "document." The same may be true for party manifestos, parliamentary bills, campaign speeches, or judicial opinions.

In other cases, however, we may need to combine different pieces of text to form a single "document." In the legislative speeches we analyze later in this chapter, for instance, the Irish parliamentary archive recorded each non-interrupted speech act separately. Because interruptions are very frequent in legislative settings—and certainly in the Irish case—we concatenated all of a single speaker's contributions in the debate into a single "document." Because this resulted in some speech "documents" for members of Parliament who did not really make speeches, but were nonetheless recorded as having delivered a short "speech" consisting only of "Hear, hear!," we also defined a threshold of words below which we simply discarded the text.

Concatenating texts into larger "documents" is very common when dealing with social media data, especially the micro-blogging site Twitter. The 140-character limit imposed on any single "tweet" means that these may be too short to analyze separately. Many researchers therefore define a document as the concatenation of all tweets of a user over a fixed period.

On the other hand, some longer texts may require segmentation to break them up into smaller units, the opposite of combining (concatenating) them. If the sentence or paragraph will form our unit of analysis, then we could use automatic methods to segment the texts based on the characters that define paragraph or sentence units.[20] In many other cases, we will use human-assigned breaks to denote meaningfully different sections of text that will define documents, possibly for later selection and analysis in groups. Slapin and Proksch,[21] for example, analyzed German manifestos on different dimensions of policy (economic, social, and foreign policy), for instance, by first segmenting manually based on which topic was being discussed.

Defining and Selecting Features

There are many ways to define features in text analysis. The most common feature is the word, although here we have used the more general term "features" to emphasize that features can be both more or less than words as they are used in the source texts. In addition, various strategies for *selecting* features may lead to some being discarded. This is a complex field, and here we describe it only in the broadest terms.

Defining features is the first step. Most approaches define words as features through a process known as "tokenizing" the texts. This language comes from linguistics, where word occurrences are known as "tokens," and unique words as word "types." Tokenization can be performed automatically and reliably by software that uses white space and few additional padding characters as delimiters.[22] Not every word type may become a feature, however, due to selection. Selection involves, very broadly speaking, two strategies: one based on combining feature types and the other based on excluding them.

Combining feature types is the strategy of treating different words as equivalent, on syntactic or semantic grounds. When we perform "stemming," we are using rules to convert morphological variations of words into their canonical or "dictionary" forms. For fiscal policy, for instance, stemmed features would treat the types "tax," "taxes," "taxing," and "taxed" as equivalent occurrences of the lemma "tax." Similar methods might be used to regularize the spellings across dialects, for instance, to treat "colour" and "color" as the same feature type. Equivalence classes may also be defined according to semantic categories. This is exactly the strategy taken by

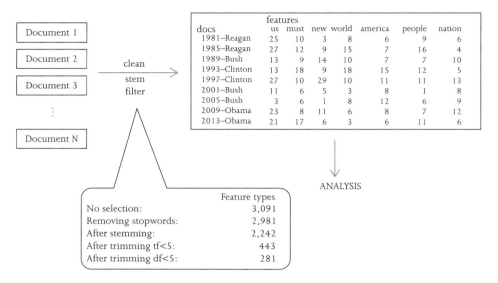

Figure 6.3. Illustration of converting presidential inaugural speeches into quantitative data using feature selection

dictionary approaches, such as the Linguistic Inquiry and Word Count, a dictionary of language and psychological processes by Pennebaker, Booth, and Francis,[23] which treats "hate," "dislike," and "fear" as members of an equivalent class labeled "Negative emotion."

Exclusion approaches for feature selection are based on dropping feature types that are deemed uninteresting for research purposes. Feature exclusion is typically done on an *ex ante* basis or on the basis of patterns of occurrence. *Ex ante*, it is quite common to exclude word features found in lists of "stop words," usually a catalog of conjunctions, articles, prepositions, and pronouns. Few analysts expect the cross-document frequencies of the word "the" (the most commonly occurring word in English) to be substantively meaningful, for instance. Stop word lists should be used with caution, however, since there is no one-size-fits-all list, although many text analysis packages provide stop word lists that are accepted as "standard" by users who seldom bother even to inspect the contents of these lists.

The other exclusion strategy is to drop features below a threshold of term or document minimum frequency: some absolute threshold of how many times a feature must occur in a document or in how many documents it must occur. In processing the corpus of inaugural speeches since Ronald Reagan illustrated in

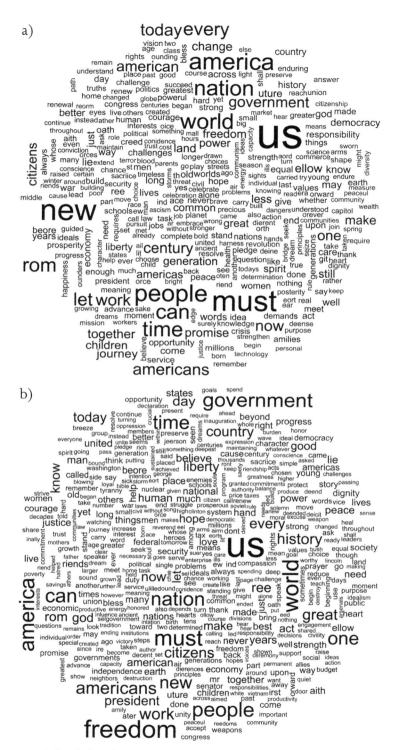

Figure 6.4. Word cloud plots for presidential inaugural speeches since 1981, by a) Democrat and b) Republican presidents

Note: Stop words have been excluded.

figure 6.3, for instance, selection strategies narrowed down an unfiltered number of features from 3,091 to 2,242 once stemming had been been applied, and a further reduction to 443 and 281 once features with feature ("term") and document frequencies less than 5 had been removed. The final feature set of 281 feature types is plotted in figure 6.4 as "word clouds" according to the political party of the president. Word clouds are common visualization tools for observing the most common word features in a text, plotting the size of the word feature proportional to its relative frequency.

A quotidian form of feature selection is known as "cleaning," the process of removing unwanted characters or symbols from text prior to tokenization into features. Almost universally, words are transformed to lowercase and punctuation symbols are discarded. It is also very common to remove numerals, although some numbers (especially years) may form substantively meaningful features depending on the research topic.

Converting Documents and Features into Quantitative Information

To analyze text as data, documents and features must be converted into a structured, numerical format. The starting point for the analysis stage of quantitative text research is the creation of a *document-feature matrix* that contains information on the number of occurrences of each feature in each document. Usually, this matrix represents documents as rows and features as columns, as depicted in figure 6.3. From this matrix, any number of analyses can be performed.

The conversion into a document-feature matrix is done efficiently by software tools designed for this purpose, in essence a large-scale cross-tabulation. When working with natural language texts with more than a trivial number of documents, many features will occur zero times in a number of documents. As a consequence, creating a simple cross-tabulation of features by documents as a *dense* matrix, or one in which zero-frequencies are recorded, becomes very inefficient. In practice, therefore, many software implementations record document feature matrices as *sparse* representations, in essence, storing only the features that occur at least once, along with their frequency indexed by document. This results in significant savings of both storage space and computational power.

Document-feature matrices are commonly transformed by either weighting features, smoothing them, or both. What we have described so far, recording a feature count, is the simplest form of weighting. Because documents differ in length, however, this will result in larger feature counts for longer documents, all other things being equal. A common remedy to this is to convert feature frequencies into relative feature frequencies, replacing the counts by the proportion of times each feature occurs in a document. Known as "normalizing"[24] the text, this process makes feature values comparable across documents by dividing each feature count by the total features per document. Many other possibilities exist[25] such as tf-idf weighting, where each feature is divided by a measure of the proportion of documents in which a term occurs to down-weight the features that occur commonly across documents.[26] Tf-idf weighting is most commonly used in information retrieval and machine learning as a way of making the results of search queries more relevant or for improving the accuracy of predictive tools.

APPLICATION TO FISCAL POLICY

We demonstrate the quantitative analysis of textual data with an analysis of budget speeches from Ireland. Government stability in parliamentary systems depends crucially on one overriding characteristic of legislative behavior: unity. Without party discipline in voting, especially on critical legislation, governments quickly come apart, formally or informally, leading to a new government or new elections. However, we know that there is a large degree of intra-party heterogeneity in policy preferences. Legislators have different preferences and often vote in spite of these, instead of because of them. Moreover, legislators often answer to more than one type of principal, and this may cause tensions when constituency representation clashes with party demands.[27] The more acute the tension between the personal interests of the legislator and the group interests of his or her party, the more we would expect the legislator's preferences to diverge.

Because of party unity, voting records tell us little about intra-party politics in legislatures where party discipline is strong. What legislators *say*, however, is typically less constrained. Legislative speeches are seldom, if ever, subject to formal sanction for those who speak out of turn. Indeed, party leaders may view floor debates as an opportunity for reluctantly faithful members to send messages to their constituents, as long as they follow party instructions when it comes to voting. For these reasons, the text analysis of parliamentary speeches has formed an important leg of the empirical study of intra-party preferences.[28] The words that legislators use can be scaled into positions providing a much more valid indicator of their preferences than the votes they cast.

In this section, we exploit this feature of parliamentary texts to measure the strain placed on party unity by austerity budgets: those splitting not only government and opposition but also governing parties and coalitions by virtue of requiring deep and deeply painful clawbacks of services, tax increases, and spending cuts. Austerity budgets are an unfortunately familiar feature of European politics since the onset of the euro zone crisis in banking and sovereign debt servicing. The challenge of passing these severe budgets, often necessitated by externally imposed conditions of emergency funding packages, has split and sometimes brought down governments. Yet even in the face of such conflict, it is seldom manifest in legislative voting, even when voting on unpopular austerity budgets. To observe the strain on governing parties, we must look at what legislators say.

Budgets and Politics of Economic Crisis in Ireland

Our case study in austerity budgets comes from Ireland, one of the first European states to experience a deep banking crisis and receive a multi billion-euro bailout with austerity conditions attached. Since 2008, the country experienced a steep decline in economic output and a sharp rise in unemployment, along with a massive debt problem caused by the financial load of recapitalizing a failing banking system. This forced the government to implement a number of severe austerity measures against growing public resentment, ultimately leading to a record low in the popularity ratings for the government parties and a breakdown in January 2011 of the coalition led by Fianna Fáil, a party that had led Ireland continuously since 1997. Addressing the crisis required an €85-billion rescue package from the European Union and the International Monetary Fund, a bailout that led to tax cutbacks in social spending equivalent to €20 billion, or 13 percent of gross domestic product (GDP),[29] including highly controversial changes to taxes and wage agreements, while leaving the public perception that the bankers who had caused the crisis were getting rescued.

We include in our analysis all annual budget debates from 1987 to 2013. During these debates, legislators are free to discuss the budget, with governing party members and ministers expressing support and opposition parties invariably criticizing the government and its budget. Given the strong party discipline in Ireland,[30] votes tend to follow strict party lines. Voting against the government's financial bill or resigning from the party are extreme measures that only a few legislators are willing to face. Party discipline in Ireland, indeed, makes the two equivalent, since voting against the party on a budget would result in expulsion from the party. In parliamentary systems such as Ireland's, where budgets are written entirely by the party in government, votes on these national fiscal plans are very much votes for or against the government itself, and, indeed, were the government to lose such a vote, it would fall and a new coalition would have to be formed.[31]

To scale the budget speeches, we used the Wordscores method of Laver, Benoit, and Garry.[32] We scaled each debate separately, training each scaling using the speech of the finance minister to represent the "pro-budget" position, and the speech of the financial spokesperson of the opposition (equivalent to the "shadow finance minister") to represent the opposition position. Representing these positions as +1 and −1, respectively, we transformed the "virgin" text scores using the rescaling proposed by Martin Vanberg,[33] a procedure that ensures that the scaled positions of the reference texts are set to the scores used to train the system (+1 and −1). While not always recommended, this transformation ensures that all other documents' scaled values are positioned relative to the reference documents,[34] an outcome we explicitly desired in our budget-by-budget comparison. Each position is then "fixed" relative to the positions of the government and opposition finance spokespersons, making the scores comparable across budgets according to a common benchmark.

Results

The results of the scaling procedure is an estimated position on the latent dimension for each speaker. Figure 6.5 displays these speaker positions for the 1999 budget debate. The figure shows that our analysis is able to recover the division between government and opposition parties: almost all members of the Fianna Fáil–Progressive Democrat coalition have positive Wordscores position, while the majority of opposition members have negative scores. Moreover, we also find interesting intra-party differences. Within the government parties, we find that, on average, cabinet members have more pro-government positions while government backbenchers are closer to the opposition.

Figure 6.6 shows estimated positions for the 2009 budget debate, which was the first austerity budget implemented by the government at the beginning of the financial and economic crisis. Compared to the budget debate during the boom years (figure 6.5), we find much more overlap between the government and the opposition—a first indication that the crisis has increased tensions with members of the government parties.

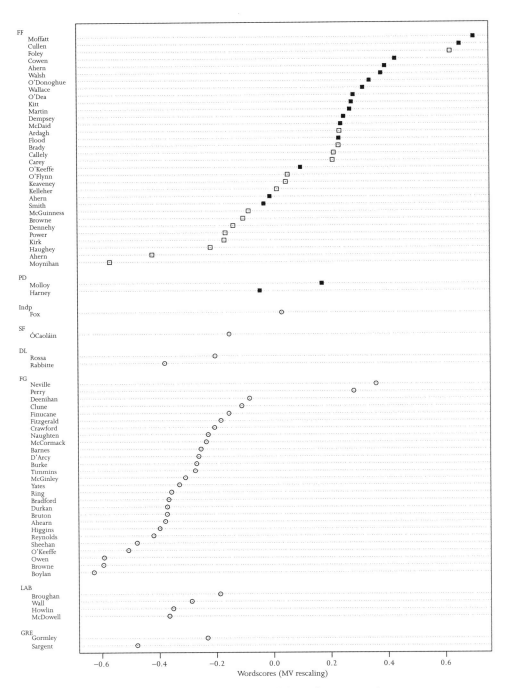

Figure 6.5. Estimated positions for 1999 budget debate (boom years)

Notes: Symbols: open squares, government members; solid squares, cabinet ministers and junior ministers; open circles, opposition members. Party abbreviations: FF, Fianna Fáil; PD, Progressive Democrats; Indp, Independent; SF, Sinn Féin; DL, Democratic Left; FG, Fine Gael; LAB, Labour; GRE, Greens.

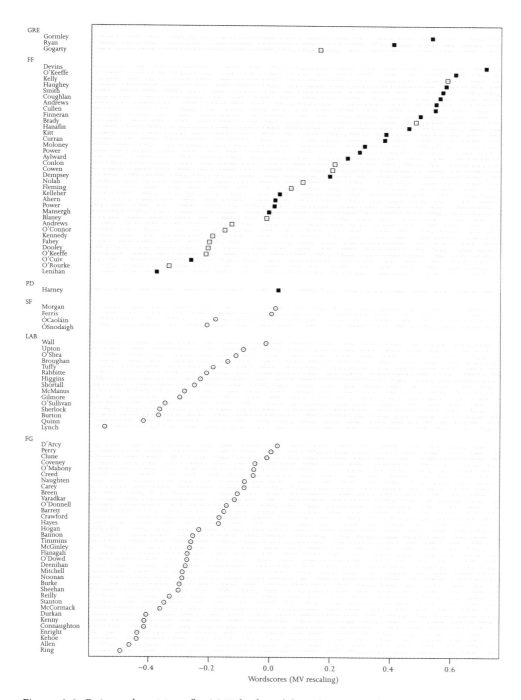

Figure 6.6. Estimated positions for 2009 budget debate (crisis years)

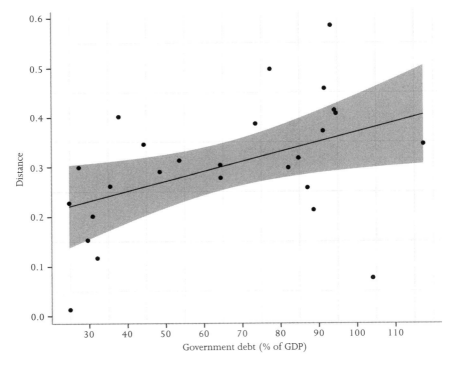

Figure 6.7. Distance between average Wordscores estimates for cabinet members and government backbenchers against government debt (percentage of GDP) with ordinary least squares (OLS) regression line and 95% confidence interval

In an attempt to explain this pattern more systematically, we plot the difference between the average positions of cabinet members and the average positions of backbenchers against government debt as a percentage of GDP, in figure 6.7. The distance between the two groups appears to be a function of the economy: the gap is relatively small in good economic times and increases as the economy worsens.

To further test the relationship between intra-government divisions and economic performance, we estimate a regression model with the distance between cabinet members and government backbenchers as the dependent variable. As controls, we include government debt, a variable that indicates years in which an election occurred, and three dummy variables that indicate an alternation in government, a change of prime minister, and a change of finance minister, respectively. Figure 6.8 summarizes the results of this regression. We find a significant effect for government debt that confirms the relationship displayed in figure 6.8: the gap between cabinet

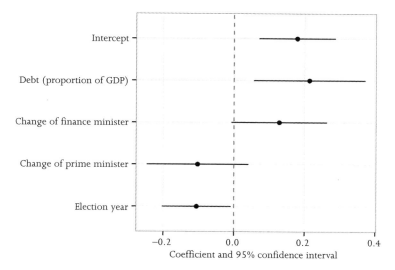

Figure 6.8. Results of OLS regression of distance between cabinet members and government backbenchers on constituency and economic variables

members and backbenchers widens during economic bad times. The anticipation of an election, in contrast, decreases the gap, possibly because government members need to demonstrate a unified front when competing in the election.

CONCLUDING REMARKS

In this chapter, we have provided readers with the basic ideas of quantitative text analysis and outlined typical challenges that readers will encounter when they apply this method to the study of public policy. This included the various file formats in which text is stored, the construction of a corpus (i.e., collection of documents), the selection of words and features on which the analysis will be based, and the transformation of unstructured data into a document-feature matrix as the starting point for the analysis of textual data. We have illustrated the application of quantitative text analysis with data from annual Irish budget debates during the period from 1987 to 2013. Our investigation of legislative positioning over austerity debates has explored the differences in preferences for austerity expressed by legislators whose votes on the budget fail to reveal any differences in their preferences due to strict party discipline.

Our results demonstrated how positional information about the relative policy preferences of individual speakers, and specifically members of the governing coalition responsible for implementing painful budget cuts, can be measured from speeches on the legislative floor using text as data. Our results have a high degree of face validity when compared to known legislative positions, with government ministers being most supportive of the budgets, opposition speakers most opposed, and government backbenchers in between. Text scaling as used here provides a valid method for measuring intra-party differences as expressed in speeches made during debates over annual budgets.

Quantitative text analysis is a new and exciting research tool that allows social scientists to generate quantities of interest from textual data. Like any method in the social sciences, the estimation of these quantities requires a theory-guided research design and careful validation of the results. One particular problem in the analysis of political texts is potential selection bias. The decision to speak or to publish a document is often the result of strategic considerations, which, if not accounted for, can bias results. In the legislative context, for example, party leaders may strategically decide who (and who is not) allowed to speak.[35] We furthermore must be careful when interpreting the results and not equate the measures we estimate with the "true" preferences of politicians, which, one may argue, are inherently unobservable. Texts produced in the policy-making process are, again, the result of strategic considerations of single politicians or groups of actors. But this is true for any method that attempts to measure policy preferences and reinforces the need to validate the results with external measures.

NOTES

This research was supported by European Research Council grant ERC-2011-StG 283794-QUANTESS.

1. Keith T. Poole and Howard Rosenthal, *Congress: A Political-Economic History of Roll Call Voting* (Oxford: Oxford University Press, 1997); and Joshua Clinton, Simon Jackman, and Douglas Rivers, "The Statistical Analysis of Roll Call Data," *American Journal of Political Science* 98, no. 2 (2004): 355–370.

2. For example, Simon Hix, Abdul Noury, and Gérard Roland, "Power to the Parties: Cohesion and Competition in the European Parliament, 1979–2001," *British Journal of Political Science* 35, no. 2 (2005): 209–234.

3. Simon Hug, "Selection Effects in Roll Call Votes," *British Journal of Political Science* 40, no. 1 (2010): 225–235.

4. Peter M. VanDoren, "Can We Learn the Causes of Congressional Decisions from Roll-Call Data?," *Legislative Studies Quarterly* 15, no. 3 (1990): 311–340; Clifford J. Carrubba, Matthew Gabel,

Lacey Murrah, Ryan Clough, Elizabeth Montgomery, and Rebecca Schambach, "Off the Record: Unrecorded Legislative Votes, Selection Bias and Roll-Call Vote Analysis," *British Journal of Political Science* 36, no. 4 (2006): 691–704; and Clifford J. Carrubba, Matthew Gabel, and Simon Hug, "Legislative Voting Behavior, Seen and Unseen: A Theory of Roll-Call Vote Selection," *Legislative Studies Quarterly* 33, no. 4 (2008): 543–572.

5. Michael Laver, Kenneth Benoit, and John Garry, "Extracting Policy Positions from Political Texts Using Words as Data," *American Political Science Review* 97, no. 2 (2003): 311–331; and Sven-Oliver Proksch and Jonathan B. Slapin, "Position Taking in European Parliament Speeches," *British Journal of Political Science* 40 (2010): 587–611.

6. For example, Michael Laver and John Garry, "Estimating Policy Positions from Political Texts," *American Journal of Political Science* 44, no. 3 (2000): 619–634; Proksch and Slapin, "Position Taking in European Parliament Speeches"; Burt L. Monroe and Ko Maeda, "Talk's Cheap: Text-Based Estimation of Rhetorical Ideal-Points" (POLMETH working paper, Society for Political Methodology, Washington University in St. Louis, St. Louis, MO, 2004); Michael Laver and Kenneth Benoit, "Locating TDs in Policy Spaces: The Computational Text Analysis of Dáil Speeches," *Irish Political Studies* 17, no. 1 (2002): 59–73; and Benjamin E. Lauderdale and Alexander Herzog, "Measuring Political Positions from Legislative Speech" (paper presented at the Text as Data Conference, Chicago, October 10–11, 2014).

7. Justin Grimmer and Brandon M. Stewart, "Text as Data: The Promise and Pitfalls of Automatic Content Analysis Methods for Political Texts," *Political Analysis* 21, no. 3 (2013): 267–297.

8. Laver, Benoit, and Garry, "Extracting Policy Positions from Political Texts."

9. For example, Laver and Benoit, "Locating TDs in Policy Spaces"; Daniela Giannetti and Michael Laver, "Policy Positions and Jobs in the Government," *European Journal of Political Research* 44, no. 1 (2005): 91–120; Michael Laver, Kenneth Benoit, and Nicolas Sauger, "Policy Competition in the 2002 French Legislative and Presidential Elections," *European Journal of Political Research* 45, no. 4 (2006): 667–697; Kenneth Benoit, Michael Laver, Christine Arnold, Paul Pennings, and Madeleine O. Hosli, "Measuring National Delegate Positions at the Convention on the Future of Europe Using Computerized Word Scoring," *European Union Politics* 6, no. 3 (2005): 291–313; Armen Hakhverdian, "Capturing Government Policy on the Left–Right Scale: Evidence from the United Kingdom, 1956–2006," *Political Studies* 57, no. 4 (2009): 720–745; Robert Klemmensen, Sara Binzer Hobolt, and Martin Ejnar Hansen, "Estimating Policy Positions Using Political Texts: An Evaluation of the Wordscores Approach," *Electoral Studies* 26, no. 4 (2007): 746–755; Young Min Baek, Joseph N. Cappella, and Alyssa Bindman, "Automating Content Analysis of Open-Ended Responses: Wordscores and Affective Intonation," *Communication Methods and Measures* 5, no. 4 (2011): 275–296; and Paul V. Warwick, "Public Opinion and Government Policy in Britain: A Case of Congruence, Amplification or Dampening?," *European Journal of Political Research* 54, no. 1 (2015): 61–80.

10. Jonathan B. Slapin and Sven-Oliver Proksch, "A Scaling Model for Estimating Time-Series Party Positions from Texts," *American Journal of Political Science* 52, no. 3 (2008): 705–722.

11. Ibid.

12. Heike Klüver, "Measuring Interest Group Influence Using Quantitative Text Analysis," *European Union Politics* 10, no. 4 (2009): 535–549.

13. Proksch and Slapin, "Position Taking in European Parliament Speeches."

14. William Lowe and Kenneth Benoit, "Validating Estimates of Latent Traits from Textual Data Using Human Judgment as a Benchmark," *Political Analysis* 21, no. 3 (2013): 298–313.

15. David M. Blei, Andrew Y. Ng, and Michael I. Jordan, "Latent Dirichlet Allocation," *Journal of Machine Learning Research* 3 (2003): 993–1022.

16. Kevin M. Quinn, Burt L. Monroe, Michael Colaresi, Michael H. Crespin, and Dragomir R. Radev, "How to Analyze Political Attention with Minimal Assumptions and Costs," *American Journal of Political Science* 54, no. 1 (2010): 209–228.

17. Justin Grimmer, "A Bayesian Hierarchical Topic Model for Political Texts: Measuring Expressed Agendas in Senate Press Releases," *Political Analysis* 18, no. 1 (2010): 1–35.

18. Brandon Stewart, Edo Airoldi, and Molly Roberts, "Topic Models and Structure" (paper presented at the Annual Meeting of the American Political Science Association, 2011).

19. Alexander Herzog and Slava Mikhaylov, "DPSI: Database of Parliamentary Speeches in Ireland," http://www.alexherzog.net.

20. Surprisingly, methods for sentence segmentation are far from perfect. Different languages use different end-of-sentence delimiters, and many delimiters (especially the period) are also used for other purposes such as to separate the decimal places in a printed number or in abbreviations (e.g., "e.g."). Detecting paragraph delimiters can be even harder.

21. Slapin and Proksch, "A Scaling Model for Estimating Time-Series Party Positions from Texts."

22. Some languages, such as Chinese, do not use inter-word delimiters, and tokenization therefore relies on rule- and statistics-based detection.

23. James W. Pennebaker, Roger J. Booth, and Martha E. Francis, *Linguistic Inquiry and Word Count*, http://LIWC.net.

24. In computer science, this is known as "L1 normalization."

25. See Christopher D. Manning, Prabhakar Raghavan, and Hinrich Schütze, *Introduction to Information Retrieval* (New York: Cambridge University Press, 2008), chap. 2.

26. If N is the total number of documents and df_t (*document frequency*) is the number of documents that contain a term t, then the *inverse document frequency* is defined for term t as $idf_t = \log(N/df_t)$. The tf-idf weight for term t in document d is then given by $\text{tf-idf}_{t,d} = tf_{t,d} \times idf_t$, where $tf_{t,d}$ (*term frequency*) is the number of occurrences of term t in document d; ibid., chap. 6.

27. For example, Kaare Strøm and Wolfgang C. Müller, "Parliamentary Democracy, Agency Problems, and Party Politics," in *Intra-Party Politics and Coalition Governments in Parliamentary Democracies*, ed. Daniela Giannetti and Kenneth Benoit (London: Routledge, 2009), 25–49; and Gail McElroy and Kenneth Benoit, "Party Policy and Group Affiliation in the European Parliament," *British Journal of Political Science* 40, no. 2 (2010): 377–398.

28. For example, Proksch and Slapin, "Position Taking in European Parliament Speeches"; Laver and Benoit, "Locating TDs in Policy Spaces"; and Lauderdale and Herzog, "Measuring Political Positions from Legislative Speech."

29. Adele Bergin, John FitzGerald, Ide Kearney, and Cormac O'Sullivan, "The Irish Fiscal Crisis," *National Institute Economic Review* 217 (2011): 51.

30. Michael Gallagher, "Making and Breaking Governments," in *Politics in the Republic of Ireland*, 5th ed., ed. John Coakley and Michael Gallagher (London: Routledge, 2009), 412–457.

31. Michael Gallagher, Michael Laver, and Peter Mair, *Representative Government in Modern Europe*, 5th ed. (Maidenhead, UK: McGraw-Hill, 2011).

32. Laver, Benoit, and Garry, "Extracting Policy Positions from Political Texts."

33. Lanny W. Martin and Georg Vanberg, "A Robust Transformation Procedure for Interpreting Political Text," *Political Analysis* 16, no. 1 (2007): 93–100.

34. Kenneth Benoit and Michael Laver, "Compared to What? A Comment on 'A Robust Transformation Procedure for Interpreting Political Text' by Martin and Vanberg," *Political Analysis* 16, no. 1 (2007): 101–111.

35. Sven-Oliver Proksch and Jonathan B. Slapin, "Institutional Foundations of Legislative Speech," *American Journal of Political Science* 56, no. 3 (2012): 520–537.

CHAPTER SEVEN

Machine Learning and Governance

Alex C. Engler

IN THIS CHAPTER

This chapter introduces machine learning, a family of tools that employ computer processing to expand on the traditional statistical methods of classification and regression analysis. Originally a branch of artificial intelligence research, the evolving methods of machine learning are having dramatic effects on improving private sector services. Just in the past few years, the public sector has begun to catch up, as machine learning has become a critical component of research methodology, predictive analytics, and big data systems. This chapter discusses the fundamental concepts and some of the most common tools in the machine learning repertoire. In addition, this text uses case studies and anecdotes to detail the nascent emergence of machine learning in public policy.

INTRODUCTION TO MACHINE LEARNING

In 1949, while working at IBM on its first commercially available computer, an engineer named Arthur Samuel came up with an ambitious idea. An alumnus of the Massachusetts Institute of Technology (MIT) and former Bell Labs employee, Samuel set out to write a checkers-playing computer program that could beat the best players in the world. In the ensuing years, Samuel wrote a series of programs that aimed to do just this and incorporated in them a new approach that profoundly expanded the role of computers in modern society.

Samuel's innovation was to go beyond developing a series of rules that defined how the computer would choose what moves to make. His program stored in memory the series of moves made by both players and the outcome of the game. Even with the limited power of computation at the time, the program could play against itself thousands of times a day—recording every game. Then, with stored examples of what moves were more likely to lead to victory and defeat, his program used its prior experience to influence its decisions.

In essence, the program was asking, "Of the available moves, which one has most consistently led to victory in the past?" Samuel eventually came to call this mechanism "machine learning."

The concept of machine learning has driven the progression of computer programs that now dominate human competitors in checkers, chess, and even *Jeopardy!* John McCarthy—noted computer scientist who is often credited with coining the term "artificial intelligence" in 1955—once wrote that playing games like checkers is to machine learning as studying the fruit fly is to the field of genetics.[1] Today, machine learning has gone far beyond games and now affects almost every interaction that we have with computers.

The process by which e-mail services filter out spam, the detection of fraudulent credit card transactions, the facial recognition that identifies people on Facebook, and automated recommendations for movies, music, and shopping—all of these are the outputs of modern machine learning algorithms. Entire businesses are based on the power of these analytics. When Capital One started as a tiny spinoff of Signet Bank in 1988, analytics were not a part of the credit card industry. Capital One's founders changed that, introducing predictive pricing and targeting algorithms as a core part of their business model, and the power of those analytics drove the company to the success it enjoys today.

The concepts and tools of this field have also begun to emerge in government and public policy. Machine learning provides unparalleled methods for prediction, which have been successfully applied to forecasting diverse outcomes:

- Probability of hospital readmission or death for patients under the care of the U.S. Department of Veterans Affairs
- Likelihood of dropping out for youth in school districts across the country
- Locations of the sale of illegal cigarettes in New York City
- Presence of lead paint in houses with young children in Chicago
- Trends in geospatial crime metrics

Machine learning is also especially adept at anomaly detection—finding individual observations that don't fit in with the corpus of data. This is particularly useful for the discovery of fraud and theft, which improves the government's ability to collect and distribute enormous sums of money. Dean Silverman, director of the Office of Compliance Analytics at the Internal Revenue Service (IRS), has implemented rigorous and cutting-edge methods for identifying mistakes in filed tax returns and for discovering fraudulent returns submitted by identity thieves.[2]

The implementations of machine learning introduced so far have all been examples of supervised learning. Supervised learning entails that for the data being analyzed, there is a known outcome variable of interest that is being modeled with the other available variables. So, concerning Samuel's checkers, the outcome variable being examined is which player won the checkers game. For the IRS examples, the outcome variable might be whether a tax return ended up being fraudulent or not.

Machine learning also encompasses unsupervised learning, in which there is no specific outcome variable of interest or that variable is unknown for the available data. The most common type of unsupervised learning is the family of clustering algorithms. Instead of trying to learn something about the relationship between a specific outcome variable and predictor variables, clustering attempts to congregate observations into similar groups. Clustering has been used with student data to look across a series of variables such as course grades, attendance, standardized test scores, discipline, socioeconomic status, and demographic information and to then group students into strata.[3] The resulting clusters of students may have similar long-term outcomes or may respond similarly to interventions. In addition, clustering of building-level data is having a burgeoning impact on urban planning, with the use of algorithms to help define sections of cities.[4]

Looking beyond applied analytics, machine learning is also a core part of the statistical researcher's toolbox—public policy research and political science are no exception. Many machine learning methods work at massive scales, make few or no assumptions about the underlying distributions of data (i.e., they are non-parametric), are rarely constrained to linearity, and have extensive applications to unstructured data such as text, audio, and video. Additionally, machine learning algorithms can be quickly and easily applied with just a few lines of code in modern data analysis tools like R, Python, and SAS.

Many different algorithms fall under the umbrella of machine learning, but their unifying characteristic is their ability to learn from their experience of performing some task—in Samuel's case, his stored history of checkers games—and to then improve their performance on that same task. Diving into an example of a machine learning algorithm will help elucidate this process.

GETTING STARTED WITH A DECISION TREE

The decision tree is perhaps the most ubiquitous type of machine learning algorithm. Decision trees are a type of supervised learning, since they necessitate the presence of a known outcome variable for some data. In the case of figure 7.1 (adapted from a *New York Times* graphic[5]), the outcome variable is which candidate won the majority vote share for that county in the 2008 Democratic primary election.

Looking at figure 7.1, we can see a hierarchy of criteria that helps describe which counties voted predominantly for Barack Obama or Hillary Clinton. Following the path to the right after the first division tells us that of the counties with more than a 20 percent black population, Obama won 383, or 84.5 percent, and lost only 70. The path to the left splits again, by whether or not the high school graduation rate exceeds 78 percent. So following the path to the left from that split (called a "node" in computer science), we can see that of the counties that are less than 20 percent black *and* have a high school graduation rate of less than 78 percent, Clinton won 704 of 793—88.8 percent.

Already, figure 7.1 has made it clear that Obama was leading in the better educated counties with higher black populations, while Clinton was more likely to win whiter and poorer counties. Following the decision tree further reveals relationships between the geography and socioeconomic status of the county with the outcome of the primaries there.

The descriptive power of figure 7.1 is somewhat obvious, but what is not as apparent is that the order of the nodes (which one goes first, second, third, etc.) and their specific cut points (why a high school graduation rate of 78 percent and not 80 percent?) are algorithmically derived. The node regarding the racial makeup of the county appears first not by chance, but because it has the most predictive power. With decision tree models, this predictive power is most often measured in the reduction of entropy.[6] Entropy is the idea of uncertainty or lack of predictability in an outcome—and so reducing entropy in a group of observations really is synonymous with improving predictive power.

To really understand this concept, it is critical to recall the fundamental concepts of conditional probabilities. Consider the textbook example of a bag of light and dark marbles. Given a bag of 10 marbles (figure 7.2), evenly split with 5 of each color, you would have a 50 percent chance of correctly guessing which shade of marble was randomly pulled from the bag. This is an example of high entropy—there is a great level of uncertainty as to what the next randomly selected marble would be.

But what if we knew something else about the marbles—for instance, if they varied in size as well as color? In the example shown on the right-hand side of figure 7.2, there are 5 each of a smaller and larger variety. By splitting our first group into two separate, smaller groups based on size, we can improve our ability to predict

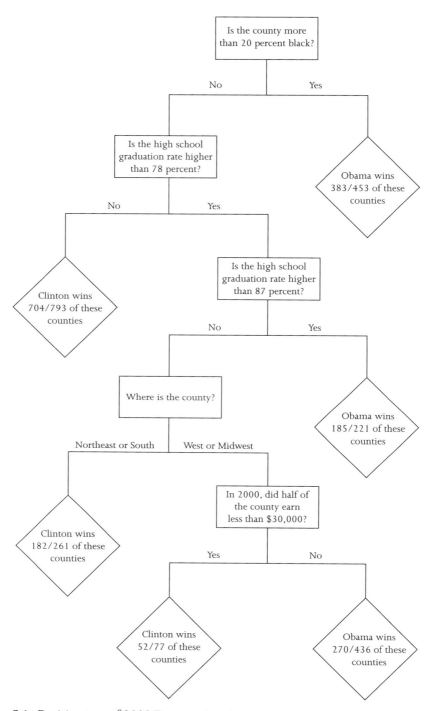

Figure 7.1. Decision tree of 2008 Democratic primary county outcomes

Source: Adapted from an original graphic by Amanda Cox, "Decision Tree: The Obama-Clinton Divide," *New York Times*, April 16, 2008, http://www.nytimes.com/imagepages/2008/04/16/us/20080416_OBAMA_GRAPHIC.html.

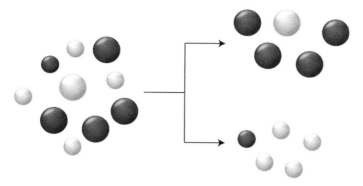

Figure 7.2. Bag of marbles

the color of a randomly selected marble. Now, when randomly choosing a random marble from the bag of small-sized marbles, there's an 80 percent chance that the marble will be light, and the opposite is true for the bag of larger marbles. This allows for much more confidence in the prediction of a randomly selected marble from either group.

This is the goal of the decision tree algorithm: to split the original, high-entropy groups into smaller, lower-entropy groups. The data scientist who designed the original *New York Times* decision tree, Amanda Cox, started with a dataset of counties that included whether Hillary Clinton or Barack Obama won the plurality vote share in that county, which is the outcome, or dependent variable—analogous to marble color. In addition, this dataset contained the other factors within the graphic: high school graduation rate, racial demographics, population density, and voting history. In classical statistics, we might refer to these variables as the "independent variables." In machine learning, these are instead called "features," though the meaning is the same.

The decision tree algorithm calculates the resulting entropy of every possible division across all the features, and then chooses the distinction that maximally reduces entropy. In this specific case, the algorithm has determined that whether a county has a black population of more than 20 percent reduces entropy more than the high school graduation rate or the geographic location of the county. The exact percentage of the population, 20, is not an accident either. The algorithm chose this value after evaluating every single possible slicing point in the percent black population feature.

This is how a decision tree algorithm explicitly works, but it may not immediately feel that closely tied to the original checkers example. However, the underlying structure of the problem is the same.

A PRACTICAL DEFINITION OF MACHINE LEARNING

By definition, a machine learning algorithm uses the experience (prior trials and outcomes) of a task to improve its performance on that same task. For Arthur Samuel, the task was the execution of an individual game of checkers with the performance measured by whether or not the game was won. So this definition is telling us what we already know—the algorithm is improving its ability to play checkers as the number of observed checkers games increases.

Although perhaps less clear at first glance, this definition does apply just as well to the voting decision tree. In this case, the task at hand is identifying the winning primary candidate for a given county based on prior information known about that county. The performance metric is whether or not the candidate identified by the model did in reality win the plurality vote share for that county. The experience is the body of available data about that county and the outcome of the primary voting in that county.[7]

It might be edifying to think about this example as though it were still ongoing. Toward the end of February 2008, Obama led Clinton by just 100 delegates. With the March 4 primaries in Rhode Island, Vermont, Ohio, and Texas looming, there was substantial interest in analyzing the likely outcomes of those races. A political strategist knowledgeable in data science (a profession that the Obama campaigns proved to be very useful) might have run this decision tree algorithm to analyze the county voting returns available at that time. This dataset of already-decided counties—in Michigan, Florida, California, and the rest—acts as the experience that this model uses to improve its ability to predict the winner of counties that haven't voted yet. Each individual county that has already been decided would be one row of data and one prior experience from which the algorithm would learn.

This is how most machine learning, at least in the supervised case, is implemented. Generally, there is data available that contains the entire set of variables, including the outcome variable. This data is called "training data," because the model learns and is ultimately defined by examining the relationships between the features and outcome variable in the training data. Then, for most purposes, the model is applied to test data—data in which the outcome variable is unknown. If the model results in a prediction of this unknown outcome variable that is categorical (as in the marble and decision tree examples), then the model is described as addressing a classification problem. The alternative is a regression problem in which the predicted outcome is a continuous variable.

This machine learning definition is important in the context of the decision tree for one more reason. It intentionally focuses on the predictive element of the model. By using this algorithm, Amanda Cox was examining the relationships between county characteristics and primary voting outcomes in a similar fashion to calculating coefficients from logistic regression. However, the principal task of the decision tree algorithm is to predict the winner of plurality vote share in the primary. The fact that the nodes inform as to the relationships between the features and the outcome variable is secondary to this predictive task.

This is the case with many other machine learning algorithms as well. Given their output, decision trees are considered to be highly interpretable as machine learning algorithms go. In addition to the predictions, a decision tree can actually help humans understand exactly what they are doing. Not all machine learning algorithms are like this—commonly used techniques such as neural nets and support vector machines are often referred to as "black boxes" because of their complete lack of interpretability. As a result, model validation is a hugely important task in machine learning.

MODEL EVALUATION

While there are many different types of machine learning algorithms with varying outputs, all supervised models do result in a prediction that can be evaluated on training data. In the case of the New York Times decision tree, the candidate who won the majority of the counties in each resulting node would be the predicted classification. Summing across all the buckets in figure 7.1, it seems that this approach would correctly identify 1,811 out of 2,241 counties, for an accuracy of 80.8 percent. Accuracy is specifically defined in this field as the number of correct predictions divided by the total number of predictions made.

Accuracy is a useful first metric for examining predictive power, but it does not go nearly far enough to wholly validate a prediction. This is foremost because accuracy in a binary classification problem assumes that the two possible outcomes are equally important and equally likely. This may happen to be true for elections between Hillary Clinton and Barack Obama, but is far from the case in many scenarios.

For instance, the Department of Veterans Affairs (VA) has a robust analytical arm within its Office of Analytics and Business Intelligence. This office has invested significant resources into predictive health modeling—including providing all VA doctors with an estimated likelihood of emergency hospital admission and death for all of their patients over the ensuing three-month and one-year periods. Suppose that, on average, patients have a 10 percent chance of emergency hospital admission over the next three months. Then consider a model that never predicts emergency hospital admission. For any patient (regardless of age, illness, line of work, medical condition), the model says this person will not be in a hospital for emergency care in the next three months. As the hospital readmission only happens in one-tenth of cases, this model would still be 90 percent accurate. So accuracy alone often does not inform very much.

To resolve this issue, statisticians have developed the confusion matrix, which helps illustrate the four distinct terms of importance in binary classification problems. These terms describe the predicted value for each observation in the data and are defined in part by the predicted value from the model (figure 7.3, left) and in part by the relationship between the predicted value and the outcome (figure 7.3, right). First, the predicted value is what the model suggests is going to happen: Did it predict the patient return to a hospital for emergency services in the next three months? If yes, then this predicted value is positive, and if not, then it is

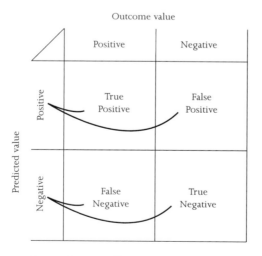
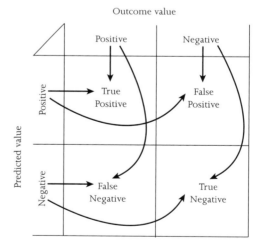

Figure 7.3. Confusion matrix explained

negative. Second, the predicted value determined by the model could have correctly determined which outcome was going to occur in reality, making the predicted value true, or it could be incorrect, making the predicted value false.

In terms of predictive modeling, the two "true" conditions for the predicted value represent success, and the two "false" conditions indicate failure. It is important to make these distinctions since some outcomes are intuitively worse than others. In this scenario (and many in health matters), the false-negative outcome is the worst-case scenario—the model has suggested this patient will not return to the hospital when that does end up being the case. Thus, the opportunity to offer interventions and improve health outcomes was missed.

Emerging from this framework are four essential metrics that help define model validity and predictive usefulness:

1. *True-positive rate*—the percentage of positive outcomes correctly identified, calculated by TP / (TP + FN)
2. *True-negative rate*—the percentage of negative outcomes correctly identified, calculated by TN / (TN + FP)
3. *False-positive rate*—the percentage of negative outcomes incorrectly identified, which is 1 minus the true-negative rate, or FP / (TN + FP)
   In classical statistics, this is often referred to as a "Type I error."
4. *False-negative rate*—the percentage of positive outcomes incorrectly identified, which is 1 minus the true-positive rate, or (FN) / (TP + FN)
   In classical statistics, this is often referred to as a "Type II error."

This is a lot of information to consider at once, so it is important to note that these rates can be boiled down to a much simpler interpretation. Because the true-positive rate is the opposite of the false-negative rate and the true-negative rate is the inverse of the false-positive rate, these terms can be placed on just two axes. The result is the receiver operating characteristic (ROC) curve, which plots the true-positive rate on the y-axis and the false-positive rate on the x-axis (figure 7.4).

So far we have discussed a scenario in which there are only a resulting true-positive rate and a false-positive rate for a model. Sometimes predictive models with machine learning produce a predicted outcome for classification as well as a level of confidence in that prediction. Using a lower threshold for confidence will increase the true-positive rate—the test will correctly identify positive outcomes—but also simultaneously increase the false-positive rate. Thus one model can be plotted

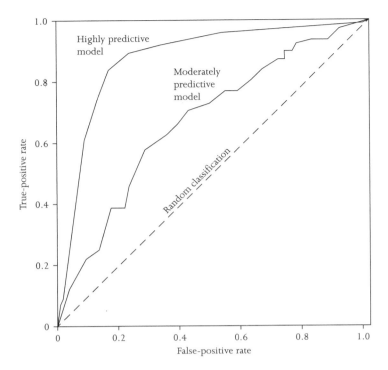

Figure 7.4. Receiver operating characteristic curve

as a curve, not just as an individual point, depending on the threshold level of confidence used.

The line cutting 45 degrees through the center of figure 7.4 reflects a model indistinguishable from random chance. Looking at the format of this plot, it is important to notice that being farther to the top left indicates a stronger model. That is the corner of the plot with a high true-positive rate and low false-positive rate. The area under the curve (AUC) metric of an ROC curve offers a single metric that indicates model quality. The AUC ranges from 0.5, equivalent to a random classifier, to 1, which would be a perfect model that identifies all positive outcomes with no false positives.

ROC curves can be used to compare across many different models, as shown in figure 7.5. The ROC curve in figure 7.5 is an adaptation depicting the improving iterations of the Wisconsin Dropout Early Warning System (DEWS) built by Jared Knowles. The model aims to identify late graduates and non-graduates before they enter high school.[8]

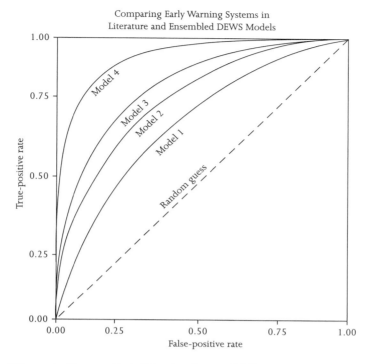

Figure 7.5. Wisconsin Dropout Early Warning System ROC curve

These metrics can be difficult to comprehend, but they are critical in that they apply to each of the numerous classification methods within machine learning. Of course, regression methods use a slew of different error metrics that different machine learning methods attempt to minimize. These metrics include mean absolute error, which is simply the average amount by which a predicted continuous value can be expected to be wrong, and root mean square error, which, in essence, gives more weight to larger errors.[9] There is some debate over which of these metrics is more consistent; however, diagnosing regression accuracy in general is more straightforward—the goal of a model is to be less wrong.

Interestingly, most machine learning algorithms can be implemented for either regression or classification—generally a methodology originally invented for one was later adapted for the other. There are a staggering number of different types of machine learning algorithms, so described in this chapter are a few of the most common and ubiquitous methods.

A TOUR OF MACHINE LEARNING MODELS

A rule-based classifier generates a collection of "if . . . then" statements, or rules, in a process very similar to a classification and regression tree. The "if" statements cover conditions of the features. In data for predictive policing, for example, this might include if the temperature is above a certain threshold, if the time is late at night, if there is a high level of activity on a street corner, or if there have been recent 9-1-1 calls on nearby blocks. Observations that meet all the criteria in the "if" statements are "then" labeled positive, in this case indicating that this block is a hot spot for crime in the near future.

The rules generated by rule-based classifiers differ from decision trees in that the rules may not cover every possible scenario in the data. This means the rules are not exhaustive, and a default classification is applied for observations that are not covered. In addition, rules are not necessarily mutually exclusive. When several different rules cover the same observation, an ordinal hierarchy of rules can be used, or, alternatively, the various triggered rules can vote for an outcome. Similar to decision trees, rule-based classifiers are among the easiest and most interpretable machine learning algorithms.

Clustering is the most common and illustrative type of unsupervised learning—in which there is no defined outcome variable. Clustering refers to a family of algorithms that attempt to group similar observations based on their characteristics within the observed data.

K-means clustering, one of the most common clustering methods, works by first randomly placing a pre-specified number (K) of centroids throughout the data. An iterative process ensues (figure 7.6), in which (1) the nearest observations to each centroid are assigned to that centroid and (2) the centroid is moved to the exact center of the observations that were assigned to it. By repeating these two steps, the algorithm shifts the centroids and the observations assigned to that cluster around until it finds a local minimum. A local minimum signifies that the algorithm can no longer change (at the same pace it has been changing) and improve the current performance of the model. This may differ from the global minimum, which signifies the location of the absolute best model fit possible for a set of data. With many machine learning problems, and clustering especially, it can be difficult to determine if the resulting model generated by an algorithm is a local or global minimum. In the example shown in figure 7.6, the algorithm has found both the local minimum and the global minimum.

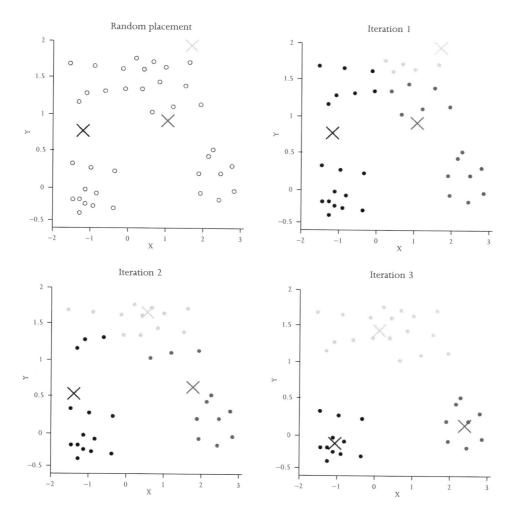

Figure 7.6. K-means clustering iterations

Clustering can take many other forms as well. While K-means clustering uses the distance between data points to form like groups, density-based clustering algorithms like density-based spatial clustering of applications with noise (DBSCAN) identify patterns in density and empty space to distinguish constellations of observations. Density-based clustering helps to properly categorize observations when it is the relationship between several variables that defines the different groups—rather than what cluster centroid is closest.

More complex applications include fuzzy clustering and hierarchical clustering. Fuzzy clustering algorithms specify the percentage likelihood that an observation will fall within a certain group or several groups rather than identifying one final cluster. Hierarchical clustering allows for clusters within larger umbrella clusters, which enables an algorithm to reflect data in which some clusters are more similar than others.

Clustering can be tremendously useful when attempting to learn about something subjectively understood that is currently unmeasured in data. The U.S. Postal Service (USPS) employs almost 500,000 people, making it the largest government employer of civilians. Working together with Elder Research, a leading government analytics firm, the USPS wanted to strategically reduce cash register theft by its employers. Although the USPS had substantial data on cash register transactions—such as the length of time the drawer was open, when it was first opened, what keystrokes were typed in, how much money was exchanged, how many and which employees were working at that time and data about those employees—it did not have any outcome data. That is, it could not tie these events to specific thefts.

Still, the USPS did have a subjective understanding of when and how cash register theft occurs—when employees were alone, near the end of shifts, masked by small purchases. So Elder Research instead ran a gambit of clustering algorithms over the register interactions data. Elder Research found significant clusters of the types of transactions that tended to happen together and thus constituted normal behavior. In doing this, the analysis also identified anomalous behaviors—very small clusters of actions that matched the subjective expectations that USPS officials had for theft. Investigations into the individuals responsible for those transactions were highly successful in discovering transgressors.

Support vector machines (SVMs) have experienced a recent growth in popularity because of their effective application in data with high dimensionality—that is, data with a large number of features. This type of algorithm maps all data into an n-dimensional space and then attempts to separate the different outcome categories by as clear and as large a margin as possible. This machination can become very complicated, but in its simplest form, SVMs are highly intuitive. When looking across only two features (e.g., x and y) and a binary outcome (e.g., light or dark), the most basic SVM is a straight line (figure 7.7). When a straight line, plane, or hyperplane[10] can effectively define the distinctions between outcomes along two or more variables, then the data is linearly separable. However, SVMs are not limited to linear models

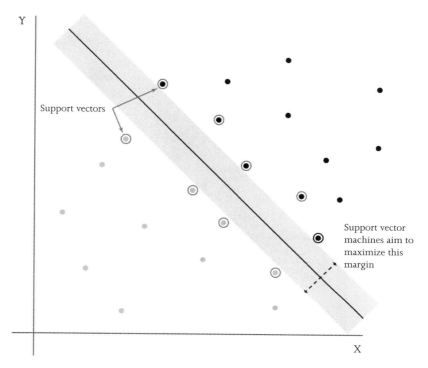

Figure 7.7. Simple support vector machine

and can use polynomial terms and other methods to accurately separate outcomes across highly complex patterns in data.

In addition, most SVMs will not perfectly model the data—thus most SVMs have soft margins, which simply means the SVM is allowed to misclassify some of the observations. In figure 7.8, several light crosses fall into the darker classified region, and a pair of dark circles fall within the lighter classified region. This is an important aspect of SVMs because these models—in fact, most machine learning models—are highly susceptible to overfitting.

ADDRESSING OVERFITTING

Overfitting describes the error of a model when random noise or variation within a dataset is interpreted as an underlying pattern. Machine learning algorithms are very powerful and generally are not limited to linear restrictions. These characteristics are both advantages of this field, but also open machine learning up to the threat of overfitting.

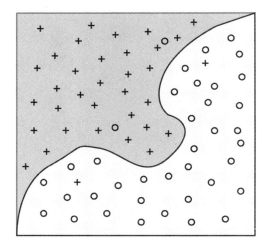

Figure 7.8. Support vector machine with soft margins

An unrestricted machine learning algorithm could get so specific as to set rules that uniquely define each observation. It might be true that a county with a median income between $40,000 and $40,010, a 74.3 percent high school graduation rate, and exactly 68 people per square mile voted for Hillary Clinton, but that does not mean this rule will extend to other counties. At times, algorithms in machine learning must be told to be less specific and less exact so that the resulting model has strong applications to future data.

Overfitting does occur in classical statistics, but it is much harder to identify in machine learning and thus a very important issue to watch out for during model specification. It often causes, and can at times be identified by, a drop in performance when a model built on training data is applied to and validated on test data for the first time.

In part because of overfitting, many leaders in this field argue that having more data is almost always more valuable than perfect algorithm selection and model specification. Having a large and robust dataset is critical to the success of meaningful machine learning, but there are other approaches to addressing overfitting and increasing the predictive accuracy of test data.

Ensemble methods act to limit the foibles of one specific algorithm by combining the results of multiple predictive systems into one output. Typically, several machine learning models will be trained independently, and the results will be combined in a voting process.

For instance, consider the researchers in Chicago trying to locate houses with lead paint and young children in order to take preventive actions (this is a real project of the Data Science for Social Good Fellowship program). The researchers might build a series of five models using a decision tree, a rules classifier, SVM, naive Bayes, a neural net, and so on. Then the researchers would take the predicted outcomes from these five models and have them vote. So, if three or more algorithms suggest that a house might have lead paint and young children, this would result in a final positive flagging of that house. Houses flagged by two or fewer models would be flagged negatively and would not be investigated further.

This is a simple example, but the concept is incredibly powerful. Using multiple models helps discover the genuine relationships within the data and greatly reduces the influence of overfitting. IBM's Watson, the famous *Jeopardy!*-playing machine, uses a highly complex ensemble method combining a large array of natural language processing algorithms. The most advanced modern ensemble methods are a critical component of the emerging field of cognitive computing.

MACHINE LEARNING FOR BIG DATA

Machine learning has tremendous implications for another powerful modern paradigm: big data. Machine learning is truly critical to the cutting-edge capacity to analyze massive datasets. There is no definitive threshold after which "big data" begins, but a reasonable working definition is data that requires specialized software and hardware beyond what is generally available on a single computer. Of course, this is an ever-changing scale, but at present this includes datasets with many billions into the trillions of rows and taking up terabytes and even petabytes of storage.

Classical statistics tend to involve mathematical operations that occur on the complete sum of the data. However, with huge scales of data, even basic calculations like the summation required by linear regression would involve so much processing power and time such as to be impractical. While data size is expanding faster than the increases in processing speed, machine learning has found many different methods for reducing the computational expense while maintaining accuracy of modeling.

One such method is stochastic gradient descent, which is a variation of a simpler machine learning method called "gradient descent." Gradient descent is an optimization function that can be used for any number of calculations. This includes familiar notions like minimizing the squared errors of linear regression.

It is sufficient for our purposes just to understand that gradient descent repeats a process to optimize some functions. This is not inherently faster than the classic method of regression, but it does have the unique benefit of being able to be broken into smaller pieces and is thus parallelizable.

This is where stochastic gradient descent (SGD) becomes truly important. Instead of working with the entire dataset, SGD involves randomly sorting the data and then analyzing one row at a time. When solving a linear regression function, SGD begins by setting all coefficients to 0. This method applies the aforementioned gradient descent optimization process to a single, randomly selected row of data and is then able to update the coefficients to be closer to the true outcome based on its result. This analysis of a single row and updating of the coefficients is then repeated for all rows in the dataset (and, for smaller datasets, should be repeated over the data multiple times). The amount by which the coefficients change between each iteration is defined by the learning rate, which can be generally described as the degree to which new information will override older information.

Notably, this algorithm will not solve perfectly for any model, but it will get indistinguishably close to the final output that would result from a classical approach. This process gives an initial estimate almost immediately and improves on that estimate as it continues the calculations. In addition, SGD can be parallelized and run in modern big data environments (like Hadoop), allowing for the running of regressions and other analyses on multibillion-row datasets with hundreds of columns. When attempting to train a logistic regression predicting the payment or default of seven hundred million rows of mortgage data, SGD implementations have been shown to exponentially reduce computation time.

This algorithm can be used to solve for linear regression, logistic regression, linear SVM, and other models. In addition, there are free and open-source tools that can be used to implement SGD and other scalable machine learning algorithms—such as Vowpal Wabbit and Apache Spark.

The public policy applications for massive-scale data analysis are everywhere. The Health Information Technology for Economic and Clinical Health (HITECH) Act passed in 2009 has incentivized a dramatic increase in the use and interoperability of electronic health records. Going forward, and to a significant historical degree, all medical patient information will be represented in data. It is easy to imagine how the scale of this data—encompassing every interaction between a patient and medical personnel for over 300 million Americans—might grow quite large.

Data-driven policy is now a huge and growing part of education as well, with longitudinal education data systems now existing in all 50 states. At present, these systems do not reach a scale that would be considered big data. However, with the increasing use of tablets and laptops in the classroom, the opportunity for data collection will increase tremendously. When many of the math problems and essay assignments given in public education are recorded electronically, machine learning will have a powerful role in improving formative assessments and developing more effective education policy.

GOING FORWARD

It may be too easy to read this chapter thus far and walk away thinking that machine learning is inherently separate from statistics, but this is not really the case. Classical statistics and machine learning cover a lot of similar ground and are really only fundamentally different in terms of origin—classical statistics developed into a field in the late 19th and early 20th centuries with the invention of standard deviations, correlation, and regression. Unlike these methods, which could feasibly be done by hand, machine learning necessitates the use of computational power—thus its discovery in the 1950s and growth into prominence starting in the 1990s. Still, both fields can and do coexist perfectly well under the umbrella term of preference: statistics, data mining, knowledge discovery in databases (KDD), and so on.

So machine learning, for all its apparent complexity, can and should be lumped together with the other applied mathematical applications that are currently taught in today's public policy schools. Open-source programming languages like R and Python offer tremendous depth in machine learning algorithms, and commercial statistical packages like SAS and Stata offer some options as well.

The scale of data is growing faster than processing power, but this is only one area in which machine learning offers critical supplements to classical statistics. Data with highly complex interactions, data with hundreds or thousands of variables or features in abnormal distributions, and data in unconventional forms like text all demand cutting-edge analytical methods. The modern data analyst in policy will soon have as much or more need for the methodologies originated from machine learning as they will from classical statistics.

These trends expand beyond the federal government as well. When Mike Flowers returned from doing logistics work in Iraq, there was no analytics office in New York City, or really in any city in the country. Overseas, Flowers had watched in awe as data-driven algorithms allowed for the directing of soldiers and troops around the most likely spots for improvised explosive devices (IEDs). Upon his return, he was convinced that the simple use of data and predictive analytics could dramatically improve city services.

Flowers did not have a mathematical background or degree in statistics, but he also knew that it did not really matter, since any predictive modeling would be dramatically better than none. In the following years, his team of young analysts identified illegal housing conversions, discovered illegal dumping of cooking oils, and modeled emergency response times in New York City. His successes, and the continued success of the Mayor's Office of Data Analytics, are now well documented. At least in part to their credit, chief data/analytics officers are emerging in cities and states all over the country.

Recent investments in city-level data collection are promising as well. The Urban Center for Computation and Data (Urban CCD) in partnership with the University of Chicago is pushing the envelope for public data collection with its Array of Things project.[11] The project aims to build sensors into many of the streetlights in downtown Chicago, measuring temperature, light, sound, motion, pollutants, and some (anonymous) foot traffic. International progress is notable as well. Studies in Japan have used cheap web cameras (and machine learning) to show that using data to change traffic lights can reduce congestion by 20 percent.[12]

With data collection and use expanding in the private sector and at every level of government, the incentives to adopt machine learning into government analytics and public policy research will only grow. Its capacity for the discovery of complex and non-linear relationships within data, its unrivaled predictive power, and its tremendous scalability to huge datasets make machine learning a critical skill for the next generation of policy analysts.

NOTES

1. Andrew Myers, "Stanford's John McCarthy, Seminal Figure of Artificial Intelligence, Dies at 84," *Stanford Report*, October 25, 2011, http://news.stanford.edu/news/2011/october/john -mccarthy-obit-102511.html.

2. Charles S. Clark, "IRS and SEC Detect Fraud Patterns in Heaps of Data," *Government Executive*, October 16, 2012, http://www.govexec.com/technology/2012/10/irs-and-sec-detect-fraud -patterns-heaps-data/58816/.

3. Saleema Amershi and Cristina Conati, "Automatic Recognition of Learner Groups in Exploratory Learning Environments," in *Proceedings of the Eighth International Conference on Intelligent Tutoring Systems*, ed. Mitsuru Ikeda, Kevin D. Ashley, and Tak-Wai Chan (Berlin: Springer-Verlag, 2006), 463–472. See also Carole Beal, Lei Qu, and Hyokyeong Lee, "Classifying Learner Engagement Through Integration of Multiple Data Sources" (paper presented at the 21st National Conference on Artificial Intelligence, Boston, 2007).

4. Zechun Cao, Sujing Wang, Germain Forestier, Anne Puissant, and Christoph F. Eick, "Analyzing the Composition of Cities Using Spatial Clustering," in *Proceedings of the Second ACM SIGKDD International Workshop on Urban Computing* (New York: ACM, 2013).

5. Adapted from an original graphic by Amanda Cox, "Decision Tree: The Obama-Clinton Divide," *New York Times*, April 16, 2008, http://www.nytimes.com/imagepages/2008/04/16/us/20080416_OBAMA_GRAPHIC.html.

6. Other measures of information gain include the Gini coefficient and misclassification error.

7. It is most frequently the case that each instance of a task will be represented in one row of data, with the known information about that task (the features and the outcome variable) in the corresponding columns.

8. Jared Knowles, "Of Needles and Haystacks: Building an Accurate Statewide Dropout Early Warning System in Wisconsin," http://jaredknowles.com/journal/2014/8/24/of-needles-and-haystacks-building-an-accurate-statewide-dropout-early-warning-system-in-wisconsin.

9. Tianfeng Chai and Roland R. Draxler, "Root Mean Square Error (RMSE) or Mean Absolute Error (MAE)?—Arguments Against Avoiding RMSE in Literature," *Geoscientific Model Development* 7 (2014): 1247–1250, http://www.geosci-model-dev.net/7/1247/2014/gmd-7-1247-2014.pdf.

10. A hyperplane is simply the generalized idea of a line or a plane extended into higher-dimensional spaces. A hyperplane is always composed of one less dimension than the space within which it exists. For example, in a five-dimensional space, a hyperplane would span four dimensions.

11. Whet Moser, "What Chicago's 'Array of Things' Will Actually Do," *Chicago Magazine*, June 27, 2013, http://www.chicagomag.com/city-life/June-2014/What-Chicagos-Array-of-Things-Will-Actually-Do/.

12. Kumiko Maeda, Tetsuro Morimura, Takayuki Katsuki, and Masayoshi Teraguchi, "Frugal Signal Control Using Low Resolution Web-Camera and Traffic Flow Estimation," in *Proceedings of the 2014 Winter Simulation Conference* (Piscataway, NJ: IEEE Press, 2014), 2082–2091.

III IMPLICATIONS FOR GOVERNANCE

CHAPTER EIGHT Governing a Data-Driven Society

Kathryn Wagner Hill

IN THIS CHAPTER

This chapter focuses on the federal government's role in data collection, use, and management and the implications of it for governance. There are two basic lenses used to examine the role of government in today's data-driven society: one focused on outcomes and the other on process. The chapter first discusses "outcomes" from the large volume of data generated by the government and the new analytics being used to assess it. Data is a public good from this perspective, and the role of the government is to be a good steward of it while making it assessable, but also utilizing it to achieve better government outcomes. The chapter then explores government's use of data from the other lens used that is focused on the "how" or process of government analytics. An overview is provided of existing policies, new ideas, and proposals regarding open government, transparency, and digital rights as they relate to "big data" and its analysis by government.

INTRODUCTION

In *Federalist* 23, Alexander Hamilton astutely refers to the federal government as "the centre of information" for the nation and argues that on that basis it will "best understand the extent and urgency" of threats to public safety. Although his immediate reference point was the matter of national defense that requires a "confined" federal government to best safeguard national interests, his discussion is remarkably applicable to contemporary concerns regarding the federal government's role in data collection, use, and management. There are two basic lenses used to examine the role of government in today's data-driven society. One is more focused on *outcomes* and the other on *process*, but both have governing implications. The questions for governance that follow from both outcome and process aspects of government's increased engagement with big data include the following: Is data best viewed as a "public good" and if so, how does the government develop the proper institutional controls to ensure its optimal use? How are transparency and access to data balanced with the need for privacy safeguards and database security? What are or should be the rights of individual citizens with respect to data about them? How can government agencies best leverage the vast amount of data continually generated today to result in better governance?

This chapter first discusses "outcomes" from the large volume of data generated by the government and the new analytics being used to assess it. The government is viewed as a platform for a level of analysis that was never possible before. Data is a public good from this perspective. Government's role is to be a good steward of data and make it assessable while also utilizing data to better design policy programs, meet objectives, and evaluate performance to improve government outcomes. The chapter will then explore government's use of data from the other lens used that is focused more on the "how" or process of government analytics. The concerns here are about rights of privacy and, more specifically, digital rights and personal data protection. How government uses data to meet public policy goals in the greater public interest while also protecting the personal digital information of citizens involves a greater articulation of privacy and other digital rights than currently exists in the United States. The chapter provides an overview of existing policies, new ideas, and proposals regarding open government, transparency, and digital rights as they relate to "big data" and its analysis by government. Concrete examples of the use of government's big data by the public and private entities are included to illustrate what government analytics means in terms of actual contemporary policy making.

As the government continues to work out how best to meet the challenges of balancing openness and access to data with protections for privacy and data security, it is also preparing itself to better use data in decision making. Government agencies in the era of "big data government" openly recognize their need for assistance in analyzing the data for policy-making purposes. President Barack Obama's Open Government Initiative includes a dominant Open Data component that over 80 other countries have subscribed to since its initiation in 2009. The United States is seen as the leading nation with respect to open data efforts, but Europe may hold that position with respect to digital privacy protections.

The Partnership for Public Service and the IBM Center for the Business of Government note that today how well an organization (public or private) is performing is largely determined by its use of analytics and that is where leaders worldwide need to focus greater attention.[1] The Federal Big Data Commission notes,

"The challenge lies in capturing the streams of Big Data that we need, effectively managing them, and extracting new and relevant insights."[2] In this still new era of "big data," huge volumes of data need analysis in government, and there is an imperative for the new field of government analytics to convert raw data into substantive information that can be used to enhance understanding of a policy problem, meet a political challenge, or improve government's overall performance.

There is evidence that academia is responding to this demand given that 7 of the top 10 most cited political science journal articles published in the 2000s related to methods and analysis.[3] Harvard political scientist Gary King points out that in the "data revolution" what is revolutionary is not so much the quantity of data now available, rather it is the new statistical and computational methods that mean "we can *do* something with the data" that was not possible before.[4] New applications, such as allocating police resources by predicting where crime is most likely to occur, attest to the power data analytics can have for governing.[5] At the same time, the amount of data now available is daunting, and as with any kind of statistical analysis, it is critically important that the limits of a particular analytical technique be carefully considered and understood when designing a specific project. New graduate-level programs are being created to help meet the demand for individuals with advanced analytical skills to be applied to the study and practice of governance. Stanford University, Northwestern University, and Johns Hopkins University have all added new programs in advanced statistical analysis, data analytics, and specifically government analytics.

OPEN GOVERNMENT AND BIG DATA

Government at both the federal and local levels has never been more committed to harnessing data to improve overall government performance.[6] President Barack Obama, dubbed the "big data president," fully embraced the idea of data as a driver for better government from his first day in office.[7] Within months, the nation's first chief information officer (CIO) was appointed and a number of new government websites launched, including www.data.gov, which is touted as "home of the U.S. Government's open data with over 112,291 data sets." Anyone can engage with the government's data through this portal for research purposes or such uses as developing web and mobile applications and designing data visualization. This puts the government at once in a powerful and precarious position to ensure that information is available and secure while used in the public's interest.

In 2012, the Office of Science and Technology Policy (OSTP) announced five science and technology policies, including one focused on big data, and is investing $200 million in this initiative. The Big Data Initiative is being implemented by six agencies: the National Science Foundation, the National Institutes of Health, the Department of Defense, the Defense Advanced Research Projects Agency (DARPA), the Department of Energy, and the U.S. Geological Survey. As John Holdren, assistant to the president and director of the OSTP, puts it, "[the Big Data Initiative] promises to transform our ability to use Big Data for scientific discovery, environmental and biomedical research, education, and national security."[8] The expectation is that the government's investment in this area will reap benefits similar to those achieved by government's investment in research and development of information technology that led to the development of the Internet and advances in supercomputing. Dozens of countries around the world followed the U.S. example and initiated their own open data initiatives. From European nations to Asian countries, such as India, the open data movement quickly gained momentum.

The premise of the open data movement is consistent with the broader goals of open government and transparency, namely, that there is an imperative for governments to "release authoritative, high quality, complete, timely data on the Web in a downloadable, non-proprietary, and license-free format."[9] The view is that the federal government needs to manage information as an asset and public good. The U.S. Open Data Action Plan, issued in May 2014, states these principals and catalogs open datasets available to the public for it to find information it wants about the government. The presumption is that this will lead to better governance while "rigorously" protecting privacy.[10] Some critics of the open data efforts point out that although most of the federal agencies are participating in the program, the agencies have discretion to decide what data to publish and well over 90 percent of the data uploaded to date comes from just three agencies: the U.S. Census Bureau, the U.S. Geological Survey (USGS), and the National Oceanic and Atmospheric Administration (NOAA).[11] The data that is uploaded is often de-contextualized because when datasets are divorced from their source records, it can mean that useful records become useless datasets.[12] Refinement of the data release strategies of agencies is an area that needs further government attention.

Open government policy as applied to big data appears to fit the "policy bubble" phenomenon. This is where there is an enthusiastic initial phase in a new area of program development with overly simplistic and self-reinforcing ideas presented and accompanied by considerable hype and promotion of them. Soon a gap between what is promised and what is achieved becomes a harsh reality check.[13] Even so, the amount of analytics being done using big government data by both government agencies and private sector organizations is increasing and is only likely to continue to do so. There is a learning curve in any new area of endeavor and while that is going on, impressive initiatives are taking hold.

OUTCOMES: HOW IS BIG GOVERNMENT DATA BEING USED?

A number of individuals and organizations are effectively using newly available government data. For example, the Sunlight Foundation (www.sunlightfoundation.com) is a non-partisan, non-profit think tank founded in 2006 which initially focused on connecting voters to information on congressional candidates, but has broadened its focus to following legislation through its OpenCongress site (now merged with GovTrack.us) and other efforts such as Follow the Unlimited Money and Influence Explorer. Another example is Code for America (www.codeforamerica.org), a non-profit group started in 2010 by Jennifer Pahlka who later served as the U.S. deputy chief technology officer in the OSTP. The goal of Code for America is to help reframe the function of government to encourage innovation and improve policy effectiveness using social media analysis and other advanced analytics to design "smart policy." An example of this is the work Code for America did with the city of San Francisco to re-design the outreach for CalFresh, the state's nutrition assistance program. Realizing that mailings or providing information about the program on a website were not effective ways to reach program recipients who often do not have a permanent address and may not have regular access to a computer, Code for America went in a new direction. It used social media analysis and experimented with different text messages, such as "Your CalFresh benefits may stop at the end of this month. Questions? Call us." to see which would track best. This approach worked and led to program revisions that kept thousands of people from inadvertently losing their benefits. Recently a group working with Code for America developed an app so citizens in Oakland, California, could influence the city's budget process. To date, Code for America has worked with 30 cities to develop 55 different apps.

A plethora of other projects and initiatives indicate the heightened focus on data and analytics by the government. For example, there is the creation of new entities such as the non-profit U.S. Open Data to facilitate agencies to publicly release datasets and the recent Office of Management and Budget (OMB) memorandum to all department and agency heads to further manage "information as an asset."[14]

These innovative uses of "open data" are what the outcome focus envisions with government as a platform for data sharing. Data is a public good, and government is to be a good steward of it. The issues of privacy discussed briefly in this chapter and in more detail in chapter 9 are not always addressed though in any comprehensive way as part of a particular policy's development or application of data analytics.

BRINGING THE POWER OF DATA ANALYTICS TO GOVERNING

Government agencies themselves are using big data and new data analysis techniques in innovative ways to improve their governing efforts. The Food and Drug Administration (FDA) initiated a project, Mini-Sentinel (www.mini-sentinel.org), which is an active surveillance system that uses existing electronic health care data by mining huge databases of medical records from insurance companies to detect if adverse events are linked to FDA-regulated drugs. Although the data exchange has been set up to protect patient privacy, there are concerns that the data from billing records means it is based on codes a doctor gives for a diagnostic test and procedure and not more nuanced descriptions of a patient's condition that might be in a chart. It is not clear how often billing data is likely to reveal negative side effects from prescribed drugs, but it took five years to build the Mini-Sentinel, and it has identified some associations between particular drugs on the market and troubling side effects.

Agencies have tremendous amounts of data that are now more accessible to the public for research. For example, the Census Bureau has a wealth of geospatial, demographic, and economic data resources available, and the National Aeronautics and Space Administration (NASA) has made earth observation data open and machine readable and is making its climate data more accessible as well. The U.S. Department of Health and Human Services (HHS), in collaboration with the U.S. Department of Veterans Affairs, the U.S. Department of Defense, and the Centers for Medicare and Medicaid Services, is leading a public-private effort called the "Blue Button Initiative." This initiative will give consumers secure access to their own health care information, which they can then more easily share with health care providers or others as they choose.

According to the U.S. Government Accountability Office (GAO), however, executive agencies need to better leverage data themselves as well as making it publicly available. There is untapped potential for agencies to use government analytics to better fulfill program missions and evaluate program performance.[15] In fact, the Office of Management and Budget is focused on encouraging agencies to increase their use of data analytics in evidence-based program evaluations.[16] Kathy Stack, advisor for evidence-based innovation at OMB, leads the efforts to encourage wider use of evidence-based policy making by government agencies. She notes that just as important as technical capabilities is the need for trust building with the agencies so that information is shared within and between agencies. If policy program offices are better linked to the research arms of agencies, data can be better utilized. Also, if agencies collaborate, they can find answers with linked databases that are not possible otherwise. For example, the Department of Education and the Social Security Administration worked together to determine which new trade school programs were most effective in securing employment related to the training students received and that provided sustainable incomes.[17]

A shift from more compliance-based evaluation to evidence-based evaluation can potentially allow for continuous evaluation and improvement of a program's efforts to achieve desired outcomes. The distinction here is that the focus is beyond merely determining if programs are being implemented as designed. Stack emphasizes the need for randomized controlled experiments to identify the causal effects of programs on stated objectives and notes examples of low-cost experiments carried out by the Department of Education and HHS that improved programs related to student financial aid and the mentorship of children of prisoners.[18] Ron Haskins, a former White House and congressional advisor on welfare issues who now co-directs the Brookings Center on Children and Families and Budgeting for National Priorities Project, recently published a book discussing the success of evidence-based policy evaluation for a number of federal social programs.[19]

PROCESS: DIGITAL RIGHTS AND OTHER GOVERNMENTAL RESPONSES TO THE DATA REVOLUTION

Designing the infrastructure of new institutional controls to ensure today's data-driven society can use "big data" to achieve policy goals is an ongoing process. Unlike the more centralized governmental responses to social and environmental problems that resulted from the Industrial Revolution, a more decentralized response is likely to the "data revolution." In fact, the response to date has been likened to a "nervous system" or an ecosystem in which big data is the driver.[20] The control framework envisioned has dual components focused on the digital rights of individuals and more sophisticated policy making. Individual citizen's "digital crumbs" (e.g., credit card transactions, global positioning system location fixes, etc.) are the valued currency which, taken in the aggregate, generate the large databases available for analysis to improve policy design, implementation, and evaluation. The idea is that there is increased capacity for the government to use data for the public good by designing and analyzing optimal policy responses to pressing problems. It follows, then, that a "successful data-driven society must be able to guarantee that [citizens'] data will not be abused—perhaps especially that government will not abuse the power conferred by access to such fine-grained data."[21]

This brings us back to Hamilton's point about the government's role as the center of information and its need to safeguard national interests, that is, broader public interests, including protecting the digital and privacy rights of citizens (see chapters 9 and 10). Personal data is referred to as the "new oil" of the 21st century while efforts to protect it are "feudal, fragmented, and inefficient."[22] Alex "Sandy" Pentland, the Toshiba Professor of Media Arts and Sciences and director of the Human Dynamics research group at the Massachusetts Institute of Technology (MIT), co-leads the World Economic Forum on Big Data and Personal Data Initiatives and is a cutting-edge thinker focused on the types of legal protections, business practices, and technical solutions necessary to ensure both digital rights and data access for our new digital economy.[23] Pentland and his team propose a "New Deal on Data," which starts with giving individuals the right "to possess, control, and dispose of copies of [their] operational data, along with copies of the incidental data collected, such as location and similar context."[24]

The fundamental idea is to rebalance data ownership in favor of the individual because it is his or her data (i.e., personal information) that is collected. Currently, the social media data generated on Twitter, Facebook, and the like leaves traces or digital crumbs that are "harvested, bought, and sold [with] an entire commercial ecosystem forming around social data with analytics companies and services at the helm."[25] Companies that resell data or perform analytics such as Gnip and DataSift believe in the value of the social data and ultimately see the promise of using advanced statistical techniques such as those discussed earlier in this book to "curb human unpredictability through information."[26] Events such as political uprisings can be detected, and reliable predictions of future outcomes such as elections or consumption patterns can be made using such analytical methods. It is not clear, however, that those who generate this data want it used by others or if they willingly would allow that if given the right and ability to control their own data crumbs. At the same time, government data is available to citizens and many believe that it can empower them.[27] As noted previously, such efforts as the Sunlight Foundation and Code for America exemplify this.

DIGITAL RIGHTS AND PRIVACY

Drawing on how English common law defines ownership rights of possession, use, and disposal, Pentland's New Deal on Data simply states:

- You have the right to possess data about yourself;
- You have the right to full control over the use of your data; and
- You have the right to dispose of or distribute your data.[28]

Both the European Union's Privacy Directive of 1995 and the U.S. Consumer Privacy Bill of Rights proposed by President Obama first in 2012 and reintroduced in 2015 were shaped by these basic ideas about ownership rights of personal data given its value as an asset in today's digital economy.[29] The U.S. Consumer Privacy Bill of Rights includes the following:

- Individual Control: Consumers have a right to exercise control over what personal data organizations collect information from them and how they use it.
- Transparency: Consumers have a right to easily understandable information about privacy and security practices.
- Respect for Context: Consumers have a right to expect that organizations will collect, use, and disclose personal data in ways that are consistent with the context in which consumers provide the data.
- Security: Consumers have a right to secure and responsible handling of personal data.
- Access and Accuracy: Consumers have a right to access and correct personal data in usable formats, in a manner that is appropriate to the sensitivity of the data and the risk of adverse consequences to consumers if the data are inaccurate.
- Focused Collection: Consumers have a right to reasonable limits on the personal data that companies collect and retain.
- Accountability: Consumers have a right to have personal data handled by companies with appropriate measures in place to assure they adhere to the Consumer Privacy Bill of Rights.[30]

Efforts to enact legislation to codify the Consumer Privacy Bill of Rights are slow to develop just as the decade-long effort to pass a comprehensive privacy law has been. Meanwhile, Europe moved ahead with a directive that gives broad protection over how citizens' data is collected and used by any private entity.

More than a decade later, data protection compliance specialists in Europe continue to work through the technological constraints to expand existing digital rights management systems to incorporate the new goals of data privacy rights. This remains a high priority and challenging endeavor on both sides of the Atlantic.[31] Indeed, U.S. technology officials in federal and state agencies when surveyed report privacy and related policy concerns at the top of the list of obstacles to better utilizing big data.[32]

The U.S. Department of Commerce is charged with leading the effort to carry out the Obama administration's plans for the Consumer Privacy Bill of Rights. As discussed in greater detail in the next chapter on privacy issues related to big data, the current patchwork of privacy laws means there is no coherent set of privacy protections for citizens. Public interest groups such as the Center for Digital Democracy and the Center for Democracy and Technology support the enactment of such privacy legislation and further implementation of the Consumer Privacy Bill of Rights. Much of the U.S. technology industry (such as Google), however, has not seriously engaged the issue. They also have not adopted primary protection policies of their own. For example, Google resists adopting such mechanisms as "do not track" options for its customers that would allow individuals to better control data collected on them by their web searches. Yet Google, along with Facebook, has had to comply with stricter privacy standards now in place in Europe. Brazil, South Africa, and South Korea have all adopted more stringent digital rights laws than the United States.[33] Legislation in the United States is unlikely, however, unless the public begins to pressure companies and the government to provide stronger personal digital privacy protection. According to a recent Pew Research Center report, over 90 percent of Americans believe they have no control over data that companies collect and use about them based on their online activities.[34] Importantly, though, Americans are not thinking in terms of personal rights yet with respect to how corporations use their personal data.

In June 2014, the National Telecommunications and Information Administration (NTIA) of the Department of Commerce issued a request for public comment on "how developments of 'big data' impact the Consumer Privacy Bill of Rights."[35] John Podesta, counselor to President Obama, at the president's request organized and led the Big Data and Privacy Working Group that engaged in a number of stakeholder activities over the course of 90 days to gather input from such interested parties as academic researchers, privacy advocates, regulators, the technology industry, and advertisers. A survey was conducted to generate public input along with the NTIA request for comments and a separate request directly from the White House for public comment on big data and privacy. In addition, the working group, in conjunction with the OSTP, held conferences at three universities (MIT, New York

University, and the University of California at Berkeley) on the topic. The President's Council of Advisors on Science and Technology also conducted a survey of the technological trends affecting the use of big data by government.

In May 2014, the culmination of the working group's effort was issued in a report from the White House called "Big Data: Seizing Opportunities, Preserving Values."[36] Also in May 2014, President Obama released his administration's U.S. Open Data Action Plan, which was a follow-up to the U.S. endorsement along with the G7 nations in June 2013 of the Open Data Charter.[37] As noted in the recently released action plan, "President Obama has articulated a vision of the U.S. Government managing information as a national asset and opening up its data, where possible, as a public good to advance government efficiency, improve accountability, and fuel private sector innovation, scientific discovery, and economic growth."[38] The focus remains on expanding government's role as a conduit for information and data while attempting to put in place privacy protections.

OPEN GOVERNMENT AND TRANSPARENCY

An interesting dynamic of the open data movement is the relationship between demands for privacy protection and for greater governmental transparency. The most basic definition of transparency is "openness to public scrutiny."[39] As Jonathan Fox, a leading expert on issues of democratization and civil society, puts it, though, "One person's transparency is another's surveillance."[40] A study of local officials in Florida found that 84 percent of them report facing "some" to "a lot" of pressure to meet demands of both ensuring transparency and protecting individual privacy rights.[41] When asked what they needed most to help them better balance government transparency goals and individual privacy, the surveyed local officials topped the list with "clear standards/procedures."[42] Often it is the lack of a clear definition of a problem and the solutions to it that derail well-intended policy efforts.

Pentland actually links transparency to the digital rights and privacy of individuals, arguing that such data transparency is essential for citizens to be able to know what data is being collected about them and to be able to control access to its use.[43] If citizens can store and manage the data being collected about them (e.g., medical, financial, insurance, etc.), it can be a powerful tool for them personally. It is less clear what the implications of that are for a "greater good" policy use of individuals' data—unless certain protections are put in place and the public trusts the overall networked system exchanging the data between consenting parties.

The World Economic Forum recognizes the need for a best practice method of "trust networking" to become more widespread as an institutional control to help form "a reliable operational framework for big data, privacy, and access."[44] A trust network is "a combination of a computer network that keeps track of user permissions for each piece of personal data, and a legal contract that specifies both what can and can't be done with the data, and what happens if there is a violation of the permissions."[45] Establishing trust between parties wanting to share personal data is a crucial underpinning to the "ecosystem" of a data-driven society. In order for information to flow freely in a networked society, data sharing with such privacy protection is essential.

A public survey taken by the Obama administration found that 80 percent of the public is "very much" concerned about the government's transparency regarding data use. Perhaps this is not surprising in the wake of the revelations of vast data collection of citizens' phone records by the National Security Agency (NSA) (see chapter 10) and which likely also accounts for the desire of 81 percent of the respondents to have proper legal standards and oversight in place. Interestingly, although trust was low for intelligence and law enforcement agencies to properly handle personal data, the public is more trusting of other government agencies and generally trusting of professionals (e.g., medical entities) and academia with respect to the handling and use of their data.[46]

From the beginning of the American republic, the health of our democratic process has rested upon the premise that citizens be informed, engaged, and actively maintaining a relationship of public trust with government. As Thomas Jefferson wrote, "Whenever the people are well-informed, they can be trusted with their own government."[47] Fundamentally, the push for transparency is motivated by the belief that it will allow citizens to be "well-informed." Some of the difficulty is that, as scholar Alon Peled cogently argues, the well-intended open data design of the government includes an unrealistic goal of furthering transparency because "compelled to live in glasshouses, bureaucratic behavior is affected by a culture of surveillance. Government officials cease to dissent, refer all decisions upward, and adopt defensive thinking and blame avoidance strategies. Rather than speaking openly to those in power, government officials learn to cover-up and to self censor their advice."[48] This means a well-defined design focused on data quality and context is needed for "genuine transparency."[49]

The government's major effort to date is the Digital Accountability and Transparency Act, the DATA Act, passed in 2014 to make data on federal expenditures more accessible and transparent by requiring all government agencies to release machine-readable, standardized appropriations and spending data to the public. In May 2015, the Treasury Department and the OMB announced government-wide data standards for all existing federal spending reports on how financial data will be captured, stored, and transmitted. This means there will be common data elements, common data formats, and common definitions of key financial data terms such as "commitments," "obligations," and "expenditures."

This level of standardizing data reporting is not only helpful for the legislation's goal of increasing the public's ability to track government spending, but it means the government itself can better make "apples to apples" comparisons with respect to spending evaluations of different government programs. Some analysts argue that the DATA Act does not go far enough and needs "to link spending to missions, not just functions" of agencies by adopting such measures as setting "standards for metadata that would help link federal finances across the life cycle of federal spending."[50] It is ironic that basic information allowing a comparison of actual spending to budget amounts for a particular government program's mission purpose is not readily attainable. This data, though, would allow appropriate comparisons of performance versus spending. The promise of the DATA Act is that it will allow government to provide "better data, better decisions, and better government," as stated by David Lebryk, fiscal assistant secretary of the U.S. Department of Treasury, for such purposes.[51]

The basic idea is that data transparency—whether financial or another measure—needs to be clear in that it reveals information about an institution's behavior such as certifying a regulated entity's compliance with, for example, environmental standards, as opposed to opaque or "fuzzy" transparency that is more of an information dump and less likely to reveal substantive information in terms of how an institution is making decisions.[52] Some scholars also define types of transparency in an effort to make the concept more operational and ensure its consistency with the openness of a free-flowing data-driven society. After all, the transparency agenda is the context within which the World Wide Web was designed, and it was built on the decentralized Internet, which itself was created by DARPA.[53] It makes sense, then, that a model of e-transparency would develop. Building on previous definitions of transparency, "e-transparency" distinguishes three categories: (1) data transparency focused on the facts and figures of government, (2) process transparency that involves making the steps involved in various processes of government known, and (3) decision/policy transparency that requires rationales and explanations for government actions.[54]

Each type of transparency addresses different kinds of questions. In turn, each type is affected differently by various technologies and involves different kinds of constraints and trade-offs. For example, the government has data on individuals, but providing that data to citizens is not without cost and some data can be misunderstood or misused. Educational data is frequently cited as being inadvertently or deliberately misused to rank schools.[55] Another issue is the inadvertent release of confidential data, and again ensuring trust is a key component of all such efforts.

The presumption is that greater trust and accountability result from increased transparency and that the asymmetrical information advantage the government has over the public can be tempered. The digital transparency movement echoes these assumptions of advocates of greater "openness" in general by government and the notion that "secrecy" in government is an administrative problem. In fact, secrecy and misuse of information or data is primarily a political issue, not an administrative one. This matters because there is not always an administrative tool that can fix an issue that is basically political in nature. This explains why, despite demands for still greater transparency, the issue of misuse of government information will remain.[56] Nevertheless, transparency is one important tool for checking governmental action. As Supreme Court Justice Louis Brandeis famously noted a century ago, "Publicity is justly commended as a remedy for social and industrial diseases, sunshine is said to be the best disinfectant, electric light the best policeman."[57] Brandeis also penned the noted essay that defined privacy as the "right to be let alone."[58] Reconciling the need for openness and protection of privacy is an ongoing dynamic in our democracy.

CONCLUDING THOUGHTS ON GOVERNING IN A DATA-DRIVEN SOCIETY

A recent report asserts that "developing a solid information strategy is the key enabler for agencies to meet their specific analytics needs and capture intelligence from all of their growing data sets."[59] A survey by the Economist Intelligence Unit (of *The Economist*) of more than 600 executives around the world found that "85 percent of the respondents believe that Big Data issues are not about volume, but the ability to analyze and act on the data in real time." The report based on this survey, *The Deciding Factor: Big Data and Decision-Making*, notes that the "inability to properly manage the information lifecycle leads to performance issues, poor data quality, and critical information gaps."[60] Government analytics means knowing how to formulate an answerable question, identify the most useful data sources, apply the appropriate tools of analysis, and present results that are substantively meaningful. In short, it is managing large data in ways that will yield sound governmental decision-making processes.

With the further development of government analytics, political scientists can make a vital contribution by supporting the growing use of analytics in the study and practice of governance. *New York Times* columnist David Brooks astutely observes that the rising philosophy of the day is "dat-ism" and ponders, "In what situations should we rely on intuitive pattern recognition and in which situations should we ignore intuition and follow the data? What sorts of events are predictable using statistical analysis and what sorts of events are not?"[61] In our data-driven politics, we assume data can sometimes better answer questions than it actually can.

Harvard's Professor King, who developed a tool for analyzing social media texts, notes that a billion social media posts are made every two days.[62] That is an enormous amount of data, but King's statistical methods analyze text messages and can provide helpful results not possible before such as where flu outbreaks are occurring or where social unrest might be rising. Yet there can be sample bias because self-selection occurs given that particular groups of individuals use the various social media platforms. Another issue can result when the broader context necessary to interpret quantitative findings is absent. For example, health care programs in different countries have been evaluated on a large scale, but sometimes the results are misleading when the data is not interpreted within the context of the particular nation or region involved. It is also the case that in data dredging (i.e., searching for patterns in large datasets) a 95% confidence level means that, in a small number of instances, you will have statistically significant results purely by chance.

The point is that there are basic limitations to any statistical analysis and, as discussed in chapter 1, results are only as good as the assumptions made in the model or within the limits of whatever quantitative tools are being used. That is, "no matter how much data exists, researchers need to ask the right questions to create a hypothesis, design a test, and use the data to determine if the hypothesis is true."[63] Asking the right questions and accurately interpreting results have never been more important than in research involving large datasets. As Lee Drutman, formerly with the Sunlight Foundation and now Senior Fellow at the think tank New America, has observed, "The important thing with data is to be humble. It's easy to over-interpret, and to generate meaningless or even wrong conclusions. But there are also tremendous insights data can provide, especially if we are careful and responsible about it."[64]

Just as the Internet did not live up to the expectation that American politics would be further democratized by it, because, in fact, it empowers a relatively small set of elites, it is not a given that big data will deliver the big results expected of it.[65] Government remains the "centre of information" and to maximize the benefits of a greater capacity for data analytics to better govern in our data-driven society, we have to be sure we are asking the right questions of our government and the data.

NOTES

1. Partnership for Public Service, *From Data to Decisions II: Building an Analytics Culture* (Washington, DC: IBM Center for the Business of Government, 2012).

2. According to the Federal Big Data Commission, "big data" is defined as "the large volumes of high velocity, complex, and variable data that require advanced techniques and technologies to enable the capture, storage, distribution, management, and analysis of the information." TechAmerica Foundation, *Demystifying Big Data: A Practical Guide to Transforming the Business of Government* (Washington, DC: TechAmerica Foundation, 2012), 10.

3. Charles Breton, "Top 10 Political Science Articles by Decade," http://charlesbreton.ca/?page_id=179.

4. Jonathan Shaw, "Why 'Big Data' Is a Big Deal," *Harvard Magazine*, November–December 2014, http://harvardmagazine.com/2014/03/why-big-data-is-a-big-deal.

5. Jennifer Bachner, *Predictive Policing: Preventing Crime with Data and Analytics* (Washington, DC: IBM Center for the Business of Government, 2013), http://www.businessofgovernment.org/report/predictive-policing-preventing-crime-data-and-analytics.

6. Minoru Nomura, "United States Government Efforts Toward Big Data Research and Development," *Quarterly Review* 46 (2013): 37–49; Rhoda Joseph and Norman Johnson, "Big Data and Transformational Government," *IT Pro*, November–December 2013, 42–43; John Miri and Caroline Brown, "Government IT Reform: Collaborating for New Solutions" (strategy paper, Center for Digital Government, Folsom, CA, 2011); and Luis Bettencourt, "The Uses of Big Data in Cities" (SFI Working Paper 2013-09-029, Santa Fe Institute, Santa Fe, NM, 2013).

7. Nancy Scola, "The Big Data President," *Washington Post*, June 16, 2013, B1; Alon Peled, "Re-designing Open Data 2.0," *Journal of eDemocracy* 5, no. 2 (2013): 187–199; and Executive Office of the President, "Memorandum on Transparency and Open Government" (White House, Washington, DC, January 9, 2009).

8. Executive Office of the President, "Obama Administration Unveils 'Big Data' Initiative; Announces $200 Million in New R&D Investments" (press release, White House, Washington, DC, March 29, 2012), www.whitehouse.gov/ostp/big_data_press_release_final_2.pdf. See also Executive Office of the President, "Executive Order—Making Open and Machine Readable the New Default for Government Information," Executive Order 13642, 78 Federal Register 28111 (May 14, 2013).

9. Peled, "Re-designing Open Data 2.0," 188.

10. Executive Office of the President, "U.S. Open Data Action Plan" (White House, Washington, DC, May 2014). Note that the U.S. Open Data Action Plan includes the following definition of government data: "structured information that is created, collected, processed, disseminated, or disposed of by or for the federal government," ibid., 2.

11. Peled, "Re-designing Open Data 2.0," 190.

12. Ibid., 191.

13. Taewoo Nam, "Citizens' Attitudes Toward Open Government and Government 2.0," *International Review of Administrative Sciences* 78, no. 2 (2012): 346–368.

14. Sylvia Burwell, Steven VanRoekel, Todd Park, and Dominic J. Mancini, "Memorandum for the Heads of Executive Departments and Agencies: Open Data Policy—Managing Information as an Asset," *Project Open Data*, 2013, http://project-open-data.github.io/policy-memo/#collect-or-create -information-in-a-way-that-supports-downstreatm-information-processing-and-dissemination -activities.

15. U.S. Government Accountability Office (GAO), *Managing for Results: A Guide for Using the GPRA Modernization Act to Help Inform Congressional Decision Making* (Washington, DC: Government Printing Office, 2012).

16. Executive Office of the President, "Memorandum to the Heads of Departments and Agencies: Next Steps in the Evidence and Innovation Agenda" (Office of Management and Budget, Washington, DC, July 26, 2013); and Council of Economic Advisors, "Evaluation as a Tool for Improving Federal Programs," in Economic Report to the President (Washington, DC: Council of Economic Advisors, 2014), 269–298.

17. Kathy Stack, "Do Data Analytics Actually Influence Government Funding and Administration Policy?" (Government Analytics Breakfast Forum, Johns Hopkins University, Baltimore, October 9, 2014), https://www.reisystems.com/Services/Pages/AnalyticsForum.aspx.

18. Ibid.

19. Ron Haskins and Greg Margolis, *Show Me the Evidence: Obama's Fight for Rigor and Results in Social Policy* (Washington, DC: Brookings Institution Press, 2014).

20. Dazza Greenwood, Arkadiusz Stopczynski, Brian Sweatt, Thomas Hardjono, and Alex Pentland, "The New Deal on Data: A Framework for Institutional Controls," in *Privacy, Big Data, and the Public Good: Frameworks for Engagement*, ed. Julia Lane, Victoria Stodden, Stefan Bender, and Helen Nissenbaum (New York: Cambridge University Press, 2014), 192–210. See also Alex Pentland's work identifying a new field, social physics, which is "a quantitative social science that describes reliable, mathematical connections between information and idea flow on the one hand and people's behavior on the other." Alex Pentland, *Social Physics: How Good Ideas Spread—The Lessons from a New Science* (New York: Penguin, 2014), 4.

21. Greenwood et al., "The New Deal on Data," 194.

22. Ibid., 196–197.

23. Ibid., 197; and Pentland, *Social Physics*, 177–182.

24. Pentland, *Social Physics*, 181. Note that the big data market is approaching $30 billion annually and is expected to top $50 billion by 2017.

25. Cornelius Puschmann and Jean Burgess, "The Politics of Twitter Data," in *Twitter and Society*, ed. Katrin Weller, Axel Bruns, Jean Burgess, and Merja Mahrt (New York: Peter Lang, 2014), 43–54, 44.

26. Ibid.

27. Brian Reich, "Citizens' View of Open Government," in *Open Government: Collaboration, Transparency, and Participation in Practice*, ed. Daniel Lathrop and Laurel Ruma (Cambridge, MA: O'Reilly, 2010), 131–138.

28. Pentland, *Social Physics*, 180–181. See also Greenwood et al., "The New Deal on Data," 195ff.

29. Pentland, *Social Physics*, 181. See European Parliament and the Council of the European Union, "Directive 95/46/EC on the Protection of Individuals with Regard to the Processing of Personal Data and the Free Movement of Such Data," *Official Journal* L 281, 23/11/1995, 31–50; and White House, "Consumer Data Privacy in a Networked World: A Framework for Protecting Privacy and Promoting Innovation in the Global Digital Economy" (White House, Washington, DC, February 2012), www.whitehouse.gov/sites/files/privacy-final.pdf.

30. Executive Office of the President, "We Can't Wait: Obama Administration Unveils Blueprint for a 'Privacy Bill of Rights' to Protect Consumers Online" (press release, White House, Washington, DC, February 23, 2012), www.whitehouse.gov/the-press-office/2012/02/23/we-can-t-wait-obama -administration-unveils-blueprint-privacy-bill-rights; and Executive Office of the President, *Consumer Data Privacy in a Networked World: A Framework for Protecting Privacy and Promoting Innovation in the Global Digital Economy* (Washington, DC: White House, February 2012), www.whitehouse.gov.sites/default/files/ privacy-final.pdf.

31. Steve Kenny and Larry Korba, "Applying Digital Rights Management Systems to Privacy Rights Management," *Computers and Society* 21, no. 7 (2002): 648–664.

32. TechAmerica Foundation, "Big Data and the Public Sector," https://www.splunk.com/content/ dam/splunk2/pdfs/fact-sheets/sap-public-sector-big-data-report-final-2.pdf.

33. Mark Scott, "Where Tech Giants Protect Privacy," *New York Times*, December 14, 2014, 5; and Zach Warren, "EU Drafting an Even Stricter Privacy and Data Security Bill," *Inside Counsel*, March 10, 2015, http://insidecounsel.com.

34. Mary Madden, "Public Perceptions of Privacy and Security in the Post-Snowden Era," *Pew Research Internet Project*, November 12, 2014, http://www.pewinternet.org/2014/11/12/public-privacy -perceptions/.

35. U.S. Department of Commerce, "NTIA Seeks Comment on Big Data and the Consumer Privacy Bill of Rights," www.ntia.doc.gov/press-release/2014/ntia-seeks-comment-big-data-and-consumer -privacy-bill-rights. See Molly Jennings, "To Track or Not to Track: Recent Legislative Proposals to Protect Consumer Privacy," *Harvard Journal on Legislation* 49 (2012): 193–206.

36. Executive Office of the President, *Big Data: Seizing Opportunities, Preserving Values* (Washington, DC: Executive Office of the President, May 2014), www.whitehouse.gov/sites/default/files/docs/big_ data_privacy_report_5.1.14_final_print.pdf.

37. Executive Office of the President, "U.S. Open Data Action Plan."

38. Ibid., 2.

39. Christopher Hood, "Transparency in Historical Perspective," in *Transparency: The Key to Better Governance?*, ed. Christopher Hood and David Heald (Oxford: Oxford University Press, 2006), 1–23; and Frank Bannister and Regina Connolly, "The Trouble with Transparency: A Critical Review of Openness in e-Government," *Policy and Internet* 3, no. 1 (2011): 1–30. See also Daniel Lathrop and Laurel Ruma, eds., *Open Government: Collaboration, Transparency, and Participation in Practice* (Cambridge, MA: O'Reilly, 2010).

40. Jonathan Fox, "The Uncertain Relationship Between Transparency and Accountability" (research paper, Center for Global, International and Regional Studies, University of California, Santa Cruz, 2007).

41. Susan MacManus, Kiki Caruson, and Brian McPhee, "Cybersecurity at the Local Government Level: Balancing Demands for Transparency and Privacy Rights," *Journal of Urban Affairs* 35, no. 4 (2012): 451–470.

42. Ibid.

43. "With Big Data Comes Big Responsibility: An Interview with MIT Media Lab's Alex 'Sandy' Pentland," *Harvard Business Review* 92, no. 11 (2014): 101–104.

44. Greenwood et al., "The New Deal on Data," 198, 203.

45. Pentland, *Social Physics*, 182; see also Greenwood et al., "The New Deal on Data," 198–199.

46. White House, "The 90-Day Review for Big Data" (White House, Washington, DC, May 2014), www.whitehouse.gov/issues/technology/big-data-review.

47. Thomas Jefferson, Letter to Richard Price, 1789, ME 7:253.

48. Peled, "Re-designing Open Data 2.0," 190.

49. Ibid., 194.

50. Jeff Myers, "Obtaining Value from DATA Act: Follow the Money," *Fedscoop*, April 14, 2015, http://fedscoop.com/obtaining-value-from-data-act-follow-the-money; Jeff Myers, "How Treasury and OMB Can Add Value to the DATA Act," *Fedscoop*, May 29, 2015, http://fedscoop.com/how-treasury-and-omb-can-add-value-to-data-act; and Jeff Myers, "The DATA Act: Make 'Following the Money' Worth the Effort," *Fedscoop*, June 5, 2015, http://fedscoop.com/the-data-act-make-following-the-money-worth-it.

51. David Lebryk, "What Analyses Do I Hope Agencies Will Make of Their DATA Act Data?" (Government Analytics Breakfast Forum, Johns Hopkins University, Baltimore, June 15, 2015), https://www.reisystems.com/Services/Pages/AnalyticsForum.aspx.

52. Fox, "Uncertain Relationship Between Transparency and Accountability," 667.

53. Aleks Krotoski, "Wikileaks and the New, Transparent World Order," *Political Quarterly* 82, no. 4 (2011): 526–530. See also Tim O'Reilly, "Government as a Platform," in *Open Government: Collaboration, Transparency, and Participation in Practice,* ed. Daniel Lathrop and Laurel Ruma (Cambridge, MA: O'Reilly, 2010), 11–39.

54. Bannister and Connolly, "Trouble with Transparency," 8.

55. Ibid., 11; and Peled, "Re-designing Open Data 2.0."

56. Mark Fenster, "The Transparency Fix: Advocating Legal Rights and Their Alternatives in the Pursuit of a Visible State," *University of Pittsburgh Law Review* 73 (2010): 443–503; Adam Candeub, "Transparency in the Administrative State," *Houston Law Review* 51, no. 2 (2013): 385–416; Rui Pedro Lourenco, *Information Polity* 18 (2013): 243–260; Lauren Rhue and Arun Sundararajan, "Digital Access, Political Networks and the Diffusion of Democracy," *Social Networks* 36 (2014): 40–53; Gianluca Misuraca, David Broster, and Clara Centeno, "Digital Europe 2030: Designing Scenarios for ICT in Future Governance and Policy Making," *Government Information Quarterly* 29 (2012): S121–S131; and Christopher Hood and David Heald, eds., *Transparency: The Key to Better Governance?* (Oxford: Oxford University Press, 2006).

57. Louis D. Brandeis, "What Publicity Can Do," *Harper's Weekly*, December 20, 1913, www.law.louisville.edu/library/collection/brandeis/node/196.

58. Samuel Warren and Louis D. Brandeis, "The Right to Privacy," *Harvard Law Review* 4, no. 5 (1890).

59. Capgemini Public Sector, "Information Strategy Is the Key to Addressing Big Data Challenges," http://www.capgemini-gs.com.

60. Economics Intelligence Unit, *The Deciding Factor: Big Data and Decision-Making,* http://www.capgemini.com/insights-and-resources.

61. David Brooks, "The Philosophy of Data," *New York Times*, February 4, 2013, http://www.nytimes.com/2013/02/05/opinion/brooks. See also David Brooks, "Death by Data," *New York Times*, November 3, 2014, http://nytimes.com/2014/11/04/opinion/david-brooks.

62. Shaw, "Why 'Big Data' Is a Big Deal."

63. Ibid.

64. Lee Drutman, "Two Principles to Avoid Common Data Mistakes," *Sunlight Foundation Blog*, http://sunlightfoundation.com/blog/2013/02/19/avoiding-data-mistakes/.

65. Matthew Hindman, *The Myth of Digital Democracy* (Princeton, NJ: Princeton University Press, 2009).

CHAPTER NINE   Big Data and Privacy

Priscilla M. Regan

IN THIS CHAPTER

In this chapter, the focus is on the privacy issues associated with big data, which exist regardless of the setting in which big data might be used, rather than the benefits or techniques of big data. The chapter first discusses the conceptualization of the privacy problems posed by "big data" based on how data practices and analytics are currently, or projected to be, used in a number of contexts. Privacy problems include controlling collection and use of information about oneself, autonomy over decision making, anonymity, choice in group associations, and "practical obscurity"—as well as related values of due process, equal protection, data security, and accountability. The chapter then identifies and evaluates a number of policy approaches for addressing these problems, demonstrating that the power of big data renders traditional information privacy policy responses obsolete and ineffective and argues for regulation and oversight on entities collecting and using big data.

INTRODUCTION

The growth of "big data" and the concomitant development of sophisticated analytical techniques for generating data, designing datasets, culling the data for patterns and trends, and identifying either individual or group prototypes of behavior raise the promise of a host of societal benefits—but also a number of more disquieting possibilities. The promised benefits include more rapid notification and understanding of epidemiological dissemination, more efficient and effective allocation of public services, more precise identification of relevant disease treatments, as well as other potential benefits. The scale and the depth of the data combined with the analytical power and sophisticated algorithms offered by modern computing enable the identification of new patterns, previously unrecognized connections, and possible new solutions for a range of social problems.

The more disquieting possibilities posed by big data, including the effects on privacy, are less obvious but nonetheless real. Big data basically depend on the collection and aggregation of small data about as many aspects of individuals' daily lives as possible—and the possibilities are increasing as individuals become more dependent on electronic devices which yield more exact and fine-tuned insight into behavior and thought patterns. Almost all this data collection and aggregation are enabled by large corporations—such as Google, Facebook, and now Nike with its FuelBand—or by government agencies such as the National Security Agency (NSA) but also by public education and health agencies.

Not only does big data entail collection and analysis of more and more refined data but big data also entail expanded power to influence, restrict, and predict individuals' actions and opportunities. Big data techniques have the potential to change much regarding how decisions about individuals, groups, and society more generally are made. The authors of a popular and influential book see "big data" as "the beginning of a major transformation," which "challenges the way we live and interact in the world" and how we "make decisions and comprehend reality."[1] Although this may ring as hyperbole, much of what they describe and analyze is valid and factual. As a society, more data are collected, in more ways, are more detailed and granular, are more easily disaggregated and re-aggregated in unexpected ways, and are distributed to more entities and over more servers. Additionally, and for many analysts more importantly, data can be analyzed with more sophisticated algorithms, increasing researchers' ability to describe patterns and correlations, offer new insights, and seemingly predict from these results. At the same time, big data are often somewhat messy, incomplete, and, still as true for data everywhere, error prone. Moreover, data encompass just about all phenomena from traditional numbers, to words, to locations and movements, to relationship networks and statuses, to activities, to attitudes and moods.[2]

The list of potential benefits that may be achieved through the use of big data is lengthy and spans many settings, from those with significant societal benefits to those with more trivial advantages. Tracking and diagnosing diseases and determining the most effective treatment may be improved by aggregating and analyzing data from pharmacies, web searches, and health care providers. Developing efficient energy use may be promoted by scrutinizing household patterns, transportation modes, and energy companies' financial records. Big data offer novel capabilities to almost all economic sectors as data can be analyzed to reveal opportunities not only to business and the individual data subjects but also, as Jules Polonetsky and Omer

Tene point out, to the community or "members of a proximate class, such as users of a similar product or residents of a geographical area" who would benefit from the knowledge yielded from the analysis enabled by big data, as well as "enhancing allocative efficiency by facilitating the 'free' economy."[3] Others, however, claim that the benefits of big data are overstated.[4] As with many new phenomena, there is a measure of hyperbole associated with big data. This chapter will not explore the benefits of big data, assuming that some of the promises are indeed quite real, but will instead focus on the privacy issues associated with big data, which exist regardless of the setting in which big data might be used.

The chapter will first offer a conceptualization of the privacy problems posed by "big data" as data practices and analytics are currently, or projected to be, used in a number of contexts. Privacy is a multifaceted concept generally including controlling collection and use of information about oneself, autonomy over decision making, anonymity, choice in group associations, and "practical obscurity"—as well as related values of due process, equal protection, data security, and accountability. The chapter will also identify and evaluate a number of policy approaches for addressing the problems posed by big data. I will demonstrate the power of big data to render the traditional policy response of "fair information practices" (collection limitation, individual notice and consent, etc.) obsolete and ineffective. Instead, I argue that policy responses would appear to require regulation and oversight on entities collecting and using big data.

BIG DATA CHALLENGES TO PRIVACY

Each step on the path of organizational shifts from the paper-based files on individuals of the 19th and early 20th centuries to the computerized mainframe dossiers of the mid-20th century to the decentralized computerized databases of the latter 20th century and now to the big data amalgams of the 21st century has raised new challenges to privacy. Each step has also required some rethinking of what privacy entails and why privacy is important. Space does not permit a detailed review of these challenges or a review of policy thinking about privacy, but some background will help provide the context for thinking about big data and privacy.

In a nutshell, the prevailing American policy approach to information privacy focuses on providing the individual with the means to "control information about oneself." This focus on control dates back to the policy framing of the late 1960s and early 1970s and is enshrined in the 1974 Privacy Act. The policy approach of this act, and others of the late 20th century, is based on the notion of "fair information practice principles"—individuals should have certain rights of notice about information collection and uses, as well as consent to those practices, and organizations should provide some level of transparency about their practices and provide individuals with some review and redress. As computerized systems and applications became more complex and integrated, and as organizations routinely shared information across programs and sectors, the policy goal of achieving individual control over information is increasingly regarded as problematical, if not obsolete and impractical.

Despite the rather relentless march of organizational and technological advances that has chipped away at individual control over information, individuals appear to still value privacy although recognizing at the same time that they have lost or are losing control over their information. A November 2014 Pew Research Center report on public perceptions of privacy revealed that 91 percent of adults "agree" or "strongly agree" that "consumers have lost control over how information is collected and used by companies."[5] At the same time, respondents viewed privacy as involving a "constellation of concepts,"[6] including security, rights, being let alone, confidentiality, personal, secret, solitude. Difficulties in conceptualizing privacy are not new; indeed, the meaning and value of privacy has been the subject of much discussion by philosophers, legal scholars, and social scientists.[7]

There are at least six components or aspects traditionally associated with privacy that are challenged by big data. These six are not intended to exhaustively cover the privacy concerns raised by big data but instead to provide some measure of logic to understand both how big data privacy issues relate to earlier privacy issues and also how big data transform these concerns.

The first is that collection of information about an individual should take place with the knowledge of the individual and that the amount of information should be minimized to that which is required for the particular purpose for which it was collected. With big data, there is more collection of information, by more parties, about more aspects of an individual's life, and with more granularity about that life. But the issue is not merely "more" or even the qualitative changes that quantity does not convey. The issue is also how much of big data collection takes place without the individual's awareness. As the President's Council of Advisors on Science and Technology (PCAST) noted in 2014, individuals "constantly emit into the environment information whose use or misuse may be a source of privacy concerns."[8] Moreover, enhancements in digital storage capacity combined with improvements in computational power and developments of more sophisticated algorithms for analyzing data have enabled organizations to probe and dissect datasets in ways unimagined even 20 years ago. As Ira Rubinstein similarly points out, big data make possible the extraction of new, potentially useful information from data—this "newly discovered information is not only unintuitive and unpredictable, but also results from a fairly opaque process."[9] The entire enterprise of big data challenges all previous ideas about how to limit data collection about individuals and how to involve the individual in the process of data collection and subsequent uses so that the individual could exercise some meaningful control.

A second concern long associated with privacy is that individuals should be able to remain anonymous or obscure if they so choose to do so. With an ever-increasing number of social relationships and practices being reduced to data points, it becomes more difficult to remain unidentified or unfindable. This concern is related to the earlier debates about privacy in public and maintaining "practical obscurity." Algorithmic searches of datasets now can rather quickly eradicate what had been high transaction costs on finding meaningful information.[10] At one point, privacy laws protected "personal information," meaning that the information was directly associated with a particular individual. As a result of technology and data collection practices, these laws were modified to address protection of "personally identifiable" information, broadening relevant information beyond that directly associated with an individual to include information that could be associated with an individual. With big data, such previous distinctions in privacy laws based on "personally identifiable information" are obviated as more and more information can be attached to a particular individual with just a bit of searching and analysis. Tene and Polonetsky advocate a continuum approach to distinguishing personally identifiable information rather than a dichotomy between identifiable and non-identifiable information. They suggest a matrix including risk, intent, and potential consequences of re-identification.[11]

With big data, anonymization of information about individuals is also more difficult, if not impossible, as big data make re-identifying data rather easy. The debate about anonymity and re-identification began in 2000 with Latanya Sweeney's study of the 1990 U.S. Census data in which she found that one's five-digit zip code, date of birth, and gender provided unique identification for 87 percent of the population, or 216 million of 248 million people.[12] In effect, few characteristics are actually needed to uniquely identify an individual, making it very difficult to anonymize databases by removing some characteristics, because the bundle of characteristics remaining will likely prove sufficient to identify individuals once a database is merged with other databases and searched using sophisticated algorithms. More recently, Sweeney and colleagues identified the names of volunteer participants in the de-identified public Personal Genome Project by linking the project's profiles to public records and data mining the results.[13]

Computer scientists and privacy policy experts and advocates continue to press for better techniques for anonymizing data, for example, by using only three digits of one's zip code or redacting year of birth or day of month. However, as databases become larger and more integrated, these attempts increasingly prove to be ineffective. After reviewing the computer science and legal literatures on anonymity and re-identification, Paul Ohm concludes that "data can be either useful or perfectly anonymous but never both."[14] This is a conclusion that is becoming more widely shared as various big data projects by companies such as Netflix, AOL, and Google reveal that individuals can indeed be identified in studies that were using supposedly anonymous data. And there is increasing recognition that data can either be useful or protective of privacy, but not both. As a biomedical researcher notes: "I can't anonymize your genome without wiping out the information that I need to analyze."[15]

A third concern involves the surveillance or tracking that provides more and more detailed information for big data analytics—and that big data require to be even more powerful. What is now being referred to as the "Internet of Things," where all our smart devices pick up and transmit detailed information, will become a key element of this surveillance. The behavioral advertising debate of the early years of the 21st century highlighted these issues, drawing attention to grouping audiences and/or consumers with particular purchasing patterns, website histories, or demographic attributes into predetermined categories. Not only does big data entail more monitoring of activities and extraction of data about those activities, but big data also involve analysis of those activities to determine likely future activities. This more sophisticated prediction that is built into many big data analytics transforms surveillance into a more omniscient phenomenon. Big data surveillance is not Foucault's panopticon, where there is one all-seeing watcher and individuals absorb the control imperatives of the controller, but big data surveillance instead is ubiquitous and prescient in ways that go beyond the individual's own knowledge, capacity, or control.

Such surveillance has entered popular culture by way of the movie *Minority Report*, which overplays the predictive power of big data but foreshadows what many see as quite possible. But such surveillance does exist in the more sophisticated behavioral advertising campaigns where retailers quite accurately predict what will entice an individual to make a future purchase based not just on past purchases, as well as shopping and spending patterns, but also on the time of day, who the individual is with, what she just ate and where, what she did last weekend and is planning for this weekend, and so on. These broadly inclusive analyses reach well beyond the expected and move from influencing behavior to forecasting behavior—much in the way meteorologists predict tomorrow's weather. Crunching big data to determine the likelihood of an individual's future actions involves a qualitative shift as it moves from surveillance of behavior to surveillance of propensities and thus raises questions about human agency and autonomy.

A fourth concern related to privacy that is challenged by big data is individual autonomy, the individual's ability to govern his or her life as that individual thinks best. Big data algorithms jeopardize autonomy by leading people in certain directions—to buy certain items or try certain routes or restaurants—and in a certain way challenge the self as defined throughout much of Western philosophy. Some have expressed this concern as being about social fragmentation into "filter bubbles," where individuals are subject to feedback loops that limit individuals' sense of their options.[16] Karen Levy distinguishes top-down data collection that may limit autonomy and a more subtle—and quite different—threat to autonomy from individuals managing and negotiating their social relationships through big data applications. As examples, she discusses the "quantified self" movement, including those tracking their own progress (e.g., FitBit and Nike FuelBand) but at the same time encouraging competition with others. She also sees friending practices on social network sites as constraining the individual's ability to manage social relationships.[17] Ian Kerr and Jessica Earle distinguish among three types of predictions that affect autonomy: consequential predictions that allow individuals to act more in their self-interest and avoid unfavorable outcomes; preferential predictions that lead one to act in a way expected from the data; and preemptive predictions that are not based on the preferences of the actor but reduce the range of options available to the actor.[18] Tene and Polonetsky point to the dangers of predictive analysis, including the perpetuation of old prejudices and the accentuation of social stratification.[19]

A fifth privacy concern associated with big data involves traditional due process for individuals, that individuals are treated fairly and equally and not discriminated against based on race, gender, age, or other personal attributes—or based on factors of which they are not aware. Big data's use of mathematical algorithms and artificial intelligence to make predictions about individuals based on conglomerates of their information and that of others raises questions about treating individuals as individuals fairly, accurately, and in ways they can understand.[20] This concern involves issues of profiling and discrimination. For example, Ohm points out that "big data helps companies find a reasonable proxy for race."[21] These issues arise whether or not the individual has consented to certain collection and uses of information—the issue of being disadvantaged or discriminated against because of information classifications (automated or not) is a separate, independent policy issue.[22] Not only are those who are included in these classificatory schemes affected, but those excluded from or ignored by them are also negatively affected as their preferences and choices are not taken into account. As Jonas Lerman points out, "The big data revolution may create new forms of inequality and subordination, and thus raise broad democracy concerns."[23]

A sixth issue that has long been part of the debate about privacy, especially information privacy, is the question of the ownership of data about an individual. Does the individual "own" the information or does the third party holding the information in a database? Although many privacy scholars question whether the property model provides a workable framework for talking about privacy,[24] the property rhetoric and rationales have become part of the policy discussion about big data, as they had been in earlier iterations of debates about privacy policy. As one moves further from either submitting personal information to one organization or clicks "I agree" on a website, any ownership in that information arguably fades. And if that information becomes part of a dataset that is then reused or reconfigured or combined with another or sold to another organization, the claim of personal ownership in that information diminishes even more.

POLICY RESPONSES—MORE OF THE SAME OR A PARADIGMATIC SHIFT?

As we move further and further into the age of big data, public concern and media attention on these six issues call into question the continued advance of big data applications and make it more important to formulate policy to address these issues. One popular way to frame the question of protecting privacy is in terms of how to ensure that "downstream" big data respect individuals' preferences about use of their data.[25] It is also widely recognized that one of the difficulties in fashioning appropriate policy solutions is what Neil Richards and Jonathan King term the "transparency paradox" because so much of the collection and analytical techniques involved in big data are secret, largely because of the complexity of the technology and proprietary concerns of business.[26]

Policy discussions about appropriate policy solutions to privacy and big data focus not on one particular type of solution but instead draw upon different forms of policy intervention, which would require more or less government action. Generally, there are four types of policy response—legal rights, regulatory requirements and oversight, technological fixes, and education. Each of these will be discussed in turn as it relates to big data and privacy. Although each will be discussed in turn, they are complementary approaches and many advocate the necessity of fashioning a policy response combining elements of several, if not all, approaches.

Legal Rights

Since the early 1970s, the most often used approach for information privacy, both in the United States and in other countries, is one that either by law or admonition requires organizations to follow a code of "fair information practice principles" (FIPPs). The genesis for these goes back to the 1973 report of a Department of Health, Education, and Welfare committee and its recommendation that there be no secret personal record-keeping systems, that individuals be informed of such records and how they are used, that individuals be able to consent to secondary uses of their information and to correct or amend information, and that organizations ensure the reliability and prevent misuse of information.[27] The FIPPs provide the core of the Privacy Act of 1974, most other information privacy laws in the United States, and European data protection policies.

Given the dominance of FIPPs in information privacy policy, discussions about big data and privacy often started with the question of whether the FIPPs approach of notice and consent could be used. The consensus among privacy policy scholars was that FIPPs, which were increasingly being recognized as ineffective for standard information collection and use practices, were undoubtedly ineffective for big data practices. Drawing upon economic analyses of consumer practices, Alessandro Acquisti concluded that FIPPs were unsuccessful because the "findings from behavioral economics document consumers' inability to exhaustively consider the possible outcomes and risks of data disclosures, due to bounded rationality."[28] Ira Rubinstein summed up analyses of FIPPs by social scientists and legal scholars with reference to the "discredited informed choice model."[29] As analysts considered the viability of the FIPPs model for big data, the shortcomings of that model quickly became apparent. Katherine Strandburg, for example, noted that consent is not meaningful with big data because the connections among particular harms to the individual, the method of data collection and handling, and the particular data handler are difficult to pinpoint and thus to assign responsibility or liability. She noted also that with big data, "harms often are societal and spread over large numbers of individuals. The privacy torts' emphasis on outrageous behavior is clearly inapropos to the privacy concerns associated with large aggregations of data."[30] Ohm also pointed out that "because big data techniques produce surprising correlations, we increasingly will find it difficult to know that we are in the presence of risky data, the kind of data that will likely lead to privacy harm."[31]

In 2014, President Barack Obama commissioned two studies on privacy and big data, both of which evaluated the effectiveness of a policy response based on FIPPs. The White House study concedes that the traditional notice-and-consent framework needs to be re-evaluated but is modest in its rethinking, largely embracing the approach of the proposed Consumer Privacy Bill of Rights, which seeks to strengthen the FIPPs, but also an approach that would entail "greater focus on how data is used and reused."[32] The President's Council of Advisors on Science and Technology (PCAST) went a bit further in its criticism of notice and consent, noting that only in "some fantasy world" did users actually give any meaningful form of consent and conceding that notice and consent was effectively "defeated by exactly the positive benefits that big data enables," but recommending that "since notice and consent is so deeply rooted in current practice, some exploration of how its usefulness might be extended seems warranted."[33]

Regulatory Requirements and Oversight

Although organizations have long held a preference for self-regulation in the area of information privacy and the government has been reluctant to interfere in ways that might constrain technological and organizational innovation, some regulatory or oversight mechanisms have been a component of information privacy policy. Most government agencies and private sector companies have "privacy officers" who provide advice and expertise on privacy issues and possible options for dealing with those issues and with raising awareness of privacy within the organization.[34] Many of these organizations also conduct privacy impact assessments, which are carried out prior to the implementation of a new electronic information system or application to identify and provide protections for possible privacy threats.[35] Although both privacy officers and privacy impact assessments have been incorporated into many organizations, in practice they are often rather weak in effectively addressing privacy issues. Privacy impact assessments, for example, are often more boilerplate and filed as yet another requirement that needs to be checked off rather than a serious exercise to identify potential threats and effective responses.[36] Likewise, the influence of privacy officers varies depending on the commitment of the organization and the respect accorded the person holding the position; in some instances, it is more symbolic and in others more effective.

Data security breach laws reflect a regulatory approach to information privacy concerns that require organizations to disclose instances when data were compromised, attempt to correct privacy violations after the fact, and also impose future-oriented requirements on organizations responsible for the unauthorized release of personal information. As a response to public concern with identity theft, a number of states adopted data security breach laws, but there is no federal law.[37] There is no question that data security measures and requirements to disclose security breaches are an essential component of information privacy policy and maintain public trust in the use of information,[38] but the concept of unauthorized releases of information is somewhat limited in the big data environment where data travel so many places and are aggregated and disaggregated so often.

Technological Fixes

Technology has often been seen as one of the causes of privacy invasions and at the same time as one of the means of curtailing or controlling such invasions. Discussions of big data and privacy similarly raise the possibility of technological fixes. One such fix that has become popular is the tagging of data with either expiration dates or the preferences of data subjects. This technological solution has conceptual roots in the FIPPs concept of individual control and the European Union's "right to be forgotten."[39] The World Economic Forum in February 2013 endorsed a policy whereby data would be tagged with a software code that specified the individual's preferences for subsequent use.[40] However, as PCAST points out, data "increasingly contain latent information about individuals, information that becomes known only if the holder expends analytical resources (beyond what may be economically feasible), or that may become knowable only in the future with the development of new data-mining algorithms."[41] The PCAST report concludes that "it is not even clear that data *can* be destroyed with any useful degree of assurance" and that policy should assume that "data, once created, are permanent" with the result that policy options must regulate use.[42]

A more traditional technological fix, and one that is particularly challenged by big data, is anonymization of data. As discussed previously, computer scientists recognize the near impossibility of effectively anonymizing data. Recent studies using census data,[43] search data,[44] movie reviews,[45] and health data reveal that despite attempts to anonymize data, people can be re-identified by merging data with other publicly available data, by purchasing other datasets, or by sophisticated analysis of the dataset itself. PCAST concluded that anonymization is not a "useful basis for policy" because of the power of re-identification methods but may be "useful as an added safeguard."[46]

Challenges to anonymization and the recognition that data can be re-identified convey the concern about big data and privacy to social science research and protection of human subjects where anonymity, along with informed consent, has been viewed as the most appropriate way of ensuring confidentiality for research subjects. A group of researchers from Harvard and MIT, who have worked on massive open online courses (MOOCs) and on data research, concluded that the conflation of anonymity and privacy is no longer a workable format for effective social science research and that a new paradigm is necessary.[47] They suggest either a technological solution, perhaps "differential privacy," or open access to data that could be re-identified but within a context where data uses were regulated and users held accountable.

"Differential privacy" has received much attention as a possible policy solution for big data and privacy. It obscures the presence or absence of a particular individual, or a small group of individuals with a similar characteristic, in a dataset. Differential privacy enables queries to statistical databases that minimize re-identification by using algorithmic methods that, in effect, introduce noise into the database without compromising the accuracy of the response. This can be achieved by "differentially private generation of synthetic data that are released to the public or in differentially private query/response systems."[48] This technological solution is better suited to some types of queries than others; for example, differential privacy does not work well for health-related or genetic queries.[49]

Another technological solution that introduces "noise" or lack of precision into disclosed data, thus protecting privacy, is "statistical disclosure limitation" techniques that alter data in some way before release, such as by aggregating data at a higher level (e.g., state rather than county), suppressing certain values, and switching data values.[50] These techniques are used primarily by large data aggregators, such as census bureaus, and their effectiveness depends on the disclosure risk assessment carried out by the data holder; these are thus not merely technological or statistical solutions but also organizational solutions. Their effectiveness is also limited because small changes will not be sufficient to protect privacy and large changes will render the data less useful for meaningful analysis.

Education

The concept of informing data subjects about collection and uses of information is part of the FIPPs notice concept and is based on the idea that if one knows what is happening with one's information, one can take measures to protect oneself. Hence, there are privacy policies posted on websites and privacy notices that are periodically sent to consumers. Their effectiveness has been questioned for decades as it is widely acknowledged, as discussed previously, that people do not read such notices or, if they do, they do not understand the full implications. The Obama White House May 2014 review of privacy and big data concluded that there was indeed a need for greater transparency and recommended that the data services industry should build a website or online portal that provides information on the data practices of various companies and the ways in which consumers can exercise some control over how their information is collected and used.[51]

The effectiveness of each of these traditional policy approaches is limited—and combining components of all four is likewise limited. Big data and privacy are not merely another case of information privacy but represent a new type of policy problem, demanding new ways of thinking about privacy and new approaches for addressing the problem. The next section begins to sketch out how we might more productively think about privacy and big data, as well as some possible policy approaches.

PARADIGMATIC SHIFT

The ubiquity and complexity of the communications and organizational systems in which much of modern life occurs and the big data that results from and fuels those systems requires that we discard the idea that we are dealing with a problem of the individual and recognize that the collective is affected by big data. I earlier argued that privacy has a collective value because technology and market forces were making it harder for any one person to have privacy without all persons having a similar minimum level of privacy. I believe there are three reasons for thinking about privacy as a collective or public good. First, privacy is not a "private good" in that one cannot effectively buy back or establish a desired level of privacy because of the non-voluntary nature of many record-keeping relationships. Second, the market will not produce an optimal supply of privacy as the calculus of large organizations is to gather more information and privacy protection is a hidden transaction cost for the individual, rendering the market an inefficient mechanism for supplying privacy. Third, the complexity and interrelatedness of the computer and communications infrastructure makes it more difficult to divide privacy as the default privacy setting is determined by the architecture of the system.[52]

I have also argued that personal information can be viewed as an overused "common-pool resource"[53] whose value to any one user is curtailed by other users. I claim that the common-pool resource system for personal information is *overloaded* in that the collection of more personal information is driving up the costs to subjects and users; is *polluted* in that inaccurate, irrelevant, and out-of-date information has contaminated the resource pool; and is *over-harvested* in that more users take similar pieces of information from the pool, reducing the unique value of that information for any one user.[54] Viewed from this perspective, privacy becomes a collective value that protects the common-pool resource of personal information.

Both of these orientations to privacy are finding traction in the current debate about privacy and big data, and both offer a better starting point to examine privacy and big data than the traditional individual-rights orientation. The idea that one can individually set one's own privacy level unaffected by others is undermined in several current contexts as illustrated by social networking sites in which others may, knowingly or unknowingly, reveal information that implicates the privacy of others. Alice Marwick and danah boyd[55] view these technological shifts in the information and cultural landscape as creating "networked publics" and necessitating a conceptualization of privacy from an individualistic frame to one that is networked. In a "networked public," it becomes much more difficult for any one person to set her own privacy standards, to monitor the flow of her information, and to establish a level of privacy without all other persons in that network having a similar level of privacy. Solon Barocas and Helen Nissenbaum refer to one of the privacy implications in such a network as the "tyranny of the minority" whereby "the volunteered information of the few can unlock the same information about the many."[56] Moreover, the methods of collecting, analyzing, and using big data have become far removed from the point at which an individual consciously provides information about herself and similarly obviate the possibility of setting one's privacy level. Steven Koonin and Michael Holland refer to the "instrumenting of society" as "big data" technologies are "producing data streams of unprecedented granularity, coverage and timeliness."[57]

Given the acknowledgment that big data have wrought a fundamental change in privacy possibilities, what policy approaches might be effective? I consider three—the first based on the idea of big data as part of an infrastructure, the second on the concept of big data as a component of a public good, and the third on the belief in individual empowerment. Each of these incorporates principles and techniques of organizational accountability and technological solutions.

Big Data as Infrastructure

If big data resources and applications have become integral to modern life, then the organizations and transmission mechanisms that support big data take on the features of an infrastructure—much as the highway, utility, water, and communications systems have. The editors of *Privacy, Big Data, and the Public Good* agree and argue that to achieve the vision of big data for the public good, "the public sector must make substantial investments in building the necessary infrastructure. If big data are the oil of the new economy, we must build the data equivalent of interstate highways."[58] Somewhat similarly, Mayer-Schönberger and Cukier recognize a more active role for government regulation to control what they call the "data barons": "We must prevent the rise of the twenty-first century robber barons who dominated America's railroads, steel manufacturing, and telegraph networks."[59] To that end, they advance the possibility of comparable measures to antitrust rules to curb abusive power and ensure the conditions for a competitive market for big data, including licensing, interoperability, and exclusion rights (similar to intellectual property rights). They also recognize that designing and implementing such a scheme "would be a tall order for policymakers."[60]

Some analysts of big data more tentatively recognize that big data has elements of an infrastructure and advocate more traditional regulatory approaches in the information privacy area, such as privacy impact assessments and privacy boards. PCAST suggests a policy solution reminiscent of previous "trusted third party" options, such as TRUSTe, which could establish and monitor privacy-preference profiles to which individuals would subscribe, and also review new data collection and use applications to determine how they fit within each of the profiles. This option is seen as correcting the problem that individuals cannot meaningfully read or discern the implications of privacy notices.[61] A somewhat similar organizational option would be data marketplaces or banks, trusted third-party holders of information, in which individuals could store their data and those who want to use that data could buy it from the bank.[62] Craig Mundie criticizes the FIPPs approach as well as the feasibility and effectiveness of data collection and retention limitations, suggesting instead that policies focus on use—and specifically a policy approach that incorporates features of "digital rights management" and relies on "digital wrappers" for data that relay the subject's restrictions and preferences for future uses of the data.[63] This would be reinforced with a system of regulation that included audits to make sure data were not misused.

Big Data as Public Good

Because individual assessments of risks become difficult as big data's externalities are not easily calculable by the individual, Katherine Strandburg suggests that "we should look to other areas in which the law has grappled with similar problems of unpredictability, probabilistic harms, and valuation difficulties . . . environmental regulation faces somewhat similar issues of balancing ephemeral broad-based values against the shorter-term benefits of private economic activity."[64] Similarly, the editors of *Privacy, Big Data, and the Public Good* suggest that "big data have many elements of a natural resource, and sensible rules must be developed in order to avoid a tragedy of the commons, and to create a commonly pooled resource for improving scientific understanding for the public good."[65]

In avoiding this tragedy of the commons, it is important to recognize that there are two values that need to be protected: the benefits to society that come from research and applications based on data and the benefits to society that come from privacy of those data. Some seem to place more emphasis on the research benefits. For example, as John Wilbanks explains, "If privacy concerns block the redistribution of data on which scientific and policy conclusions are based, then those conclusions will be difficult to justify to the public who must understand them. We must find a balance between our ability to make and produce identifiable data, the known failure rates of de-identification systems, and our need for policy and technology supported by 'good' data. If we cannot find this balance we risk a tragedy of the data commons in which the justification for social, scientific, and political actions are available only to a select few."[66]

How and by whom that balance is calibrated, as well as who monitors or oversees its implementation, is a critical policy decision. One such public goods approach, the "commons-based framework," has been developed for health data and is based on "the reuse of the information as a higher goal than the guarantee of privacy or the prevention of re-identification."[67] Such a framework was developed as part of the Personal Genome Project and then later adapted to a "portable" approach to informed consent in which individuals could give consent to a range of data researchers with some understanding of the risks involved and the responsibilities the users were obligated to provide.[68] In effect, these seem to comprise more sophisticated individual consent models with the caveat that the individual may withdraw consent at a later time, although whatever data have been revealed may still exist. It would seem that such commons-based frameworks would need to be sector based, which is somewhat difficult to implement given the flow of big data.

Also adopting a public goods perspective and recognizing that our data are worth more when shared, Greenwood and colleagues advocate a *New Deal on Data*, which describes workable guarantees that the data needed for public good are readily available while at the same time protecting the citizenry."[69] This New Deal, discussed in more detail in the previous chapter, requires both secure technology and regulation. Greenwood and colleagues suggest that the establishment of a "trust network" as a system of data sharing, "elegantly integrating computer and legal rules, allows automatic auditing of data use and allows individuals to change their permissions and withdraw data."[70] Under such a network, data would not remain under the exclusive control of siloed private sector companies nor would it be the exclusive domain of government.

Individual Empowerment

Some analysts of privacy and big data still cling to the hope that the individual can become the controller of his or her information. For example, Ira Rubinstein suggests big data and privacy policy "combine legal reform with the encouragement of new business models premised on consumer empowerment and supported by a personal data ecosystem." He sees this as "making the FIPPs efficacious" in the big data environment. Tene and Polonetsky adopt a similar approach seeking to rebalance the relationship between individuals and data holders by providing individuals access to their information in a machine-readable, usable format. They believe this will spark the growth of a new personal information ecosystem or market that will be friendlier to individuals and will "share the wealth" made possible by big data applications. Their scheme is derived in large part from the notion of "vendor relations management" (VRM) whereby the customer, rather than the business, sets the terms of how information is used in the marketplace.[71] Rubinstein and others see potential in such personal data services as a solution to privacy issues[72] but are cautious about the technical feasibility of tagging every unit of data or providing information on the digital rights of data, the intellectual coherence of this model as it relies on property conceptions of information privacy,[73] and the existence of business incentives.

CONCLUSION

Although each of the approaches discussed previously contains elements of an effective policy to protect privacy in the era of big data, the fundamental elements are independent institutional control to provide real accountability and simplicity to achieve trust. Controls that rely on the goodwill of organizations or appeal to organizations' market potential will not be effective. Self-regulation has no place in the complicated and highly technological environment of big data. Similarly complicated schemes will fail as they will be too difficult to implement given the scale of big data. The arena of big data and privacy requires government regulation, along the lines encompassed in the concept of a public trustee.

NOTES

1. Viktor Mayer-Schönberger and Kenneth Cukier, *Big Data: A Revolution That Will Transform How We Live, Work, and Think* (New York: Houghton Mifflin Harcourt, 2013).

2. Ibid., 73–97.

3. Jules Polonetsky and Omer Tene, "Privacy and Big Data: Making Ends Meet," *Stanford Law Review Online* 66 (September 3, 2013): 25–33.

4. Paul Ohm, "The Underwhelming Benefits of Big Data," *University of Pennsylvania Law Review* 161 (2013): 339.

5. Pew Research Center, *Public Perceptions of Privacy and Security in the Post-Snowden Era* (Washington, DC: Pew Research Center, November 2014), 31, http://www.pewinternet.org/files/2014/11/PI_PublicPerceptionsofPrivacy_111214.pdf.

6. Ibid., 13.

7. See, for example, Priscilla M. Regan, *Legislating Privacy: Technology, Social Values, and Public Policy* (Chapel Hill: University of North Carolina Press, 1995); Beate Rossler, *The Value of Privacy* (Cambridge: Polity, 2005); Julie E. Cohen, *Configuring the Networked Self: Law, Code, and the Play of Everyday Practice* (New Haven, CT: Yale University Press, 2012); Helen Nissenbaum, *Privacy in Context: Technology, Policy, and the Integrity of Social Life* (Stanford, CA: Stanford University Press, 2010); and Daniel J. Solove, *Understanding Privacy* (Cambridge, MA: Harvard University Press, 2008).

8. President's Council of Advisors on Science and Technology (PCAST), *Big Data and Privacy: A Technological Perspective* (Washington, DC: Executive Office of the President, PCAST, May 2014), 38, http://www.whitehouse.gov/sites/default/files/microsites/ostp/PCAST/pcast_big_data_and_privacy_-_may_2014.pdf.

9. Ira S. Rubinstein, "Big Data: The End of Privacy or a New Beginning?," *International Data Privacy Law* 3, no. 2 (2013): 74–87, http://idpl.oxfordjournals.org/content/early/2013/01/24/idpl.ips036.full.pdf+html.

10. Woodrow Hartzog and Evan Selinger, "Big Data in Small Hands," *Stanford Law Review Online* 66 (September 3, 2013): 81–88; and Woodrow Hartzog and Evan Selinger, "Obscurity: A Better Way to Think About Your Data Than Privacy," *The Atlantic*, January 17, 2013, http://www.theatlantic.com/technology/archive/2013/01/obscurity-a-better-way-to-think-about-your-data-than-privacy/267283/.

11. Omar Tene and Jules Polonetsky, "Big Data for All: Privacy and User Control in the Age of Analytics," *Northwestern Journal of Technology and Intellectual Property* 11, no. 5 (2013): 239–273, 258, http://scholarlycommons.law.northwestern.edu/cgi/viewcontent.cgi?article=1191&context=njtip.

12. Latanya Sweeney, "Uniqueness of Simple Demographics in the US Population" (Working Paper LIDAP-WP4, Laboratory for International Data Privacy, Carnegie Mellon University, Pittsburgh, PA, 2000), http://dataprivacylab.org/projects/identifiability/index.html.

13. Latanya Sweeney, Akua Abu, and Julia Winn, "Identifying Participants in the Personal Genome Project by Name" (White Paper 1021-1, Data Privacy Lab, Harvard University, Cambridge, MA, April 24, 2013), http://dataprivacylab.org/projects/pgp/1021-1.pdf.

14. Paul Ohm, "Broken Promises of Privacy: Responding to the Surprising Failure of Anonymization," *UCLA Law Review* 57 (2010): 1701–1777, 1704.

15. John Quackenbush, quoted in Jonathan Shaw, "Why 'Big Data' Is a Big Deal," *Harvard Magazine*, March–April 2014, 30–35, 74–75, 34, http://harvardmagazine.com/2014/03/why-big-data-is-a-big-deal.

16. Eli Pariser, *The Filter Bubble: How the New Personalized Web Is Changing What We Read and How We Think* (New York: Penguin, 2011).

17. Karen E. C. Levy, "Relational Big Data," *Stanford Law Review Online* 66 (September 3, 2013): 73–79.

18. Ian Kerr and Jessica Earle, "Prediction, Preemption, Presumption: How Big Data Threatens Big Picture Privacy," *Stanford Law Review Online* 66 (September 3, 2013): 65–72.

19. Tene and Polonetsky, "Big Data for All," 253.

20. Danielle Keats Citron and Frank Pasquale, "The Scored Society: Due Process for Automated Predictions," *Washington Law Review* 89 (2014): 101–133.

21. Paul Ohm, "General Principles for Data Use and Analysis," in *Privacy, Big Data, and the Public Good: Frameworks for Engagement*, ed. Julia Lane, Victoria Stodden, Stefan Bender, and Helen Nissenbaum (New York: Cambridge University Press, 2014), 96–111.

22. Cynthia Dwork and Deidre K. Mulligan, "It's Not Privacy, and It's Not Fair," *Stanford Law Review Online* 66 (September 3, 2013): 35–40.

23. Jonas Lerman, "Big Data and Its Exclusions," *Stanford Law Review Online* 66 (September 3, 2013): 55–63, 60.

24. Paul M. Schwartz, "Property, Privacy, and Personal Data," *Harvard Law Review* 117, no. 7 (2004): 2055–2128; and Julie E. Cohen, "Examined Lives: Informational Privacy and the Subject as Object," *Stanford Law Review* 52 (2000): 1373–1438.

25. For one way in which this question was framed, see William McGeveran, "Revisiting the 2000 Symposium in Light of Big Data," *Big Data and Privacy: Making Ends Meet* (workshop, Future of Privacy Forum and Stanford Center for Internet and Society, Stanford, CA, September 10, 2013), http://www.futureofprivacy.org/2013/03/24/september-event-on-big-data-and-privacy-making-ends-meet/.

26. Neil M. Richards and Jonathan H. King, "Three Paradoxes of Big Data," *Stanford Law Review Online* 66 (September 3, 2013): 41–46.

27. Secretary's Advisory Committee on Automated Personal Data Systems, U.S. Department of Health, Education and Welfare, *Records, Computers, and the Rights of Citizens* (Washington, DC: Government Printing Office, 1973).

28. Alessandro Acquisti, "The Economics and Behavioral Economics of Privacy," in *Privacy, Big Data, and the Public Good: Frameworks for Engagement*, ed. Julia Lane, Victoria Stodden, Stefan Bender, and Helen Nissenbaum (New York: Cambridge University Press, 2014), 87.

29. Rubinstein, "Big Data."

30. Katherine J. Strandburg, "Monitoring, Datafication, and Consent: Legal Approaches to Privacy in the Big Data Context," in *Privacy, Big Data, and the Public Good: Frameworks for Engagement*, ed. Julia Lane, Victoria Stodden, Stefan Bender, and Helen Nissenbaum (New York: Cambridge University Press, 2014), 31.

31. Paul Ohm, "Changing the Rules: General Principles for Data Use and Analysis," in *Privacy, Big Data, and the Public Good: Frameworks for Engagement*, ed. Julia Lane, Victoria Stodden, Stefan Bender, and Helen Nissenbaum (New York: Cambridge University Press, 2014), 100.

32. Executive Office of the President, *Big Data: Seizing Opportunities, Preserving Values* (Washington, DC: Executive Office of the President, May 2014), 61, http://www.whitehouse.gov/sites/default/files/docs/big_data_privacy_report_5.1.14_final_print.pdf.

33. PCAST, *Big Data and Privacy*, 38.

34. Justine Brown, "Rise of the Chief Privacy Officer," *Government Technology*, May 30, 2014, http://www.govtech.com/state/Rise-of-the-Chief-Privacy-Officer.html.

35. For background, see Federal Trade Commission, *Privacy Impact Assessments*, http://www.ftc.gov/site-information/privacy-policy/privacy-impact-assessments.

36. Priscilla M. Regan and Torin Monahan, "Fusion Center Accountability and Intergovernmental Information Sharing," *Publius* 44, no. 3 (2014): 475–498.

37. Priscilla M. Regan, "Federal Security Breach Notifications: Politics and Approaches," *Berkeley Technology and Law Journal* 24, no. 3 (2009): 1103–1132.

38. Peter Elias, "A European Perspective on Research and Big Data Analysis," in *Privacy, Big Data, and the Public Good: Frameworks for Engagement*, ed. Julia Lane, Victoria Stodden, Stefan Bender, and Helen Nissenbaum (New York: Cambridge University Press, 2014), 182.

39. Viktor Mayer-Schönberger, *Delete: The Virtue of Forgetting in the Digital Age* (Princeton, NJ: Princeton University Press, 2009).

40. World Economic Forum, *Unlocking the Value of Personal Data: From Collection to Usage* (February 2013), http://www.weforum.org/reports/unlocking-value-personal-data-collection-usage.

41. PCAST, *Big Data and Privacy*, 39.

42. Ibid., 40.

43. Sweeney, "Uniqueness of Simple Demographics in the US Population."

44. Michael Barbaro and Tom Zeller Jr., "A Face Is Exposed for AOL Searcher No. 44177749," *New York Times*, August 9, 2006, A1, http://www.nytimes.com/2006/08/09/technology/09iht-aol.2431152.html?pagewanted=all&_r=0.

45. Arvind Narayanan and Vitaly Shmatikov, "How to Break the Anonymity of the Netflix Prize Dataset," arXiv, October 16, 2006.

46. PCAST, Big Data and Privacy, 39.

47. Jon P. Daries, Justin Reich, Jim Waldo, Elise M. Young, Jonathan Whittinghill, Daniel Thomas Seaton, Andrew Dean Ho, and Isaac Chuang, "Privacy, Anonymity, and Big Data in the Social Sciences," ACM Queue 12, no. 7 (2014): 2, http://queue.acm.org/detail.cfm?id=2661641.

48. Cynthia Dwork, "Differential Privacy: A Cryptographic Approach to Private Data Analysis," in Privacy, Big Data, and the Public Good: Frameworks for Engagement, ed. Julia Lane, Victoria Stodden, Stefan Bender, and Helen Nissenbaum (New York: Cambridge University Press, 2014), 301.

49. John Wilbanks, "Portable Approaches to Informed Consent and Open Data," in Privacy, Big Data, and the Public Good: Frameworks for Engagement, ed. Julia Lane, Victoria Stodden, Stefan Bender, and Helen Nissenbaum (New York: Cambridge University Press, 2014), 239–240.

50. Alan F. Karr and Jerome P. Reiter, "Using Statistics to Protect Privacy," in Privacy, Big Data, and the Public Good: Frameworks for Engagement, ed. Julia Lane, Victoria Stodden, Stefan Bender, and Helen Nissenbaum (New York: Cambridge University Press, 2014), 276–279.

51. Executive Office of the President, Big Data.

52. Regan, Legislating Privacy, 212–243.

53. Elinor Ostrom, Governing the Commons: The Evolution of Institutions for Collective Action (Cambridge: Cambridge University Press, 1990).

54. Priscilla M. Regan, "Privacy as a Common Good," Information, Communication and Society 5, no. 3 (2002): 382–405, 400.

55. Alice Marwick and danah boyd, "Networked Privacy: How Teenagers Negotiate Context in Social Media," New Media and Society 16, no. 7 (2014): 1051–1067.

56. Solon Barocas and Helen Nissenbaum, "Big Data's End Run Around Anonymity and Consent," in Privacy, Big Data, and the Public Good: Frameworks for Engagement, ed. Julia Lane, Victoria Stodden, Stefan Bender, and Helen Nissenbaum (New York: Cambridge University Press, 2014), 61.

57. Steven E. Koomin and Michael J. Holland, "The Value of Big Data for Urban Science," in Privacy, Big Data, and the Public Good: Frameworks for Engagement, ed. Julia Lane, Victoria Stodden, Stefan Bender, and Helen Nissenbaum (New York: Cambridge University Press, 2014), 137.

58. Julia Lane, Victoria Stodden, Stefan Bender, and Helen Nissenbaum, Privacy, Big Data, and the Public Good: Frameworks for Engagement (New York: Cambridge University Press, 2014), 135.

59. Mayer-Schönberger and Cukier, Big Data, 183.

60. Ibid.

61. PCAST, Big Data and Privacy, 41.

62. Wilbanks, "Portable Approaches to Informed Consent and Open Data," 241–242.

63. "All electronic personal data would have to be placed within a 'wrapper' of metadata, or information that describes the data without necessarily revealing its content. That wrapper would describe the rules governing the use of the data it held. Any programs that wanted to use the data would have to get approval to 'unwrap' it first. Regulators would also impose a mandatory auditing requirement on all applications that used personal data, allowing authorities to follow and observe applications that collected personal information to make sure that no one misused it and to penalize those who did." Craig Mundie, "Privacy Pragmatism: Focus on Data Use, Not Data Collection," Foreign Affairs, March–April 2014, http://www.foreignaffairs.com/articles/140741/craig-mundie/privacy-pragmatism.

64. Strandburg, "Monitoring, Datafication, and Consent," 33.

65. Lane et al., *Privacy, Big Data, and the Public Good.*

66. Wilbanks, "Portable Approaches to Informed Consent and Open Data," 234.

67. Ibid., 244.

68. Ibid., 244–247.

69. Dazza Greenwood, Arkadiusz Stopczynski, Brian Sweatt, Thomas Hardjono, and Alex Pentland, "The New Deal on Data: A Framework for Institutional Controls," in *Privacy, Big Data, and the Public Good: Frameworks for Engagement*, ed. Julia Lane, Victoria Stodden, Stefan Bender, and Helen Nissenbaum (New York: Cambridge University Press, 2014), 194.

70. Ibid., 198.

71. Tene and Polonetsky, "Big Data for All," 266.

72. Rubinstein, "Big Data," 9–13.

73. See Schwartz, "Property, Privacy and Personal Data," 2055, arguing against a property-based theory of information privacy because it will exacerbate privacy market failures, it neglects important social values (information is a public good—privacy commons is at stake), and it invites free alienability of personal data. Schwartz advocates a hybrid model.

CHAPTER TEN

Reflections on Analytics

Knowledge and Power

Benjamin Ginsberg

IN THIS CHAPTER

We tend to assume that good data lead to better governance. But the efficient collection and improved analysis of data should not simply be seen as exercises in good government. Governments do not seek knowledge merely in order to provide better services to their citizens. The political philosopher Thomas Hobbes famously observed that the end or purpose of knowledge is power.[1] That is, both citizens and rulers require and seek knowledge about one another in order to exercise or resist the exercise of power. This Hobbesian observation becomes especially significant if we consider the role of knowledge in the context of popular government in an age of big data.

INTRODUCTION

Popular government requires that citizens possess a good deal of knowledge about the actions of the state. Knowledge is necessary to permit citizens to evaluate rulers' claims and to hold rulers accountable for their conduct. In essence, citizens must undertake their own surveillance of the government and its officials as a precondition for exerting influence over them. This idea is captured in the ancient Athenian practice of the audit (*euthyna*) in which all civil and military officials, including even priests and priestesses, were periodically required to undergo detailed public examinations of their actions.[2] The results might then be debated in the popular assembly (*ecclesia*) that was, of course, open to all male citizens who had performed the requisite period of military service. In this way, surveillance through the audit directly empowered the citizenry.

At the same time, citizens' ability to exercise power also requires that they have considerable protection from the state's scrutiny. In point of fact, privacy may be a prerequisite for effective popular political action. To begin with, those intent on expressing anything but support for the groups in power need privacy to plan, organize, and mobilize lest their plans be anticipated and disrupted. Terrorists are hardly the only ones who need privacy. Even in the mundane realm of partisan politics, the efforts of the party out of power can certainly be compromised if the government becomes privy to its plans. Recall that the Nixon administration thought its surveillance activities, including the work of the infamous "plumbers' squad," could help it to undermine Democratic campaign plans in 1972.

Known political dissidents, moreover, always face some risk of official reprisal. Accordingly, at least some citizens may refrain from acting upon their political beliefs for fear that they will draw attention to themselves and become targets for tax audits and other government efforts to find evidence of criminality, cupidity, or other misconduct that can be used against them. Privacy for political activities is, like the secret ballot, an important element of political freedom.

Indeed, this notion of the relationship between privacy and freedom of political expression is at the heart of the Constitution's Fourth Amendment, prohibiting unreasonable searches. While many currently see the Fourth Amendment as related to evidence in mundane criminal cases, the framers were well aware of the fact that government intrusions into private homes were often aimed at identifying papers, manuscripts, and books that might point to nascent efforts to foment political dissent.[3] Individuals whose private papers evinced dissenting political opinions might then be prosecuted for the crime of seditious libel, that is, criticism of Crown officials, to forestall any public expressions of their views. As Justice William Brennan wrote for a unanimous court in the 1961 case of *Marcus v. Search Warrant*, "The Bill of Rights was fashioned against the background of knowledge that unrestricted power of search and seizure could also be an instrument for stifling liberty of expression." In her dissent in a recent case, Justice Ruth Bader Ginsburg called attention to this original purpose and meaning of the Fourth Amendment as an instrument for protecting liberty of political expression.

Thus, popular government requires a combination of government transparency and citizen privacy. To exercise influence over the government, citizens must know what it is doing. At the same time, citizens seeking to exercise influence over the government need protection from retaliation and intimidation. Unfortunately, however, objective conditions in the United States today are far from these ideals. Today, indeed, the state keeps more and more of its activities secret while the citizenry has less and less privacy.

Government surveillance of communications, travel, and personal conduct has become a fact of American life. Revelations of extensive electronic surveillance by the National Security Agency (NSA) in the summer of 2013 caused considerable consternation in Congress and in the news media. Such surveillance, however, is not an entirely new phenomenon in the United States. As early as 1920, the Cipher Bureau, remembered today as the "Black Chamber," an office jointly funded by the Army and the State Department, and arising from a World War I program, secretly inspected telegrams in the Western Union system.

Today, Americans find themselves subject to more or less constant government surveillance via electronic interception of telephone calls, examination of e-mail communications and social media postings, to say nothing of ubiquitous security cameras now tied to crowd-scanning software, traffic monitoring, airport searches, and so forth. And, while Black Chamber staffers sifted through transcripted telegrams by hand, peering at their contents, today the work is done by computers and analytic methods that allow the government to process and analyze enormous quantities of data looking for possible indications of illicit activity among seemingly disparate bits of information.[4]

Some in Congress and in the media are concerned with citizens' privacy, as well as their own, while police and intelligence agencies aver that their surveillance activities are of critical importance in the nation's ongoing struggle against crime and, of course, terrorism. Testifying before Congress in 2013, NSA officials declared that the agency's eavesdropping program had averted dozens of possible terrorist attacks. Needless to say, since the matters were highly classified, no actual proof of these assertions was proffered, and many members of Congress, including Senate Intelligence Committee chairman Patrick Leahy of Vermont, expressed doubts about the agency's claims. Later the NSA conceded that its domestic surveillance programs had possibly thwarted only one terrorist plot, rather than the dozens initially claimed.[5]

Many Americans seem satisfied to believe that they are the beneficiaries rather than the potential victims of government surveillance. Those who have nothing to hide, goes the saying, have nothing to fear.[6] This view is, of course, rather naive. As law professor Daniel Solove shows, surveillance can entrap even the most innocent individuals in a web of suspicions and allegations from which they may find it extremely difficult to extricate themselves.[7] To couch the issue of government surveillance purely in terms of the conflict between security and privacy interests is to miss the larger question of political power in which this debate is embedded.

SURVEILLANCE: THE NSA

Between the 1930s and 1960s, domestic surveillance activities were mainly the province of the Federal Bureau of Investigation (FBI). During the 1960s, at the behest of President Richard Nixon, the Central Intelligence Agency (CIA) began to play a role in this realm. During the years that J. Edgar Hoover was expanding the FBI's surveillance activities and the CIA was being asked to target domestic groups, another federal agency was developing a capacity to monitor Americans through their communications. This was the National Security Agency (NSA) created by President Harry Truman in 1952 and assigned primary responsibility for American signals intelligence. Eventually, NSA capabilities would dwarf those of the FBI and CIA.

Over the years, the NSA developed a variety of systems designed to intercept satellite-based communications throughout the world. One of these systems, code named ECHELON, was deployed by the NSA in cooperation with several American allies, including the United Kingdom, Canada, New Zealand, and Australia, though the American role was primary. By the 1990s, through ground-based listening stations and its own satellites, the NSA had the potential to intercept much of the world's telephone and fax traffic.[8] In the late 1990s, however, the communications industry's shift from satellites to buried fiber-optic cables rendered ECHELON's systems obsolete. In cooperation with industry scientists, the NSA was able to develop mechanisms for intercepting and reading communications sent through fiber-optic systems. These devices were called "PacketScopes," and they allowed the NSA to tap into fiber-optic networks and record the contents of messages, including e-mails, which could then be stored and analyzed. By 2001, the NSA had secured the cooperation of much of the telecommunications industry for the installation of its PacketScopes and had the capacity to intercept and examine all the data flowing through their worldwide systems.

THE CHURCH COMMITTEE AND FISA

In 1974, in the aftermath of the Watergate affair, the various surveillance activities conducted by the FBI, CIA, NSA, and other federal agencies came under scrutiny by a number of congressional committees. Perhaps the most important of these was the Senate's Select Committee to Study Governmental Operations with Respect to Intelligence Activities, chaired by the late senator Frank Church of Idaho. In its report, the committee found that numerous individuals had been subjected to surveillance and subsequent action based solely on their political beliefs. As the report stated, "Too many people have been spied upon by too many government agencies and too much information has been collected. The government has often undertaken the secret surveillance of citizens on the basis of their political beliefs even when those beliefs posed no threat of violence or illegal acts on behalf of a hostile or foreign power."[9] Senator Church added:

> The [NSA's] capability at any time could be turned around on the American people, and no American would have any privacy left, such is the capability to monitor everything: telephone conversations, telegrams, it doesn't matter. There would be no place to hide. [If a dictator ever took over, the NSA] could enable it to impose total tyranny, and there would be no way to fight back.[10]

It is worth noting that when Senator Church expressed these fears in 1975, the NSA could read telegrams and listen to phone calls. Along with other security agencies, it might also open mail but, in practice, only a tiny fraction of the hundreds of millions of letters sent each year could be examined. Thus, Church's remarks embodied a bit of exaggeration at the time. The advent of e-mail and social media, however, greatly enhanced the volume of information available to federal agencies and made the senator's comments more prescient.

In response to the findings of the Church Committee and other congressional inquiries, Congress in 1978 enacted the Foreign Intelligence Surveillance Act (FISA) designed to place limits on electronic surveillance by government agencies. Of course, these selfsame agencies, as well as successive presidents, had ignored or circumvented previous legal restrictions on electronic surveillance, such as those embodied in the 1968 crime control act. Nevertheless, members of Congress hoped that by mandating stricter judicial supervision and stiff penalties for violators, government surveillance of American citizens might be curtailed and controlled.

FISA stipulated that in order to undertake electronic surveillance of Americans, the government would be required to apply for a warrant from a special court created by the statute. This was called the Foreign Intelligence Surveillance Court (FISA Court) and initially consisted of seven federal district court judges appointed for seven-year terms by the chief justice of the U.S. Supreme Court. In 2001, the FISA Court was expanded to 11 judges. A second court created by the act, the Court of Review, consisted of a three-judge panel empowered to hear appeals by the government resulting from negative decisions by the FISA Court. In practice, the Court of Review has been relatively quiescent since the government has had reason to appeal only a handful of the FISA Court's decisions. Both the FISA Court and the Court of Review deliberate in secret and the content of their decisions is not made public.

FISA also stipulated that the court would issue a warrant only if it found probable cause to believe that the target of the surveillance was acting in concert with a foreign power or agent. The 1978 act defined a foreign power as a nation-state, but this was subsequently amended to include non-state actors such as terrorist groups. The act also allowed the president to authorize warrantless surveillance within the United States if the attorney general certified to the FISA Court that the target was a foreign intelligence agent, and there was little chance that the privacy of any American citizen would be violated.

The effectiveness of the FISA process has been debated. On the one hand, between 1979 and 2012, only 11 of the nearly 34,000 requests for warrants made by government agencies, primarily the NSA and FBI, were turned down by the FISA Court.[11] This datum might suggest that the court was lax in its procedures. However, it may be that the FISA process forced the government to exercise at least some measure of caution in its surveillance activities, knowing that requests would need to withstand judicial scrutiny. Support for this latter view might be derived from the fact that in the aftermath of the 9/11 terror attacks, in its determination to expand electronic data collection, the Bush administration deemed it necessary to ignore the FISA process and launch a large-scale program of warrantless wiretapping.

What would later be called the President's Surveillance Program (PSP), launched in 2001, involved warrantless monitoring of virtually all telephone calls and e-mail messages between the United States and foreign countries. As in previous major surveillance efforts, the NSA, in collaboration with several other federal agencies, was able to secure secret cooperation from the major telecommunications companies for this purpose. The result was that millions of telephone and e-mail conversations were monitored. In some instances, voice intercept operators actually listened to the calls. More often, the information was stored and subjected to keyword searches, but, with the advent of the Defense Advanced Research Projects Agency (DARPA) Total Information Awareness program in 2002, the NSA began analyzing intercepted communications in conjunction with other data such as credit card usage, social network posts, traffic camera photos, and even medical records to search for suspicious patterns of activity.

Information not available electronically could be obtained by the FBI which, via secret national security letters (NSLs) authorized by the 2001 Patriot Act, has compelled a variety of institutions ranging from universities to gambling casinos to turn over student or customer information without informing the subject. Congress ended DARPA funding for the Total Information Awareness program in 2004, but by then the methodology had become well developed. In addition, tens of thousands of NSLs have been issued annually since 2001 providing data that, particularly in conjunction with communications intercepts, allow federal authorities to learn an enormous amount about the activities of any individual or group.

In response to *New York Times* articles published in 2005 revealing the existence of the PSP, several members of Congress expressed outrage at what they saw as violations of FISA and vowed to fully investigate the matter. The Bush administration, however, was able to convince Congress that its actions had been necessary if not entirely legal means of thwarting terrorism. After some deliberation, Congress enacted the Protect America Act of 2007, which amended FISA to loosen restrictions on electronic surveillance and, in effect, retroactively codified the legally questionable actions of previous years.[12] Thus, under the amended act, the government was empowered to intercept communications that began or ended outside the United States without any supervision by the FISA Court. Moreover, telecommunications companies, whose cooperation had previously been voluntary, were directed to lend assistance to federal agencies engaged in electronic surveillance if ordered to do so by the government, and were immunized against any civil suits that might arise from providing such assistance.

The 2007 act contained a sunset provision requiring Congress to reconsider the surveillance issue in 2008. The resulting FISA Amendments Act of 2008 was similar to the 2007 act but did place restrictions on the power of the NSA and other intelligence agencies to target Americans. At President Barack Obama's behest, the act was renewed in 2012 for another five years. Between 2008 and 2013, the government insisted that it was not engaged in spying on Americans either at home or abroad. In March 2013, for example, James Clapper, the director of national intelligence, testifying before the Senate, indignantly denied reports that the government was collecting data on millions of Americans. Similarly, NSA director General Keith Alexander denied charges by a former NSA official that the agency was secretly obtaining warrantless access to billions of records of Americans' phone calls and storing the information in its data centers. General Alexander piously declared that doing such a thing would be against the law.[13]

In June 2013, however, an NSA contractor named Edward Snowden leaked classified documents describing the NSA's theretofore top secret PRISM surveillance program, which had operated since 2007. Snowden's disclosures were published in the *Guardian* and the *Washington Post* and revealed that, through PRISM and several other programs, the NSA had been collecting data on its own as well as collaborating with virtually all major telecommunications companies to intercept, examine, and store the electronic communications of millions of Americans These included e-mail, social network posts, Internet searches, and even local telephone calls. In essence, the NSA appeared to have the capacity to monitor all forms of electronic communication.

While the NSA's goal is said to be monitoring communications between the United States and foreign countries, officials acknowledge that some purely domestic communications have been accidentally accessed but said they did not keep records of the number. Communications among Americans nominally cannot be viewed without a warrant from the FISA Court, but, in practice, this rule is frequently violated said one official who did not wish to be named. The NSA essentially is responsible for policing itself; according to one telecommunications executive formerly involved in the NSA program, whatever the nominal legal restrictions, "There's technically and physically nothing preventing a much broader surveillance."[14] A lawsuit that brought about the declassification in 2013 of a 2011 FISA Court opinion revealed that the NSA had been accessing as many as 56,000 "wholly domestic" communications each year without warrants. In an angry opinion, the then chief judge of the FISA Court, Judge John D. Bates, wrote, "For the first time, the government has now advised the court that the volume and nature of the information it has been collecting is fundamentally different from what the court had been led to believe."[15]

In an August 2013 speech, President Obama addressed public concerns about the government's surveillance programs. The president pointed to the importance of interdicting terrorist attacks, declared himself to be confident that Americans' rights had not been abused, and said he hoped ways could be found to make the public more "comfortable" with government surveillance activities. Unfortunately, given the history of government surveillance, there is little reason for Americans to feel a sense of comfort. Using methods that seem so primitive today, J. Edgar Hoover's FBI collected information that made and broke political careers, disrupted dissident groups, and interfered with ordinary partisan politics. And much of what Hoover did was undertaken at the behest of the various presidents whom he served. From Franklin Roosevelt to Richard Nixon, presidents could not resist the chance to collect information to be used against their political foes as well as dissident political forces.

Should we believe that no possible future president would be willing to use today's surveillance capabilities against his or her opponents? To believe this idea is comparable to believing in Santa Claus and the Easter Bunny. The framers of the Constitution certainly understood this point. James Madison wrote, "If angels were to govern men neither external nor internal controls on government would be necessary. In framing a government which is to be administered by men over men . . . experience has taught mankind the necessity of auxiliary precautions."[16]

And, as to the terrorist threat against which massive electronic surveillance is nominally directed, one former federal prosecutor commented that, "upon scrutiny," traditional surveillance of particular phone numbers or e-mail addresses for which warrants could easily have been obtained was a far more important tool than massive data collection programs.[17] It appears that security, alone, may not require surrendering citizens' privacy and power to Big Brother.

SECRECY

Popular government requires a measure of government transparency as well as citizen privacy. Yet every government seeks to shield various actions from public view. In many instances, the major instrument used for this purpose is official censorship. In the United States, however, the First Amendment has made it difficult for the government to restrict press coverage except in wartime. Thus, while the courts did not interfere with official censorship during World War I or with the actions of the Office of Censorship during World War II, most government efforts to block press reports of sensitive material have been struck down on constitutional grounds. In the 1971 *Pentagon Papers* case, for example, the Supreme Court refused to condone the government's efforts to block publication of classified information leaked by a whistle-blower.[18] Of course, in a small number of other cases such as those involving former CIA agents Victor Marchetti and Frank W. Snepp, the judiciary did grant government requests to suppress publication of at least some facts the authors wished to disclose.[19]

The U.S. government does not have much power to censor press publication of material that comes into reporters' or publishers' possession. It lacks the equivalent of Britain's Official Secrets Act allowing prior restraint of publications. However, an enormous quantity of allegedly sensitive information is classified so that anyone who makes it public or reveals it to the media is subject to criminal penalties. This is little more than censorship by another name.

Governmental secrecy in the United States takes two main forms. These are the official classification system and delay and obfuscation. The official classification system was established by presidential order and nominally designed to protect national security information. The classification system creates three "classes" of sensitive information. These are confidential, secret, and top secret, each governed by its own set of rules. Once information is classified, it can be viewed only by those with the requisite level of security clearance. Access to information classified as top secret, defined as potentially causing "grave damage" to the United States, is limited to a small number of individuals and then on a need-to-know basis. That is, even those with top secret security clearances are only allowed access to top secret information relevant to their own work. Information is classified as secret when its disclosure might threaten "serious damage" to the United States, and information is classified as confidential when its disclosure might threaten "damage" to the United States.

A number of federal defense and security agencies are authorized, by presidential order, to classify information. Within those agencies, several thousand officials are designated "original classifiers" with the authority to classify material. The number of individuals possessing such authority is linked to the level of classification. Reportedly, only several hundred officials, including the president and vice president, can order a top secret classification. Perhaps as many as 2,500 are authorized to order lower levels of classification.[20] Information is usually classified for a specified period of time, usually 10, 25, or 50 years depending on its sensitivity, and then subject to declassification or a downgrade of its classification.

In addition to the formal secrecy system, information that one or another agency does not wish to release is shielded by the general opacity of government bureaucracies, which have many procedures designed to impede public scrutiny of their actions. Indeed, in recent years, several federal agencies have, without any statutory or presidential authorization, adopted their own classification schemes, labeling information "sensitive but unclassified," or "sensitive security information," or "critical program information," and restricting access to it.

The Classification System

The beginnings of formal document classification in the United States can be traced to an 1857 law concerning the management of American diplomatic and consular offices in which the president is authorized to "prescribe such regulations, and make and issue such orders and instructions ... in relation to ... the communication of information ... as he may think conducive to the public interest."[21] The current classification system dates from 1940 when President Roosevelt issued Executive Order 8381 declaring that the existing tripartite classification system would apply to all military and naval documents. Roosevelt cited national defense as the justification for protecting information and, for the most part, only the Army and Navy departments were given authority to classify information. Subsequent presidents have issued their own executive orders refining and expanding the classification system. The most sweeping change was instituted by President Truman who in place of the term "national defense" declared that the broader concept of "national security" was the underlying justification for the classification system. Upon taking office in 2009, President Obama asserted his support for government transparency but issued executive orders instituting only one major change in classification policy. Obama established the National Declassification Center (NDC) within the National Archives to speed the declassification of older documents deemed to be of historic interest but posing no security risks.

The precise number of documents currently classified by federal agencies is not known. It is clear, however, that the number is enormous. During each of the past several decades alone, some 200,000 documents per year, totaling tens of billions of pages, have been newly classified by various federal agencies.[22] Since 2009, pursuant to Obama's executive order, the NDC has hastened the declassification of several million pages of older documents.[23] During the same period, though, tens of millions of pages of new documents were classified. Several agencies, particularly the CIA, have resisted declassification of documents and have, indeed, sought to reclassify documents that had already been declassified.

Leaked Information

Of course, there are legitimate and proper reasons for classifying information. America's security is threatened by foreign foes, terrorists, and even criminal enterprises. However, much that is declared secret or even top secret seems to pose less of a threat to the nation's security than to the security of various politicians and bureaucrats. This is one of the lessons of the various leaks of information that have so troubled official Washington in recent years.

Take, for example, the top secret Pentagon Papers, whose release was labeled by President Nixon's national security advisor, General Alexander Haig, as "a devastating security breach of the greatest magnitude."[24] Published in 1971, the documents leaked by Daniel Ellsberg represented a history of America's involvement in Vietnam from 1945 to 1967. The history and supporting documents had been developed by a Defense Department study group created by Secretary of Defense Robert McNamara and tasked with writing a detailed history of the Vietnam War. Ellsberg had briefly worked as a staffer for the study and was able to photocopy most of the information contained in the study's 47 volumes.

The Pentagon Papers provided a fascinating look at an important episode in American history, but all their information was historical and the only secrets they revealed concerned lies, evasions, and cover-ups by successive presidents and other government officials. Former solicitor general Erwin Griswold argued before the Supreme Court in 1971 that publication of the papers would cause great and irreparable harm to the nation's security. Writing in the *Washington Post* some 15 years later, Griswold conceded, "I have never seen any trace of a threat to the national security from the publication."[25] One might say that the threat was to the reputations of political leaders and the credibility of the government, not the security of the nation.

For another example, take the WikiLeaks case. In 2010, a U.S. Army private named Bradley Manning downloaded more than 700,000 classified documents from military servers and sent them to WikiLeaks, which shared the documents with a number of newspapers.[26] Some of the leaked documents arguably deserve to be classified if only to protect American intelligence sources. Others seem to have been classified to hide evidence of wrongdoing by the United States and its allies or to avoid embarrassing one or another government entity. As in the case of the Pentagon Papers, many documents were classified less to protect the nation's security than to prevent the public from glimpsing the truth behind official facades. Perhaps the American people might have benefited from knowing some of these facts.

Support for an unflattering view of the classification program can also be gleaned from the ongoing tug-of-war over the declassification of documents. In 2005, for example, the CIA reclassified a dozen documents that had been declassified and were publicly available in the National Archives. For the most part, these documents reveal foolish agency projects or missteps sometimes going back a half century. One document detailed an abortive CIA effort to drop propaganda leaflets into Eastern Europe by hot-air balloon. Other documents described the intelligence community's faulty analysis of the Soviet nuclear weapons program in 1949. Still another document shows that the CIA was terribly wrong in its analysis of whether or not China would intervene in the Korean War in the fall of 1950.[27] Why were these now-ancient documents reclassified? Perhaps because they caused the agency some embarrassment and this, sometimes more than national security, is deemed by the government to be an adequate reason to keep information from the public.

Congressional Access to Information

The Constitution assigns Congress the power to make the law. Presidents, however, have sought to limit congressional access to information. To begin with, every president since Franklin Roosevelt has taken the position that the presidentially established system of security classification applies to members of Congress and their staffs as well as to the general public. In the Intelligence Oversight Act of 1980, however, Congress explicitly required the president to keep congressional intelligence committees fully and currently informed of all intelligence activities. The act also requires the director of national intelligence to provide any information required by these committees "consistent with the protection of sources and methods." Congress has taken this phrase to mean that classified information will be given only to members of the intelligence committees and that staff members of those committees must possess requisite security clearances to receive classified information.[28]

Since 1980, intelligence agencies have briefed congressional committees on many of their undertakings. There is, however, reason to be concerned about the accuracy of the information given to Congress. For example, in March 2013, while testifying before the Senate Intelligence Committee, James Clapper, the director of national intelligence, responded to a question by saying that the NSA was not "wittingly" collecting information on millions of Americans. Subsequent revelations showed that Clapper's testimony was disingenuous. Leaving aside the question of veracity, some members of Congress have complained that intelligence briefings are usually filled with jargon and designed to be confusing. Because of security restrictions, moreover, members are usually barred from consulting expert advisors who might challenge or at least more fully explain the programs being discussed. And, by failing to disclose significant information in the first place, intelligence agencies make it difficult for members of Congress to ask questions or request briefings. President Obama, for example, averred that any member of Congress could have asked for a briefing on the PRISM program. This claim, however, seems a bit dubious. "How can you ask when you don't know the program exists?" asked Senator Susan Collins of Maine, speaking on National Public Radio.[29]

Executive Privilege

On a number of occasions, presidents have explicitly refused to provide Congress with documents requested by lawmakers. In some instances, there may be valid reasons for this refusal, but in most cases the aim seems to be to hide evidence of foolish or illegal activity. When refusing, presidents generally claim "executive privilege." A related claim, used when the executive refuses to turn over documents to the courts, is called the "state secrets privilege," and was recently cited by the Obama administration in seeking to block a suit involving the targeted killing of a U.S. citizen suspected of terrorist activities in Yemen.[30]

Delay and Obfuscation

Though hundreds of thousands of pieces of information are classified every year, this represents only a tiny fraction of the information generated by federal agencies. The fact, however, that most information is not classified does not mean that it is made available to the public or even to the Congress. Most secrets are easily kept by federal agencies because they are hidden in an ocean of information and no outsider even knows of their presence. Occasionally, however, a whistle-blower, a clever reporter, or sheer accident will offer a glimpse of the existence of knowledge the agency would prefer to hide. If this happens, agencies will almost invariably seek to avoid fuller disclosure of information that does not present their actions in the most positive light and will vigorously resist efforts by the media or the Congress to pry loose their secrets, which sometimes turn out to include fraud, waste, abuse, illegal conduct, and poorly conceived plans. Whistle-blowers, nominally protected by law, are almost certain to face agency retaliation to serve as a warning to others.[31] There are many recent examples of agency efforts to hide embarrassing secrets.

In 2009, for example, agency whistle-blowers revealed that the Arizona field office of the U.S. Bureau of Alcohol, Tobacco, Firearms and Explosives (ATF) had managed a poorly conceived "sting" operation code named Fast and Furious that allowed licensed firearms dealers in the United States to sell weapons to illegal buyers. The ATF apparently planned to trace the weapons back to Mexican drug cartel leaders. Unfortunately, most of the some 2,000 weapons involved in the case were not recovered though several were linked to subsequent crimes and murders, including the killing of a U.S. Border Patrol agent. In response to the revelations, ATF officials refused to provide documents pertaining to the operation and, instead, sought to retaliate against the agents who revealed its existence. Similarly, in 2013, the Environmental Protection Agency (EPA) granted one gasoline refinery (out of hundreds in the nation) an exception to the rule requiring a certain amount of ethanol to be blended into gasoline. This exception is worth millions to the refinery and, after it was noted by a *Wall Street Journal* reporter, the agency refused to explain why it had been granted. Some in Congress and the media suggested that perhaps some political motivation had been involved. Also in 2013, when conservative groups voiced suspicions that they had been subjected to extra scrutiny by the Internal Revenue Service (IRS), the agency refused to provide relevant documents.

Two of the main tools that can be used to force government agencies to make documents public are the congressional subpoena power and a public request under the Freedom of Information Act. As to the first of these tools, congressional committees have the power to order federal officials to produce desired documents. An official who refuses may be cited for contempt of Congress, which may, in principle, result in a prison term. Generally speaking, though, efforts by congressional committees to secure information from the executive do not reach the point of confrontation produced by the Fast and Furious case. Typically, agencies go through the motions of cooperating with Congress while delaying, providing only limited responses to congressional demands, and hiding facts that would enable Congress to focus on or even learn of the existence of the most pertinent pieces of information. As one critic noted, an agency may provide tens of thousands of pieces of information, assert that it has complied with congressional demands, and fail to find other pieces of information or, in the event that Congress learns of their existence, take the position that these were not covered by the subpoena.[32]

Similar problems can blunt the impact of a second tool of governmental transparency, the Freedom of Information Act (FOIA), enacted in 1966 as a mechanism for reducing agency discretion to withhold records from the public. With the advent of FOIA, agencies could no longer arbitrarily declare that a release of documents would not be in the public interest, as had been their typical practice. FOIA requires that all federal agencies must make their records available to any person upon request within 20 days unless the documents fall within one or more of nine exemptions, which include classified documents, trade secrets, sensitive law enforcement records, and personal or medical records. If a requested document contains some information that falls under one of the exemptions, FOIA requires that the non-exempt portions of the record must still be released with an indication of the location of the deleted portion of the document. Requestors who believe that their FOIA requests have been improperly denied may ask a federal court to order the relevant agency to comply.

Federal agencies, however, have learned to undercut FOIA in a variety of ways. To begin with, FOIA requires that only documents that qualify as "agency records" can be requested. Agencies tend to construe the term "records" narrowly and take the position that records of meetings that took place somewhere other than agency property are not agency records, that e-mails sent via officials' personal e-mail accounts are not agency records, and that records maintained by non-agency personnel are not agency records. Agencies, moreover, may delay responding to requests; delete much of the requested information; provide information in dribs and drabs, necessitating multiple FOIA requests; assert that the requested information does not exist or cannot be found; and so forth. FOIA also exempts those records that are "necessarily withheld to encourage the deliberative process." In other words, records of deliberations leading to a final decision do not have to be produced in response to a FOIA request. Agencies are inclined to classify their most important records as "deliberative" and to refuse access to them.

After taking office in 2009, President Obama promised a more transparent government. In an experiment, however, *Bloomberg News* sent rather mundane FOIA requests to 57 federal agencies. The requests asked for a list of trips taken by agency heads and a breakdown of their travel expenses. Twenty-seven agencies ignored the requests altogether, and only eight complied within the 20-day period specified by the FOIA statute.[33] Reporters or individuals seeking more sensitive information than travel schedules typically find that turning on the FOIA spigot will produce a few droplets from the vast and ever-growing federal sea of information.

Information and Popular Government

Without information, popular government is an impossibility. Citizens would have little choice but to believe what they were told, and the unfortunate fact of the matter is that politicians and public officials tend to be practiced liars, viewing what is useful or convenient as far more important than the truth. "I have previously stated and I repeat now that the United States plans no military intervention in Cuba," said President John F. Kennedy in 1961 as he planned military action in Cuba. "As president, it is my duty to the American people to report that renewed hostile actions against United States ships on the high seas in the Gulf of Tonkin have today required me to order the military forces of the United States to take action in reply," said President Lyndon Johnson in 1964 as he fabricated an incident to justify expansion of American involvement in Vietnam. "We did not, I repeat, did not, trade weapons or anything else [to Iran] for hostages, nor will we," said President Ronald Reagan in November 1986, four months before admitting that U.S. arms had been traded to Iran in exchange for Americans being held hostage there. "Simply stated, there is no doubt that Saddam Hussein now has weapons of mass destruction," said Vice President Dick Cheney in 2002. When it turned out that these weapons did not exist, Assistant Defense Secretary Paul Wolfowitz explained, "For bureaucratic reasons, we settled on one issue, weapons of mass destruction (as justification for invading Iraq) because it was the one reason everyone could agree on." After leaks showed that his 2013 congressional testimony denying the existence of the NSA's surveillance program was false, Director of National Intelligence James Clapper declared, "I responded in what I thought was the most truthful or least untruthful manner by saying, 'No.' "

The Athenians subjected their officials to the *euthyna* because, without a public audit of their actions in office, how would anyone know whether they deserved praise or censure? Surely officials could not be trusted to judge their own performance and give an accurate account of their activities. This seems quite reasonable, but the government of the United States, while practicing secrecy and concealment, exhorts its citizens to show trust.

SURVEILLANCE, SECRECY, AND POPULAR GOVERNMENT

Popular government requires transparency on the part of the government and privacy for the citizenry. Citizens can hardly exercise influence over a government whose actions are hidden from them. And, as the authors of the Fourth Amendment knew, citizens are inhibited from criticizing or working against officials who monitor their political activities. Unfortunately, the government of the United States has reversed this democratic formula of governance in favor of secrecy for itself and transparency for its citizens. How appropriate that the government currently views as the worst of all possible traitors an individual whose actions had the effect of exposing this new formula of governance in action. By revealing the government's secret program of surveillance, Edward Snowden's leaks to the media illustrated the manner in which secrecy and surveillance, two of the chief antitheses of popular government, are closely intertwined in the current American state. Even, or perhaps especially in the age of analytics, the purpose of knowledge is power.

NOTES

1. Jean Hampton, *Hobbes and the Social Contract Tradition* (New York: Cambridge University Press, 1988), 46. Hampton indicates that this quote is "after Bacon" whom Hobbes served as a secretary.
2. Matthew Dillon and Lynda Garland, eds., *Ancient Greece: Social and Historical Documents from Archaic Times to the Death of Alexander* (New York: Routledge, 2010), 18.
3. Thomas P. Crocker, "The Political Fourth Amendment," *Washington University Law Review* 88, no. 2 (2010): 303–379, 347.

4. James Bamford, "They Know Much More Than You Think," *New York Review* of Books, August 15, 2013, 4–8.

5. Ellen Nakashima, "Skepticism Deepens About NSA Program," *Washington Post*, August 1, 2013, 1.

6. Daniel J. Solove, *Nothing to Hide: The False Tradeoff Between Privacy and Security* (New Haven, CT: Yale University Press, 2011).

7. Ibid.

8. James Bamford, *The Shadow Factory* (New York: Anchor, 2009).

9. Quoted in Solove, *Nothing to Hide*, 10.

10. James Bamford, "The Agency That Could Be Big Brother," *New York Times*, December 25, 2005, http://www.nytimes.com/2005/12/25/weekinreview/25bamford.html?pagewanted=all&_r=0.

11. Electronic Privacy Information Center, "Foreign Intelligence Surveillance Act Court Orders 1979–2012," http://epic.org/privacy/wiretap/stats/fisa_stats.html.

12. Bamford, "They Know Much More Than You Think," 4.

13. Ibid.

14. Siobhan Gorman and Jennifer Valentino DeVries, "HSA Reaches Deep into U.S. to Spy on Net: Fresh Details Show Programs Cover 75% of Nation's Traffic, Can Snare Emails," *Wall Street Journal*, August 21, 2013, A8.

15. Ellen Nakashima, "NSA Collected Thousands of Domestic E-mails," *Washington Post*, August 22, 2013, 1.

16. James Madison, *The Federalist*, No. 51.

17. Bamford, "They Know Much More Than You Think," 6.

18. *New York Times v. United States*, 403 U.S. 713 (1971).

19. Gabriel Schoenfeld, *Necessary Secrets: National Security, the Media and the Rule of Law* (New York: Norton, 2010), chap. 10.

20. Kenneth Jost, "Government Secrecy," *CQ Researcher*, December 2, 2005, 1009.

21. 11 Stat. 60 (1857).

22. OpenTheGovernment.org, *2011 Secrecy Report* (Washington, DC: OpenTheGovernment.org, 2012).

23. National Archives and Records Administration, *Bi-annual Report on Operations of the National Declassification Center* (Washington, DC: National Archives and Records Administration, July 1, 2012–December 31, 2012), http://www.archives.gov/declassification/ndc/reports/2012-biannual-july-december.pdf.

24. Schoenfeld, *Necessary Secrets*, 175.

25. Ibid., 185.

26. Peter Walker, "Bradley Manning Trial: What We Know from the Leaked WikiLeaks Documents," *The Guardian*, July 30, 2013, http://www.theguardian.com/world/2013/jul/30/bradley-manning-wikileaks-revelations.

27. Matthew M. Aid, "Declassification in Reverse," National Security Archive, George Washington University, Washington, DC, February 21, 2006.

28. Kate Martin, *Congressional Access to Classified National Security Information* (Washington, DC: Center for National Security Studies, March 2007).

29. Dan Nosowitz, "Congress Was Not Really Briefed on PRISM," *Popular Science*, June 12, 2013, http://www.popsci.com/technology/article/2013-06/obama-said-all-congress-was-briefed-prism-nonsense.

30. Ryan Devereaux, "Is Obama's Use of State Secrets Privilege the New Normal?," *The Nation*, September 2010, http://www.thenation.com/article/155080/obamas-use-state-secrets-privilege-new-normal#axzz2cWH5ZitX.

31. Dana Milbank, "The Price of Whistleblowing," *Washington Post*, August 21, 2013, A17.

32. Christopher C. Horner, *The Liberal War on Transparency: Confessions of a Freedom of Information Criminal* (New York: Threshold, 2012).

33. *Bloomberg News*, "Testing Obama's Promise of Government Transparency," September 27, 2012, http://go.bloomberg.com/multimedia/bloomberg-checks-obama-transparency/.

Contributors

Jennifer Bachner is Director of the Master of Science in Government Analytics at Johns Hopkins University. She is the author of *What Washington Gets Wrong* (with Benjamin Ginsberg; Prometheus) and *Predictive Policing: Preventing Crime with Data and Analytics* (IBM Center for the Business of Government). She holds a Ph.D. from Harvard University, Department of Government.

Kenneth Benoit is Professor of Quantitative Social Research Methods in the Department of Methodology at the London School of Economics and Political Science. He received his Ph.D. from Harvard University, Department of Government. His current research focuses on computerized and statistical methods for analyzing text as data, mainly political texts and social media, on small and large scales. His other methodological interests include general statistical methods for the social sciences, especially those relating to measurement.

Joshua D. Clinton is Abby and Jon Winkelried Chair and Professor of Political Science at Vanderbilt University, where he studies political processes and outcomes using statistical methods. He has won several awards for his scholarship and published multiple articles in the *American Political Science Review*, *American Journal of Political Science*, and *Journal of Politics*, among others. He is also editor in chief of the *Quarterly Journal of Political Science*.

Lee Drutman is a senior fellow in the program on political reform at New America. He is the author of *The Business of America Is Lobbying* (Oxford University Press). He teaches in the Center for Advanced Governmental Studies at Johns Hopkins University. Drutman was also a senior fellow at the Sunlight Foundation. He has also worked in the U.S. Senate and at the Brookings Institution. He holds a Ph.D. in political science from the University of California, Berkeley, and a B.A. from Brown University.

Alex C. Engler is a statistician at the Urban Institute, where he specializes in data visualization and big data analytics. He is also an adjunct professor in the Master of Science in Government Analytics program at Johns Hopkins University, where he teaches data visualization and data science as they relate to public policy. Previously, he has worked in data and policy at the Sunlight Foundation and the Congressional Research Service, and in local education policy in Washington, DC. He graduated from American University with a B.A. in economics before earning a Master of Public Policy at Georgetown University.

Justin Esarey is Assistant Professor of Political Science at Rice University. His scholarly work has been published in the *American Journal of Political Science, Journal of Politics, Political Analysis*, and other outlets. He is currently the editor of *The Political Methodologist*.

Alexander Furnas is a Ph.D. student in political science at the University of Michigan. His work applies network methods to the study of interest group representation and lobbying. He holds an M.Sc. in the social science of the Internet from the University of Oxford, and he spent several years as a research fellow at the Sunlight Foundation.

Benjamin Ginsberg is David Bernstein Professor of Political Science and Chair of Governmental Studies at Johns Hopkins University. He is the author or co-author of a number of books, including *The Fall of the Faculty* (Oxford University Press), *Presidential Power: Unchecked and Unbalanced* (Norton), *Downsizing Democracy: How America Sidelined Its Citizens and Privatized Its Public* (Johns Hopkins University Press), *Politics by Other Means* (Basic), *The Fatal Embrace: Jews and the State* (University of Chicago Press), *American Government: Freedom and Power* (Norton), *We the People* (Norton), *How the Jews Defeated Hitler* (Rowman & Littlefield), *The Value of Violence* (Prometheus), and *The Captive Public* (Basic). Ginsberg received his Ph.D. from the University of Chicago in 1973. Before joining the Johns Hopkins University faculty in 1992, Ginsberg was Professor of Government at Cornell University. He currently has two books in press, *Presidential Government* (Yale University Press) and *What Washington Gets Wrong* (with Jennifer Bachner; Prometheus).

Alexander Herzog is a postdoctoral researcher in the Social Analytics Institute at Clemson University. His research focuses on the development and application of methods to analyze large amounts of textual data, such as political documents, speeches, social media, and newspaper articles. His work has appeared in the *European Political Science Review* and at various conferences.

Ryan T. Moore is Assistant Professor of Government at American University in Washington, DC. He spent two years as a Scholar in Health Policy Research, funded by the Robert Wood Johnson Foundation, at the University of California, Berkeley. His work focuses on American politics, social policy, and statistical political methodology, especially causal inference, the design of randomized experiments, and geolocated data. His work has appeared in *Political Analysis*, *American Journal of Public Health*, and *The Lancet*, among other places.

David W. Nickerson is Associate Professor of Political Science at Temple University. He uses experiments to study how campaigns mobilize, engage, and persuade voters in the United States and Latin America. He works with campaigns, non-profit organizations, and government agencies and has published articles in the *American Political Science Review*, *American Journal of Political Science*, *Political Analysis*, *Psychological Science*, and *Journal of Economic Perspectives*.

Andrew Reeves is Assistant Professor of Political Science at Washington University, St. Louis, and a research fellow at the Weidenbaum Center on the Economy, Government, and Public Policy. He is the author of *The Particularistic President: Executive Branch Politics and Political Inequality* (with Douglas Kriner; Cambridge University Press). He has held research fellowships at the Hoover Institution at Stanford University and at the Center for the Study of American Politics within the Institution for Social and Policy Studies at Yale University. His work has appeared in the *American Political Science Review*, *American Journal of Political Science*, and *Journal of Politics*, among other outlets.

Priscilla M. Regan is Professor of Government and Politics in the School of Policy, Government, and International Affairs at George Mason University. She is the author of *Legislating Privacy: Technology, Social Values, and Public Policy* (University of North Carolina Press) and co-editor, with Deborah Johnson, of *Transparency and Surveillance as Sociotechnical Accountability: A House of Mirrors* (Routledge), as well as over 40 journal articles and book chapters.

Kathryn Wagner Hill is Director of the Center for Advanced Governmental Studies at Johns Hopkins University. She is the editor of *Environmental Management in Healthcare Facilities* (Saunders), as well as the author of journal articles and book chapters on policy research, environmental regulation, government analytics, and curriculum development. She holds a Ph.D. from Cornell University and a B.A. from Oberlin College.

Index